UNCIVIL DEMOCRACY

Uncivil Democracy

HOW ACCESS TO JUSTICE
SHAPES POLITICAL POWER

JAMILA MICHENER

MALLORY E. SORELLE

PRINCETON UNIVERSITY PRESS

PRINCETON & OXFORD

Copyright © 2026 by Princeton University Press

Princeton University Press is committed to the protection of copyright and the intellectual property our authors entrust to us. Copyright promotes the progress and integrity of knowledge created by humans. By engaging with an authorized copy of this work, you are supporting creators and the global exchange of ideas. As this work is protected by copyright, any reproduction or distribution of it in any form for any purpose requires permission; permission requests should be sent to permissions@press.princeton.edu. Ingestion of any PUP IP for any AI purposes is strictly prohibited.

Published by Princeton University Press
41 William Street, Princeton, New Jersey 08540
99 Banbury Road, Oxford OX2 6JX

press.princeton.edu

GPSR Authorized Representative: Easy Access System Europe - Mustamäe tee 50, 10621 Tallinn, Estonia, gpsr.requests@easproject.com

All Rights Reserved

ISBN: 9780691264462
ISBN (e-book): 9780691264455

Library of Congress Control Number: 2025945897

British Library Cataloging-in-Publication Data is available

Editorial: David McBride and Alena Chekanov
Production Editorial: Jaden Young
Production: Erin Suydam
Publicity: James Schneider
Copyeditor: Cindy Milstein

Jacket images: Lev Mel / Gearstd / iStock

This book has been composed in Arno

Printed in the United States of America

10 9 8 7 6 5 4 3 2 1

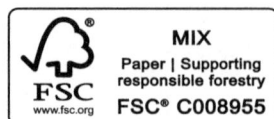

For Justin and Carrie

CONTENTS

ACKNOWLEDGMENTS

UNCIVIL DEMOCRACY is, at its core, a story about people. And it would not exist without the generous engagement and support of many people who have influenced our writing journey. We began separate paths toward what would become this joint endeavor to understand the politics of the civil legal system: Jamila as a summer intern at Queens Legal Services, and Mallory as a research assistant at the National Consumer Law Center—a former backup center for the Office of Economic Opportunity's Legal Services Program described in chapter 4. Our experiences, while distinct, inspired us to ask a similar set of questions about politics, power, and precarity in the civil justice system. We are grateful for those early experiences, and the kind and generous colleagues with whom we worked at Queens Legal Services and the National Consumer Law Center, for helping to chart our path toward writing *Uncivil Democracy*.

This project would not have been possible without the opportunity to learn from the 124 thoughtful, tenacious, brave people who shared their time, stories (including moments of pride and pain), and prescient insights with us. We offer them our deepest gratitude and the hope that we have done justice to their contributions in the pages that follow.

We also benefited from the work of an amazing team of research assistants from Cornell University, Duke University, and Lafayette College, without whom we would undoubtedly still be toiling through the data collection and analysis for this project. Kels Bowman, Ryana Jones, Lesley Idrovo-Pauta, and Fayola Fair were instrumental in helping to assemble the federal policy dataset used in chapter 4. Kanika Khanna, Grace Beals, Amanda Chen, Jordan Shannon, Whitney Taylor, Vanessa Navarro Rodriguez, Colin Cepuran, Arlenny Taveras, and Ben Finegan each contributed to some part of this research (and some to multiple parts), including the state policy data featured in chapter 2, background research on civil legal institutions and actors that informed the broader project, and the collection of qualitative interview data featured throughout the book.

Many colleagues and friends have provided intellectual support and community critical to our book's development. We are grateful to Suzanne Mettler who, knowing of our separate interests in studying the politics of civil legal representation, served as a scholarly matchmaker, encouraging us to work together to bring this project to life. Nick Carnes was generous enough to read and provide detailed feedback on the entire manuscript. Delphia Shanks, Sarah Maxey, and Tamar Malloy all supplied invaluable feedback over the course of this project on everything from survey question wording to the book proposal. Thanks are owed to the many other colleagues who have offered feedback on various parts of the manuscript, including Carolyn Barnes, Vesla Weaver, Hannah Walker, Serena Laws, Hahrie Han, and participants at the many conferences, talks, and workshops where we presented parts of this work (too many to name). Thank you also to the anonymous reviewers whose incisive feedback has undoubtedly strengthened this manuscript. Finally, many wonderful colleagues and friends have provided support and intellectual community along the way, including Andrew Clarke, Kristin Goss, Jay Pearson, Angelika von Wahl, Anna Haskins, Julilly Kohler-Hausmann, Jill Frank, David Bateman, Carolyn Barnes, Neil Lewis Jr., Jeff Niederdeppe, and Joe Margulies.

Of course, *Uncivil Democracy* would not have been possible without financial, research, and editorial support. Thank you to the Center for the Study of Inequality at Cornell, the Sanford School of Public Policy at Duke, and the Robert Wood Johnson Foundation for providing funding to facilitate both our quantitative and qualitative data collection. We are also grateful for the help of the archivists at the LBJ and Clinton Presidential Libraries for their research support. Dixie Franklin, Katie-Rose Repp, Lynette Edgerton, Rebecca Stoker, and Laurie Dorsey have provided essential administrative support throughout. We have also benefited from an excellent editorial team at Princeton University Press, including Bridget Flannery-McCoy, David McBride, Alena Chekanov, Eric Crahan, and our copyeditor, Cindy Milstein.

Finally, we are both incredibly grateful to our partners—Justin Michener and Carrie Baldwin-SoRelle—to whom this book is dedicated and without whom it would not have come to fruition. One challenge when writing the acknowledgments for a second book is not to simply repeat oneself when thanking the spouses who have continued to provide unlimited support, love, and patience for a project like this. Justin and Carrie have, once again, made their imprint on our work through countless conversations shared, dinners made, housework managed, schedules accommodated, family needs met, and editorial assistance rendered. We couldn't have done this without them.

Jamila and Mallory

UNCIVIL DEMOCRACY

1

"If the Community Isn't Doing Good, You're Not"

POWER, POLITICS, AND ACCESS TO JUSTICE

JOSEPHINE, A Black woman and grandmother in her late fifties, has lived in the same New York City building for more than thirty years.[1] She "absolutely loves" the Manhattan neighborhood where her family has "the benefit of Morningside Park and Central Park, and every bus and train that you can imagine." Josephine and her (now deceased) husband raised their children in a modest, but meticulously well-kept apartment. When their kids grew up and moved into their own homes, Josephine embraced her role as a grandmother, frequently caring for her disabled granddaughter.

A few years before her husband died, the building Josephine lived in started changing for the worse, deteriorating in ways that she and her neighbors could scarcely bear. To meet the challenge posed by the corrosion of her living conditions, Josephine changed too—but for the better. She mobilized legal resources, organized her neighbors, and fought back against the degradation of her housing and her humanity. Over the course of an hour-long interview, Josephine described all of these changes in harrowing detail. We elaborate the specifics at length in the pages to follow because the arc of Josephine's

---

1. We use pseudonyms throughout this book. The names (and sometimes locations) of research participants are masked to ensure their privacy. Some research subjects asked for this. Others did not. Some even preferred to be named. But since our research participants are sometimes connected to one another (via networks, personal relationships, or word of mouth), the most feasible way to prevent unanticipated or inadvertent harm, and be considerate to those who felt most vulnerable, was to mask the names and identities of all participants.

experiences parallels the trajectory of this book, concretizing the meaning of *Uncivil Democracy*. We learn from Josephine how a fundamentally unequal political economy puts marginalized people in positions of precarity and exposes them to predation. We see how traditional levers of political power often fail to address the most pressing problems that plague the lives of such people. We observe the ways that civil legal interventions—a lawyer representing one's interests in housing court, for example—can offer some recompense and bolster individual feelings of efficacy. Yet we discern the limits of individualistic legal approaches for solving collective problems of precarity. Finally, through the lens of Josephine's experiences, we grasp the transformative possibilities that emerge when individuals organize—acting collectively to oppose and alter the daunting realities of an unjust political economy. All of these lessons—reflected in Josephine's experiences and reinforced throughout this book—have implications for the prospects of a just and equitable democracy in the United States.

———

In 2018, Josephine's building was sold "to a hedge fund." Per her accounting, the new owners' goal was "to make a profit . . . not to think about humanity and think about the tenants. To make a profit." Without prompting, Josephine explained exactly why she was convinced that her building's current owner did not care about tenants:

> I have experienced my elevator broken from December all the way until February. . . . One of my grandkids is in a wheelchair. I brought her up one day and couldn't bring her back down. So we had to carry her [and] an eighty-five-pound wheelchair downstairs. . . . I've experienced no fire alarms functioning in the hallway. Just a beep, beep, beep, which clearly tells you it needs to be changed, which is a fire hazard. We had somebody get shot directly in front of our building, and the cops told the landlord, "If you had a real camera instead of this little fake stuff sitting up here, we could see who the perpetrator was." We've had people sleeping on the roof, whole families. We've experienced a scaffolding that's been on top of my building for eleven years . . . and it's a haven for drug dealers, drug sellers, people on drugs. . . . We have to dodge rats. . . . I [used to] come in this building any time I wanted to and maybe encountered one or two rats. Now you get fifty.

This only scratched the surface of the problems Josephine and her fellow tenants experienced. In conversation, Josephine noted much more: a hole in her roof due to water damage that left her exposed to infestation, a broken window that forced her to contend with a constant draft, the periodic loss of heat and hot water ("We didn't have heat and hot water from Christmas to New Year's"), and the unremitting refusal of the owner to make vital repairs.

Josephine's abysmal living conditions ran deeply counter to her character, desires, and personal standards. So when the hole in her roof lingered for longer than she could abide and a broken lock caused her to fear for her life, she acted decisively.

> That's what made me go to the state. I'm not OCD, but I like a clean place. My mom had eleven kids. It was thirteen people in the house, and she said, "If you ever lived in a matchbook, keep it clean." I have to have a clean environment or I go crazy. And that big hole that was sitting up in there, I'm scared of rats. I'm scared of rodents. I didn't know what was going to come through that hole ... [then] I [tried] to go out of the building one day and I couldn't get out. And it scared me to death because what if there's a fire. I have a granddaughter in a wheelchair ... to not be able to get out because of a broken lock that needs to be fixed ... it's ridiculous because the people who run this building don't live like that. So what makes you think we want to? ... I went to the Division of Housing and Community Renewal. They came and they inspected everything ... and the process is you have to write to the landlord and tell him all these conditions, and they give them a certain amount of time to fix it. And when they don't, that's when [the state] steps in.

Once Josephine identified, through Google, a state agency that could help her, she brought her neighbors on board. To ensure a favorable response from the Division of Housing and Community Renewal, Josephine convinced all the people in her building to sign the requisite forms. Though everyone came from different backgrounds, they shared the common experience of substandard housing conditions. Josephine leveraged that commonality to garner the needed signatures: "I was working with every tenant in this building—it's twenty-eight apartments in my building and twenty-eight people signed it because we all couldn't get out the building. We all know somebody was sleeping on the roof. We all know that the smoke alarms weren't working."

Eventually, Josephine succeeded in mobilizing the state to act. The Division of Housing and Community Renewal issued a letter to the owner of Josephine's building ordering them to make the necessary repairs. The owner did not comply. As a result, everyone in the building got a rent reduction of $100 per month for three years. Notwithstanding the reduced rent, the violations of standards of habitability continued.

Still insistent on seeking redress, Josephine turned to the civil legal system. She again found a satisfying but inadequate victory. Here is her description of what happened:

> JOSEPHINE: My recent experience was I woke up one day . . . [and] I heard this gurgling sound. I go in my bathroom, and my bathroom is—the toilet is sewage—raw sewage is coming up out of the toilet. . . . I called [the property management company] and I said, "You have two hours to send somebody here to fix my toilet or I will hire a plumber, a licensed plumber, get the receipt, and you will be paying for it." And that's exactly what I did. I personally took them to court. . . . I found a free lawyer . . . right up on [Washington] Avenue. . . . He was amazing too. Legal services. He was amazing. He was amazing.
>
> JAMILA: What did he do?
>
> JOSEPHINE: Well, he gave me good advice. He went with me to court. He made sure I had court dates. He made sure I didn't do anything that will make me lose my apartment. Like, I was going to get the ceiling fixed myself, but I wasn't going to fix it exactly like they had it. I figured since I'm going to get it fixed, if I want stucco, let me get stucco. And he was like, "No, because in your lease it says, if you alter the apartment, they can put you out." And I didn't think about that stuff. "The walls need to be white." So he told me. He said, "When they come in here, [Josephine], the walls need to be white, or they can say you altered the apartment and charge you. You don't want that stuff to backfire." He was humane. *My thing is, just treat me like a person.* Don't treat me like a thing. Treat me like a person. Understand that I have concerns . . . that's my thing with [the property management]. Don't just dismiss it and say, "Oh, she could go a month without a toilet," when number one, you're not [going without]. Number two, it's not legal. And number three, why should I have to do that if I sent you my rent?
>
> JAMILA: So how many times did you go to court? Have you had your court date?
>
> JOSEPHINE: One time. It was on Zoom [during the pandemic]. I won, and that was that.
>
> JAMILA: You won?
>
> JOSEPHINE: Oh, yeah. I got my $187.37. Yes. Yes, ma'am.

Though a court victory that netted less than $200 might not seem like much, it was meaningful to Josephine. It signaled her ability to confront a wealthy, irresponsible landlord—a veritable David and Goliath scenario—and win. It buoyed her confidence and confirmed her belief that something could be done to improve her living situation. But the court case was only a triumph for Josephine. It did nothing for the other tenants in her building who faced similar problems. It did nothing to solve the deeper issues that necessitated her court battle in the first place. And that did not sit right with Josephine. She had grown up with a deep-seated sense of responsibility to those around her. That ethos rendered her win hollow.

> My mom was a humanitarian. My mom had thirteen people in my household, and she still managed to feed other people, have rent parties, made sure that Sam had a pair of shoes. And I watched that. And she always told us, "Listen, if the community isn't doing good, you're not." So I always took that.

With "the community" looming large in her mind, Josephine met Aiden, and the opportunity emerged to do more. Aiden was a young White man from across town who lived in one of the other buildings owned by the company, which we will call Stonehill, that owned Josephine's building. Stonehill had acquired more than one hundred buildings across the city, and the tenants in those other properties suffered similarly appalling situations as Josephine and her neighbors. Aiden was attempting to organize Stonehill tenants throughout the city so that they could fight together. Somewhere along the way, Aiden heard about Josephine; word had gotten around about her reputation for being a force of nature. So Aiden found her and brought her into the coalition of tenants he was forming. He asked Josephine to organize the tenants in her building as part of the larger coalition of all Stonehill tenants.

> Aiden came to me in the embryonic stages of [the coalition]. . . . I went out the building one day, and Aiden introduced himself to me and said that somebody had given him my name. . . . When Aiden came to me, I was definitely on board. It was right after we had the rat problem, which we still have. . . . When he came to me, I was full of complaints, and he was full of complaints. . . . I said, "I'm tired of talking to people about my complaints [when I] can't do anything about them. It doesn't make any sense. If we're going to sit down and complain over tea every day, we're still going to be complaining fifty years from now. I want a resolution. I want to know if I join this coalition—it's like protesting and protesting and protesting. At some point, you have to stop protesting and go to step two."

That honest conversation was the start of Josephine's pivotal role in the Stonehill Tenants Coalition. The work she's done since has been wide-ranging, but one core element has been organizing people in her building:

> And some of the people in this building were willing. Then you have some that's scared. Then you have some that's immigrants. Then you have some that think it's going to interfere with their public assistance and their Section 8. And then you have some that just settle—if this is what they're giving me, this is what I'm going to take—whereas with me, I want what I pay for. . . . Since I've been involved with [canvasing for the coalition], we're trying to make people aware . . . and organizing, getting more people—two voices is louder than one. So getting people organized, getting people on board, finding out what their complaints are, finding out what they want, and what they need. How long have you been complaining about this, and what do you want to do about it? If they're turning this place into co-ops, which was one of the rumors we heard, let us know so that we can buy in if we want to, that kind of stuff, but don't try to push us out like we don't belong here. Don't try to push us out because you want to sell the apartment at market rate to make your profit.

The Stonehill Tenants Coalition gave Josephine an avenue for putting her mother's wisdom into practice ("if the community isn't doing good, you're not"). She helped to build the coalition by deepening her ties to community. She got people out to meetings, listened carefully to their struggles, and worked alongside them to develop concerted political strategies addressing the problems that emerged: "The coalition is growing, and I am so proud that Aiden called me and told me that my building had the most tenants at the meetings. And my building has the least apartments. . . . So people are involved."

The coalition met weekly, at first on Zoom during the pandemic and then in person. Listening to the struggles of Stonehill tenants was moving and motivating. As Josephine described it:

> [The meetings] are explosive, and they're emotional. I mean, some of these people, when you hear—we had a girl talk to us about rat mites. And I had never in my life heard of a rat mite. . . . I guess they're similar to bedbugs. And when she told her story, I wanted to cry. I wanted to cry. She had to go to the hospital. She had to take antibiotics, and they did not care. They didn't care.

Frequent meetings helped Josephine and her fellow tenants to develop empathetic relationships, a crucial springboard for collective action. Stonehill tenants met with local elected officials, challenged hedge fund managers, and initiated a rent strike, withholding their rent and keeping it in a secure escrow account until their landlord responded (a tactic that provides them with legal protection from eviction). As Josephine so wittily explained, "My rent money is on vacation at Chase Manhattan Bank, and it's staying in hotel escrow." In all of these ways and more, Josephine and her neighbors pursued a transformative vision of a humane political economy:

> The goal is to have us live like human beings on a consistent basis without having to go jump through hoops. . . . We pay our rent. We're human. We don't want to walk through piss in the elevator and be scared to come in our building. . . . I want to see . . . humanity play a role.

―――

This book is about people like Josephine. People who face problems that bring them into the orbit of the civil legal system: into courtrooms where they struggle against predation and grasp (often fruitlessly) for amends; into legal aid offices where they seek representation from those with expertise in navigating complex, adversarial legal processes; and into community organizations where they find support, mutuality, and—most vitally—prospects for building and exercising power to improve and change the conditions that precipitate their problems.[2] In the pages to follow, we lay out the core research questions that motivate this work, the methods we use to answer those questions, and the scholarly contributions we make by doing so. But we begin with Josephine because this book is most fundamentally about people—those who are subjugated at intersections of race, gender, and/or class; those who are essential for realizing the aspiration of US democracy but marginalized within democratic politics; and those who are most affected by the quality and nature of civil legal systems.

A person-centered approach drives our analysis of US civil legal institutions, their role within the broader American political economy, and their

―――

2. We define power as the capacity of individuals, groups, communities, and organizations to influence the structural conditions that affect them and others (Rosino 2016; Michener 2023c).

implications for democracy.[3] Building on multiple scholarly literatures, we use a variety of methods (policy mapping, historical analysis, surveys, ethnography, and in-depth interviews) to systematically illuminate the processes that produce civil legal inequality and the politics surrounding it. We do this with a central purpose: to understand how civil legal systems structure the political lives of racially and economically marginalized people, and thus shape their power.[4]

All along the way, we center people like Josephine because their experiences warrant being heard, seen, and understood; because the profoundly uncivil realities of the civil justice system matter for their lives; and because US democracy cannot thrive (or even exist) without them. In *Uncivil Democracy*, we argue that legal representation vitally protects people like Josephine and can incrementally strengthen their sense of individual efficacy and trust in the legal system. But we also reveal the limits of this kind of procedural fairness. Increasing access to justice through an ever-growing *supply* of lawyers elides the structural problems that generate the *demand* for lawyers in the first place. Problems like poverty, racial inequality, lack of affordable housing, and inadequate health care come to manifest as legal problems, especially when more effective political routes to resolution are foreclosed. These troubles, though, are rooted in an unequal, precarious, and sometimes predatory political economy. Only collectively organizing to exercise power holds promise for more fundamental change. Ultimately, civil legal representation is necessary but woefully insufficient. As Josephine so clearly recognized, people like her need more than a lawyer; they need the power to alter the conditions that create their precarity.

3. Political economy approaches focus on how economic and political systems are linked. Many aspects of civil legal systems reflect dynamic interactions between markets and politics. As we will describe in detail throughout the book, the most distinctive features of the American political economy—multilevel, multivenue governance, unique interest organization, and systematic racial division (Hacker et al. 2022)—are also pivotal elements of the politics of civil legal institutions.

4. By "structure" and "shape," we do not mean "effect." In this book, we focus less on identifying cause and effect, and more on understanding *what* people experience when they navigate civil legal institutions, *how* such institutions are embedded within the American political economy, and *how* civil legal experiences come to have meaning for political life. The latter is what we mean when we say "structure." This is similarly what we mean when we say "shape." Generally, we do not intend to denote or imply causal relationships unless we explicitly say so. For more details on our methodological approach along these lines, see the qualitative appendix.

In addition to taking a person-centered approach, *Uncivil Democracy* orients primarily around the case of housing and the process of tenant organizing. Civil justice issues are myriad—too vast for one book to cover comprehensively. Attempting to study every civil legal domain would have made it difficult for us to dig deeply and richly enough into any given arena. Concentrating on housing enabled us to develop a thematically connected set of narratives that reflect struggles related to one of the most fundamental aspects of the American political economy.[5] As the biggest expense for most families, housing is a site of perennial crisis in the United States (Bureau of Labor Statistics 2024).[6] The problems of housing affordability, quality, and accessibility have only intensified over time. As home prices soar to record highs, climate change threatens housing stock, and housing cost burdens intensify, staggering numbers of people find themselves struggling to keep a roof over their heads (Joint Center for Housing Studies of Harvard University 2024). The financialization of housing through the increased role of private equity, venture capital, and other extractive actors has only worsened such problems (Fields 2017; Fields and Uffer 2016; Kohl 2021; Lima 2020).[7] Market conditions and government policies disadvantage all but the wealthiest, and do so in racially disparate and politically polarizing ways (Fields and Raymond 2021; Lewis 2022; Michener 2025c; Robinson 2021). As a result, housing unaffordability, substandard quality, commodification, and inaccessibility are core features of political-economic relations in the United States.

Navigating housing in this unequal political economy pushes many marginalized people into the web of the civil legal system—necessitating that they fight evictions, inhumane living conditions, incursions of their legal rights, and much more. At the same time, these conditions create incentives for political action. Consider Josephine, whose story initiated this chapter. Housing was the fulcrum around which her political participation and community organizing pivoted. This is in line with a lengthy history of struggle within racially and economically marginalized communities, where contestation over housing has long persisted (Feldman and Stall 2004; Fields 2015; Karp 2014; Madden and Marcuse 2016; Michener 2019b; Michener and SoRelle 2022; Moffett-Bateau

5. Our focus on housing emerges via our qualitative interview and ethnographic data. Our quantitative and historical analyses account for a fuller breadth of civil legal problems.

6. Housing accounted for 32.9 percent of all consumer expenditures in 2023.

7. "Financialization" refers to the increased dominance of financial markets and actors in the housing sector (Wijburg 2021).

2023, 2024; Rodriguez 2021; Taylor 2013; Thurston 2018; Williams 2004; Wolfinger 2009). The political economy of housing is marked by racialized oppression
through processes of exclusion or predatory inclusion (Rothstein 2017; Taylor
2019; Thurston 2018; Trounstine 2018).[8] Racially marginalized communities
have struggled against such oppression, leveraging political institutions ranging
from legislatures and courts to community organizations and social movements
(Baranski 2007; Feldman and Stall 2004; Juravich 2017; Karp 2014; Rodriguez
2021; Williams 2004). This makes housing an instructive and compelling case
for understanding the workings of civil legal systems as well as the flow of politics and power in the lives of marginalized people.

Civil (In)justice in the United States

People like Josephine face hundreds of millions of new civil justice problems
each year in the United States (Hague Institute for Innovation of Law and the
Institute for the Advancement of the American Legal System 2021; Sandefur
and Teufel 2020). Many of these involve the stuff of everyday life: disputes surrounding housing, health care, wage theft, debt collection, access to public benefits, child custody, and the like. These "justiciable events"—problems that raise
legal issues, but may or may not receive legal attention (Genn 1999; Sandefur
2007)—can have devastating repercussions: displacement, houselessness, loss
of income, family separation, diminished health, poverty, and too much more
(Sandefur and Teufel 2020). Despite the weight and consequences of civil legal
problems, most people face them alone, and as many as 120 million US civil
justice issues remain unresolved (Hague Institute for Innovation of Law and
the Institute for the Advancement of the American Legal System 2021).[9]

One of the most widely touted ways for policymakers to address civil legal
problems is to provide access to counsel in civil courts for lower-income litigants—a form of governmental support that is sometimes hailed as the balm
to soothe the wounds inflicted by enduring civil justice inequalities. Indeed,

8. "Predatory inclusion" refers to the "process whereby members of a marginalized group
are provided with access to a good, service, or opportunity from which they have historically
been excluded but under conditions that jeopardize the benefits of access" (Seamster and
Charron-Chénier 2017).

9. Throughout this book, we will refer to justiciable events, whether they formally enter the
realm of the civil legal system or not, as civil legal problems or civil justice problems,
interchangeably.

Senator Walter Mondale once deemed the federal program of financial support for legal services "the most effective poverty program, dollar for dollar," in the United States. Mondale's assertion reflected a sober awareness of the importance of the legal system in the lives of low-income people and the difficulties they experience in navigating it. The US polity is simultaneously characterized by a reliance on legal contestation for dispute resolution *and* limited access to the courts for those making rights-based claims (Burbank and Farhang 2017; Kagan 1991, 2019; Staszak 2015). Many areas of civil law—housing, public benefits, immigration, and debt collection—concern the relationship between denizens and the state.[10] Navigating the civil legal system is thus necessary (though, as we will show, not sufficient) to receive the benefits and protections nominally guaranteed by government policies (Michener 2023a). Given this, access to civil legal representation is a fundamental aspect of a free and fair society that remains out of reach for many of the most vulnerable.

Notwithstanding the immense importance of the protections enshrined by civil law, there is no constitutionally guaranteed right to civil legal counsel.[11] While the Legal Services Corporation (LSC) Act of 1974 acknowledged that "providing legal assistance to those who face an economic barrier to adequate legal counsel will serve best the ends of justice and assist in improving opportunities for low-income persons," there is a yawning chasm between the ideal established by this law and the reality that has materialized since its enactment. This "justice gap"—the difference between the level of legal assistance necessary to meet the needs of low-income people and the level of legal assistance available to them—is striking. Between 50 and 80 percent of people living in poverty in the United States have difficulty obtaining civil legal representation to address their problems, leaving them without a critical tool to protect their rights and livelihoods (Chu et al. 2013; Rhode 2004).

10. Scholars often distinguish between private law—disputes between private individuals or entities—and public law—disputes that involve questions of constitutional or administrative law in which government entities are implicated. The civil legal system encapsulates both types of proceedings, but most civil justice problems of the type we describe in this book are matters of private rather than public law. Despite that designation, government policies and benefits are frequently implicated in private law disputes (e.g., housing vouchers in eviction cases), as the examples throughout the book will demonstrate.

11. In *Gideon v. Wainwright* (1963), the US Supreme Court found a right to counsel in criminal cases involving felony charges. In *Argersinger v. Hamlin* (1972), the Supreme Court supported the right to counsel in criminal cases involving misdemeanor charges. No equivalent federal rights exist for civil cases.

The justice gap is especially imperative because low-income people are both disproportionately in need of civil legal safeguards and significantly less likely to have recourse to them. In 2022, 74 percent of low-income households in the United States experienced at least one civil legal problem, and nearly 40 percent experienced five or more such problems. Among a vast array of reported problems, the LSC (2022) estimates that 92 percent of eligible problems received inadequate or no legal attention. While scholars rightly challenge the notion that all such problems are best served through formal legal processes (e.g., see Sandefur 2019), this still represents a massive disconnect between the frequency with which people experience justiciable civil problems and their capacity to get legal help for those problems.

The high demand for civil legal representation combined with its limited supply means that for every person who receives publicly funded legal assistance, there is at least one applicant turned away because of insufficient capacity. In fact, there is less than one civil legal aid attorney to help every ten thousand people living in poverty in the United States—a rate deemed the minimum for adequate access to justice (National Center for Access to Justice 2016). As a result, low-income litigants frequently appear in court without lawyers, and vast numbers of people do so because they cannot afford one. These patterns unfold unequally across social groups. In 2022, 71 percent of LSC (2023) clients were women and nearly 60 percent were people of color—32 percent Black, 17 percent Latinx, 3 percent Asian and Pacific Islander (AAPI), and 2 percent Native American.[12]

Racially and economically differentiated need for and access to civil legal representation has meaningful consequences. Evidence indicates that having civil counsel can help to narrow health disparities, bolster wealth (through increased property values), improve communication between public institutions and impoverished communities, and reduce poverty (Cunningham 2016; Houseman and Minoff 2014; Powers 2015; Teufel et al. 2015). Unrepresented or self-represented litigants are at a dramatic disadvantage in the convoluted and highly specialized US court system (Fleming-Klink, McCabe, and Rosen 2023). People who are denied access to legal representation have more negative experiences of the courts (Bezdek 1991; Tyler and McGraw 1986; Zimmerman and Tyler 2009).

---

12. The LSC collects race and ethnicity data on clients served by grantees as a single identity (where race and ethnicity are not considered separate identities). Note that 3.9 percent of these clients identified as multiracial and 2.1 percent were of unknown racial background.

Despite the value of legal aid as a policy tool, policymakers at both the federal and state level have failed to maintain a robust program of civil legal service provision for those in need. As a result, civil legal resources, and the prospects for access to justice they entail, are distributed scarcely and inequitably. Even more significant than the failure to provide access to civil justice is the broader failure to reckon with how the justice gap follows from and exacerbates existing inequalities within the larger political-economic system (Michener 2023a).

The Political Economy of Civil Justice

Notwithstanding the scope and significance of civil legal systems in the lives of racially and economically marginalized people, the dynamics of the justice gap are seldom considered core to the American political economy or welfare state (Michener, SoRelle, and Thurston 2022; Rahman and Thelen 2022).[13] Yet civil courts are inundated precisely because they function as a stopgap in the face of an insufficient and unequal infrastructure for public goods provision. As noted by Colleen Shanahan and colleagues (2022, 1473), civil litigants

> do not end up behind that door by coincidence. Rather, this is a foreseeable consequence of the absence of affordable and adequate housing, health care, childcare, and education, the absence of fair and equal wages, and the presence of mass incarceration in our society. State civil cases involving debt, family relationships, and children have different names on the courtroom door but similar stories behind those doors.

US civil legal processes are embedded within economic and political structures that generate as well as perpetuate economic precarity (Callison, Finger, and Smith 2022; Hepburn et al. 2021; Sandefur 2019). Inequality has grown as federal, state, and local policies neglect rising housing costs, flattened wages, predatory consumer practices, meager social welfare supports, and much more (Brady, Blome, and Kleider 2016; Franko 2021; Franko and Witko 2018; Petach 2022; SoRelle 2020; Taylor 2019).

The culprit lies in policy design and implementation choices (e.g., Michener 2018; SoRelle 2020; Soss, Fording, and Schram 2011) as well as in a larger political unwillingness to rein in poverty and inequality (Brady, Finnigan, and Hübgen 2017; Partridge and Weinstein 2013). Ineptly mitigated

13. For some exceptions, see Farhang 2010; Melnick 2010; Tushnet 2009.

market excesses have proliferated economic deprivation that overflows into the civil legal system. But civil legal processes were not designed to tackle structural inequality and thus have proven inadequate to the task (Michener 2023a). Indeed, a reliance on litigation often does just the opposite, prioritizing the individual economic nature of people's problems at the expense of addressing their collective political dimensions.[14] The spillover of economic and social needs into the legal system creates what Shanahan and colleagues (2022, 1474–75) call an "institutional mismatch":

> We see an *institutional mismatch*: state civil courts are institutions where people bring their social needs more than their [legal] disputes. The work of state civil courts is a daily manifestation of the failure of the executive and legislative branches to disrupt structural inequality or invest in systems of care to mitigate it. These courts operate in the breach to address social needs because they cannot decline the cases presented to them. Thus, the social needs people bring to court are framed as disputes in order to access social provision. . . . This leaves state civil courts attempting to address—within the constraints of their dispute resolution design—the social needs of litigants.

Institutional mismatch indicates a political economy of civil justice characterized by an inability or refusal, as quoted above, "to disrupt structural inequality or invest in systems of care to mitigate it."

A long tradition of law and political economy scholarship charts how the broader judicial system creates as well as enforces rules that structure pervasive inequalities in a capitalist economy—more often in ways that benefit elite economic interests (e.g., Brown 2015; Culpepper 2010; Fraser 2014; Galanter 1974; Sabbeth 2021; Streeck 2011).[15] The civil legal system plays a critical role

---

14. There is a robust debate among scholars about the degree to which private law can be mobilized to shape public or collective outcomes (e.g., see Burstein 2017; Zemans 1983). But considerable work from political theorists and critical legal scholars demonstrates how a reliance on private law and regimes based on individual rights can undermine incentives to address the collective nature of social problems (e.g., Brown 1995; Marx [1844] 1926; Smith 1997; Spade 2015; Waldron 1993).

15. For example, scholars who study the political economy of litigation and administrative law have demonstrated how the legal system can privilege business interests (Culpepper 2010) and "repeat players" (Galanter 1974), who over time, accumulate the advantage of expertise, relationships, and resources that allow them to prevail over those who navigate the courts with less frequency.

in enforcing the contract and property rights that undergird a capitalist system. But it does so in a systemically coercive, extractive manner that disadvantages low-income, racially marginalized litigants. Most race-class-subjugated litigants do not appear in civil court voluntarily.[16] Josephine—who successfully initiated proceedings against her landlord—is anomalous in this sense. In contrast, most people are forced into legal proceedings by landlords, debt collectors, and other well-resourced actors. Once there, the courts invoke a variety of both formal and informal strategies—from a reliance on default judgments to a lack of discovery or equitable presentation of evidence—to quickly and efficiently dispossess assets from already marginalized litigants and redistribute them to economic elites (Brito et al. 2022; Fleming-Klink, McCabe, and Rosen 2023; Hanley, Howell, and Teresa 2024; Kepes and Kempler 2024; Sabbeth 2023; Sudeall and Paociuti 2021). In the process, the civil courts both maintain and deepen existing inequalities in economic power.

Employing a political economy perspective to explore the justice gap illuminates the collective dimensions of the individual claims that flow through the civil legal system, and highlights the importance of power relations in structuring both the precursors to and ramifications of civil legal inequality (Michener 2023a).[17] Figure 1.1 illustrates the complex set of factors at play in a political economy approach to the justice gap.

To date, scholars and practitioners have primarily focused on understanding and addressing the substantive elements of the justice gap (noted in the top layer of each square in figure 1.1). The prevalence of material hardship gives rise to civil justice problems and thus generates demand for civil legal representation (Michener 2023a; Shanahan et al. 2022). Relatedly, substantive concerns about the supply of civil legal representation dominate both historical scholarly accounts and proposed solutions to inequalities in access to justice (see Michener 2025b; Sandefur 2019). Finally, a growing literature considers

16. We draw on the insights of Joe Soss and Vesla Weaver (2017, 567) in using the "race-class-subjugated" construction, which recognizes that "race and class are intersecting social structures . . . that defy efforts to classify people neatly."

17. Political economy means different things to different scholars. We do not use political economy to refer to the application of rational, public choice models or formal theory to study judicial politics, although there is a robust literature in this vein (e.g., de Figueiredo and de Figueiredo 2002; Eskridge and Ferejohn 1992; Gelly and Spiller 1990; McNollgast 1990, 1994; Weingast 2002). Instead, we employ the substantive meaning of political economy as work that explores the interplay of US market, political, and policy institutions along with their varied material and political repercussions.

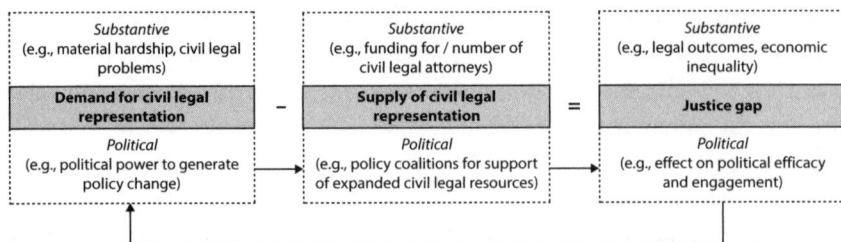

Substantive (e.g., material hardship, civil legal problems)		Substantive (e.g., funding for / number of civil legal attorneys)		Substantive (e.g., legal outcomes, economic inequality)
Demand for civil legal representation	−	**Supply of civil legal representation**	=	**Justice gap**
Political (e.g., political power to generate policy change)		Political (e.g., policy coalitions for support of expanded civil legal resources)		Political (e.g., effect on political efficacy and engagement)

FIGURE 1.1. Political economy of the US civil legal system

the negative legal and socioeconomic ramifications that the justice gap produces in the lives of marginalized litigants. While attention to the socioeconomic determinants and consequences of inadequate civil legal representation is important, both scholars and practitioners too often overlook critical dimensions of the justice gap: politics and political power.[18] We contend that comprehensively examining access to civil justice requires addressing the distribution and configuration of power in the American political economy.

Though civil law has sometimes been optimistically envisioned as a mechanism "by which power may be diffused throughout society" (Zemans 1983, 693), civil litigants are often on the losing end of power imbalances. Charting the political economy of the justice gap necessitates grappling with how power asymmetries operate within and beyond courts and other civil legal spaces. The ebb and flow of structural inequality is contingent on power relations. This is why we center on the role of power resources—organizations and actors that can both build and channel the influence and capacity of people with civil legal problems—in shaping the structural drivers of civil legal outcomes (Korpi [1978] 2022).

As figure 1.1 illustrates, questions of political power emerge for each element of the justice gap equation (noted in the bottom layer of each square). *Demand* for legal services is generated in large part by a political economy of scarcity wherein the people with the fewest resources lack the power to change the

---

18. Scholars of public law and judicial politics have long argued that the US courts are inherently politicized (e.g., Cameron et al. 2000; Hasen 2013; Kagan 2019; Melnick 1983; Sessa-Hawkins and Perez 2017). Moreover, the courts have played a critical role in the political development of the US state (Gerstle 2017; Skowronek 1982; Tushnet 2011) and continue to shape the politics of policymaking in critical ways. We build on these insights by extending the emphases on politics and power into the literatures that examine access to justice in civil legal contexts.

policies that impede their well-being (Michener 2023a). Many people facing civil justice problems are grappling with continuous threats of deprivation that they have limited ability to deter. Such constrained power both engenders the circumstances that create civil legal problems and reduces political pressure on policymakers to be responsive to those problems. Since legal needs are a function of power, the justice gap cannot be bridged without deploying power in ways that reduce the scale of legal needs (e.g., decrease demand).

Political dynamics also shape the *supply* of civil legal representation available for those who seek out or are forced into the civil legal system. In the absence of sufficient political pressure from those who stand to benefit most from expanded access to representation, policymaking elites lack the political incentives to provide adequate funding to support civil legal representation for low-income litigants, particularly, as we will show in chapter 4, in the face of growing conservative opposition to such efforts. Instead, their actions reflect the concerns of economic elites, such as landlords and property owners, government agents, and even legal professionals, who are invested in harnessing the coercive and extractive elements of the civil legal system for their benefit.

Finally, our political economy approach acknowledges that the justice gap has significant repercussions for political life. As the following section outlines in greater detail, we contend that civil legal problems and institutions structure experiences in ways that have meaningful implications for how people perceive political efficacy, citizenship, and governing institutions, as well as how they make decisions about individual and collective political action.

Civil Injustice and Political Power

Uncivil Democracy marshals a variety of original evidence to show how experiences of the civil legal system are politically meaningful. We pay particular attention to the varied processes through which individual and collective power can be expanded or contracted when people come into contact with the civil legal system. Figure 1.2 presents an overview of the pathways along which we argue the civil legal system can structure political power for those in positions of precarity.

As we have described in this chapter, the underlying social policy infrastructure generates economic precarity that produces a wide-ranging set of civil justice problems. These problems can alter the resources a person has available to them as well as their sense of political efficacy, democratic belonging, and institutional trust. For those whose civil justice problems are funneled

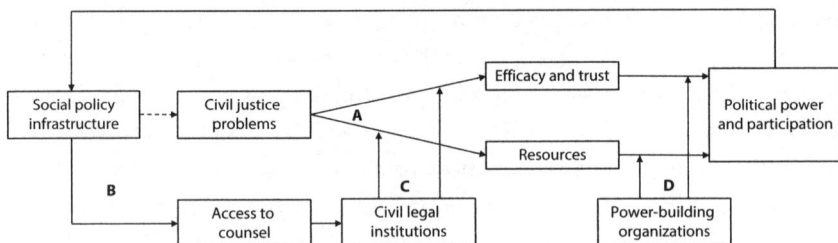

FIGURE 1.2. Pathways of political power in the civil legal system

through the legal system, interactions with civil legal institutions—with and without counsel—can further structure resources, efficacy, and trust in distinct ways. When civil justice problems and interactions with the court bring people like Josephine into the orbit of power-building organizations, like tenant groups, those experiences also bear on the relationship between civil legal problems and political power. Each chapter of this book delves into the theoretical and empirical underpinnings of these processes along with the consequences for racially and economically marginalized people trying to navigate them.

As we explore the pathways of political power laid out in figure 1.2, we intentionally avoid making causal arguments.[19] We rely on multiple kinds of evidence interwoven throughout each chapter.[20] Some of this evidence is

19. We refer here to a conceptualization of causation that is aligned with the potential outcomes framework (also known as the Rubin causal model), which supposes "that every subject has multiple outcomes that could have been observed, corresponding to each possible treatment . . . even though only one outcome was ultimately observed," and posits causal effects as "the difference between what actually happens in a given case and what would have happened had that case been assigned to a different treatment category" (Keller and Branson 2024, 575; Seawright 2016b, 19).

20. We do not assume that multiple triangulated methods inherently or inevitably improve on the quality of evidence. Rather, we thoughtfully integrate distinct methods based on what we seek to know and how best to learn it. While we share some of J Seawright's (2016a, 49) criticism of triangulation as insufficient insofar as it "provides multiple, somewhat incommensurable answers to causal questions," we do not follow Seawright's (2016a, 47) exhortation toward "integrative multimethod research" in which "two or more methods are carefully combined to support a single, unified causal inference" where "additional methods are used to test or reframe the assumptions behind the central causal inference." While there is certainly value in an integrative approach of this sort, it diverges from our own in that we do not center or fixate on causal inference as our core aim. In contrast, our central research goals orient around offering

quantitative, identifying associations that corroborate our rendering of the pathways of power. Some is historical, situating civil legal processes within a broader arc to help us understand how and why they operate. Much of our evidence is based on qualitative experiential accounts that describe the nature of people's interactions with civil legal institutions (courts, legal aid organizations, and tenant groups) and the politically relevant meaning they make in response to encounters with those systems.

We employ quantitative methods when useful, but not in strict service to a causal explanation. Instead, we remain focused on generating descriptive knowledge of *what* is happening within civil legal systems, *how* people are making sense of it, and *what* this means for US democracy. While this lays a rich foundation that can be built on by scholars seeking to estimate causal relationships, we commit primarily to the first-order tasks of describing how civil legal processes operate within people's lives; mapping the micro-, meso-, and macro institutional realities those processes are embedded within; and surfacing the implications for politics and power in marginalized communities.

The Racialized Political Economy of Civil Justice

As we explore dynamics of politics and power, one of the most significant themes that emerges is that the political economy of access to justice produces racialized outcomes. From the political development of policy to the community organizing efforts to combat civil justice problems, racialized political dynamics are a force that pervades the civil justice landscape. This does not mean civil legal problems only affect people of color (though they do so disproportionately).[21] Instead, it means that civil legal processes take on racial meaning and significance, despite having no inherent racial valence (Omi and Winant 1986). Notwithstanding this reality, scholars of the civil courts lament how the "relationship between race and civil courts has been understudied

---

deep description of experiences and processes, capturing the ways potential causal mechanisms unfold in practice, developing noncausal explanations to support constitutive arguments (Navarrete 2024; Pacewicz 2022), and charting political possibilities (as opposed to probabilistic likelihoods). In the qualitative appendix, we elaborate on these aims and the ideas underlying them.

21. While many of the experiences we center in the book are those of Black women, we intentionally include the voices of a broad swath of people from different geographic locations and with distinct backgrounds (racially and otherwise).

and undertheorized" (Brito et al. 2022, 1244). We rectify this oversight by paying particular attention to the racialized political dynamics of the development and consequences of access to civil justice.

A primary reason why civil justice is racialized is because it is tethered to and built on institutions with long and well-documented histories of racism (e.g., courts, housing markets, and regulatory regimes). These institutions have driven the processes that give the construct of "race" social and political meaning (e.g., Bell 1980; Crenshaw 1988; King and Smith 2005; Lopez 1996; Novkov 2002; Smith 1997, 2003). Moreover, when public institutions and policies are designed in ways that disproportionately allocate benefits and burdens to groups based on social systems of racial classification, while simultaneously decentralizing control over those policy institutions (as is the case for programs to support access to counsel), racialized patterns are a likely outcome (Michener 2019b). Indeed, scholars have demonstrated disparate racial impacts in several domains of civil law (e.g., Brito et al. 2014; Roberts 2009, 2014).

The political economy of civil justice is also consistent with the expectations of racial capitalism and racial authoritarianism that operate within the broader American political economy (Brito et al. 2022; Libgober 2025; Robinson 1983; Soss and Weaver 2017; Weaver and Prowse 2020). *Uncivil Democracy* details a decades-long process by which economic and political power have accumulated to elites in ways that enabled as well as intensified predation and exploitation among predominantly race-class-subjugated communities—a hallmark of racial capitalism (Robinson 1983; Táíwò et al. 2021). For example, chapter 4 details how both the extension and retrenchment of federal support for civil legal counsel is frequently driven by efforts to preserve an underlying racialized power structure. From attempts to remove control over federal grants from the hands of community action agencies that require participation in decision-making from the diverse constituents they represent, to modest extensions of access to counsel as a tool to "civilize" restive urban, predominantly Black and Latinx communities and prevent their collective mobilization, the suppression of economic and political power among racially marginalized groups features prominently in this book.

Racial capitalism also emerges in our archival historical work and as a theme reflected in people's experiences navigating the civil legal system. Theorists of racial capitalism "tie race and class together with the broader system of capitalism that determines how income, wealth, and social advantages are produced and distributed" (Táíwò et al. 2021, 17). In a similar vein, we repeatedly demonstrate that racialized inequality is a glaring and widespread feature of civil legal experiences, hardening existing economic and political hierarchies. The people whose voices inform this research relay how this happens in excruciating detail. They describe how state institutions and actors like courts and judges, together with economic elites, such as landlords and property managers, generate and deepen the racialized power differentials that emerge in the civil justice system. They often portray these outcomes not as individualized experiences but rather as collective patterns of structurally rooted racism. Such observations are particularly notable because we rarely prompted interviewees to talk about race. Instead, racialized accounts emerged organically from people's own evaluations of their experiences.

It is clear in the words of those most harmed that the racially marginalized people at the proverbial bottom of US power structures bear the weight of disproportionate detriment. Consider the perspective of Ali, a leader of a tenant organization in the Deep South:

> My organizing was rooted out of struggles from my own family, my own struggles with housing insecurities and housing instabilities, and lack of access to housing, *the whole historical way that housing has been used to racialize generations in my own personal history.* We [organize] because the need is so great. . . . What do we want to do to change these systems and the systematic use of housing, and how it's used for other people's capital gains and our losses? . . . [Change] is not going to come because we want it to. It's not going to come because they feel that they need to do something out of good faith. . . . It's going to come because we organized really well to make it happen.

Ali, and so many of the other people whose perspectives we center in the pages to follow, experienced unequal civil legal processes that disproportionately extract from and punish people of color. By highlighting such experiences and contextualizing them in relation to the American political economy, *Uncivil Democracy* contributes to existing scholarship on access to justice and racial capitalism.

A Road Map for *Uncivil Democracy*

For nearly two decades, political scientists have increasingly turned their attention to the punitive politics of the criminal justice system. This has yielded important research on the political development of the carceral state, role of public opinion in shaping that trajectory, and participatory consequences of carceral experiences (Burch 2013; Enns 2016; Forman 2017; Fortner 2015; Gott-schalk 2006, 2011, 2016; Lerman and Weaver 2014; Murakawa 2014; Walker 2020; Weaver 2007). Contrastingly, political scientists have been less attentive to the other half of the US legal system: the realm of civil law.[22] Focusing specifically on the political economy of the justice gap, *Uncivil Democracy* comprehensively explores the historical trajectory of the justice gap, its con-temporary upshots, the ways that inequitable access to legal representation structure political life, and the implications of all of this for how we understand pathways to more fundamental political transformation.

Our entry into these tasks begins in chapter 2 with an overview of how the civil legal system and access to civil legal representation works in the United States, paying particular attention to policy variation across states. We analyze original data on nearly thirty years of state policymaking alongside evidence from lawyers and tenants describing challenges navigating legal problems with housing. Together, these data contextualize crucial institutional realities that shape the ebb and flow of the justice gap across states, and situate the political economy of civil justice within an unequal federated polity.

With a clearer picture of the civil legal system, chapter 3 turns to under-standing the nature of demand for civil justice. It looks at the landscape of civil justice problems in the United States, concretizing the political repercussions of those problems and their democratic implications. The chapter begins by using original, national survey data to show the magnitude and scope of civil

22. To be sure, scholars—predominantly from political theory and public law—have studied many aspects of administrative and constitutional legal development, with a focus on civil rights and discrimination (e.g., Farhang 2010; Law 2010; Novkov 2001, 2002; Smith 1997). While these studies ask important questions about how aspects of civil law shape social, political, and eco-nomic citizenship in the United States, they concentrate primarily on macrolevel development within the realm of public law. A separate literature attends to elements of private civil law, ex-amining the political economy of litigation and torts with a primary focus on the economic costs of litigation (e.g., Danzon 1984; Jacobi 2009; McIntosh 1990). While these literatures have much to add to our understanding of civil law broadly construed, neither pays much attention to the political economy of the justice gap. Nor do they address the political consequences for individuals navigating civil legal processes. Furthermore, the work on the political economy of litigation and torts is largely inattentive to questions of race. The existing scholarship on the politics of the broader civil legal system mainly revolves around the role of elite actors—policymakers, judges, lawyers, and so on—with less attention to the perspectives of the indi-vidual litigants—particularly low-income, racially marginalized ones—who are navigating these systems. These are the voids of knowledge we seek to fill.

legal problems as well as the variation in those experiences across hierarchies of class and race. The chapter then turns to the political consequences of civil legal problems. Building on theoretical frameworks that show how resources, negative life events, and interactions with governing institutions shape political behavior, we demonstrate how civil justice problems translate to feelings of trust (or distrust) in legal and political institutions along with evaluations of individual political efficacy (path A in figure 1.2). Analyzing our survey data alongside ethnographic observations and over one hundred in-depth qualitative interviews with people navigating housing challenges, the chapter shows how experiences with civil justice problems can undermine trust, efficacy, and engagement, eroding political power for communities that are already marginalized.

Having registered the demand for civil justice   and the political implica tions of that demand, chapters 4 and 5 turn to the politics of supply in the justice gap equation. Specifically, chapter 4 details the rise and retrenchment of federal efforts to provide access to civil legal representation for low-income people (path B in figure 1.2). Drawing from archival and legislative records as well as an original dataset of all federal bills proposed to address access to civil legal counsel from 1966 through 2020, the chapter explains how the politics of civil legal aid became entangled with a larger, racialized debate over who deserves power in the United States. Going further, chapter 4 demonstrates how three main groups of policymakers emerged in the debate over civil legal representation, each with a distinct vision for the distribution of economic and political power in the United States. For proponents of a structural transformation approach, the provision of civil legal representation provided an opportunity to transform economic and power relations, leading to a more equitable political economy. Procedural justice advocates, by contrast, pursued carefully circumscribed access to counsel as an opportunity to offer individual procedural justice to beneficiaries deemed deserving of assistance. These advocates did not espouse aspirations to reshape the underlying inequalities in socioeconomic or political power. Finally, a third and growing contingent of welfare opponents pursued the complete elimination of federal support for civil legal representation as part of their larger efforts to undermine the welfare state. By examining the push and pull among these three groups, we chart the development of a policy equilibrium that maintains widespread but underresourced programs of legal representation for low-income people, limiting the prospects for robust access to justice and thwarting the potential to rebalance power relations.

Continuing to examine the politics of supply, chapter 5 asks how the provision of legal counsel—for the few who receive it—is understood by those who experience civil justice problems. In essence, chapter 5 investigates the political consequences of a procedural justice approach to the civil legal system—one that is designed to facilitate a fairer process for individual claim making (e.g., see Thibaut and Walker 1975; Tyler 1988) without providing recourse to collective, transformative power. Drawing on insights from the policy feedback literature, which contends that people's interactions with public institutions like the courts can influence their trust and sense of political efficacy, we show how access to counsel can improve litigants' experiences of the civil legal system, with modest positive consequences for individual political efficacy. We demonstrate how access to counsel is associated with moderately increased trust in the civil legal system.

Nevertheless, the limits of access to counsel—both in scope and efficacy—have been well-documented (e.g., see Sandefur 2016, 2019; Wallat 2019). And while the provision of procedural justice might improve outcomes for individual litigants, it also bolsters the legitimacy of the courts without sufficiently ameliorating the problems that drive people into them. Thus in chapter 6, we extend our consideration of access to civil justice beyond courts and lawyers to investigate the possibilities that emerge when robust community organizing builds legal as well as political power within marginalized communities (path D in figure 1.2). Drawing on qualitative interviews with members and leaders of tenant organizations across the country, chapter 6 explores the relationship between the civil legal system and collective organizing in the context of housing. It charts how attorneys and organizers can work together to both get individuals the legal support they need and identify pathways for change in the absence of efficacious civil legal remedies. This chapter more closely reflects the ambitions of those poverty lawyers and law reform proponents who saw in the civil legal system a way to transform the American political economy into a more equitable, less precarious system for people who have been historically marginalized at the intersection of race and class.

The book concludes with a holistic view of the political economy of access to justice, postulating that the underlying structural and institutional processes described in the preceding chapters perpetuate economic precarity and engender demand for civil justice. It then considers how civil legal issues can be addressed within and beyond legal frameworks. By focusing on how community organizations build power among people navigating civil justice problems, this concluding chapter looks at the potential to move from a system that individualizes legal problems (and solutions) without addressing underlying conditions of precarity toward more transformative, collective enactments of community power and politics. Taken together, these chapters offer a novel and necessary account of the political economy of the justice gap.

––––––––

It is not possible to fully comprehend the political causes and consequences of US legal institutions without accounting for the substance, meaning, and effects of access to civil justice. Nor is it possible to fully make sense of the American political economy without considering how civil justice problems and their attendant legal remedies construct political power for people in positions of precarity. Perhaps most important, civil legal benefits and protections are essential mechanisms mediating the relationship between denizens and the state (Michener, SoRelle, and Thurston 2022). As such, a thorough accounting of democratic citizenship in the United States demands recognition of the politics of access to civil justice.

Uncivil Democracy sits at the nexus of several distinct scholarly literatures, contributing to our understanding of access to justice, policy feedback, racial politics, and political economy.[23] Bridging these important but disparate literatures as well as integrating them into bottom-up empirical research on civil legal institutions offers a distinctive account that charts pathways of power in the civil legal system, illuminates the racialized political dynamics of the justice gap, incorporates collective organizing into an account of power building within the civil legal system, and gives primacy to the voices and experiences of people at the proverbial bottom of civil legal power structures.

Uncivil Democracy has critical implications for politics, policies, and people. Policymakers at all levels of government have identified access to justice as a key issue in the contemporary political landscape (although as chapter 4

23. The existing sociological and legal scholarship on access to justice places limited emphasis on political economy or politics more broadly, while the existing American political economy literature in the field of political science is largely devoid of direct insights on civil legal systems. Moreover, the interdisciplinary literature on the political economy of civil law overlooks the racialized, individual-level political consequences of people's interactions with civil justice institutions. Relatedly, while racialized processes overdetermine civil legal outcomes, research on US racial politics and racialized policy feedback offer little by way of systematic attention to the civil legal domain (Libgober 2025; Michener 2019b; Michener, SoRelle, and Thurston 2022).

demonstrates, those priorities are often contingent on shifts in political administration). In 2023, for the first time ever, the federal government allocated funds for medical-legal partnerships—unique institutional configurations that merge social policy and legal aid. Increasingly popular "right to counsel" efforts continue to gain steam across cities and states (Benfer et al. 2025). Perennial debates on the relationship between the welfare state, courts, and economy are coming into sharper relief than ever, particularly in the aftermath of COVID-19 emergency policies like the federal eviction moratorium and the state moratoriums on civil debt collection cases (Michener 2023c). We offer an analysis of civil justice, power, and democracy that can meaningfully inform these policy debates.

Uncivil Democracy speaks to some of the most salient, pressing, and practically important policy and political issues in the United States. It also points to a path forward. Beyond simply observing the experiences that people have with civil justice problems, civil legal institutions, and the political ramifications thereof, this book foregrounds power and highlights organizing as a pathway to change.

2

"Every State Has Their Own Kind of System"

MAPPING THE CIVIL LEGAL LANDSCAPE

LEO, A Black man in his fifties who grew up in Alabama, has lived in many different places. By the time he was interviewed for this research in late 2024, Leo had settled in Boulder, Colorado. Despite having lived there for only one year, Leo liked Boulder and anticipated staying for the remainder of his life ("I'm at my resting place"). Notwithstanding his contentedness in Colorado, the "journey" that got him there had been harrowing at times. Leo was a spiritual man who saw good even in his troubles. He believed that he was "blessed" and appreciated the hardships that "allow me to value where I'm at today." But Colorado was a reprieve for Leo precisely because there had been so few other places where he experienced support and security.

Over the course of our conversation, Leo explained how he ended up in Colorado, what he went through in other places, and how he made sense of the systems that structured his cross-country travails. As we recount Leo's experiences, consider what his struggles reveal about the heterogeneity of civil legal institutions across the country and the significance of federalism as a feature of the racialized American political economy.[1] Like Josephine— and all the people whose stories animate the pages of this book—Leo's narrative is not merely an illustrative vignette underscoring points we make in the text. Instead, Leo's experience constitutes compellingly instructive

---

1. Federalism refers to a system of government in which political power is divided both within and across central and regional jurisdictions (e.g., the federal, state, and municipal governments).

evidence broadly reflective of core aspects of processes of civil legal inequality. For this reason, Leo's insights provide a poignant grounding for this chapter's descriptive analysis of the civil legal landscape in the United States.

———

At the start of his interview, Leo almost immediately pointed out Jamila's New York accent. He explained that he was able to identify accents because he has

> traveled a lot of places . . . traveled a lot of states. . . . I can tell if you from Texas. If you're from Mississippi, I can hear your Mississippi. If you from Arkansas, I can hear Arkansas. If you're from Detroit, Michigan, I can hear Detroit. If you from Chi, I can hear Chicago. I can [hear] if you from Queens.

Jamila did indeed grow up in Queens, a borough of New York City. Though many years of living away from Queens has dulled her accent, Leo picked up on it right away. It was an auspicious start to a conversation that came to revolve around Leo's varied experiences living in different parts of the country.

Before moving to Boulder, Leo was "put out" of his home in Alabama. He expressed gratitude that his eviction "pushed" him to explore new opportunities and ultimately led him to Colorado. Still, he admitted that it was a "bad experience" because of "how they handled the situation." In summer 2023, Leo and his (former) partner were surreptitiously removed from their residence, with no notice, the day before his birthday. Just days prior, Leo had paid his landlord $5,000 to get caught up on his rent ($2,500 for back rent plus an astounding $2,500 in fees). Having paid what he owed, Leo thought things were settled. But he was on a month-to-month lease in a state that did not require good cause for eviction and where leases can include clauses exempting landlords from having to give any notice before evicting tenants (LSC 2021).[2] In this context, Leo's landlord had considerable power and faced little

2. Good cause (also known as just cause) statutes protect tenants from eviction, displacement (nonrenewal of lease agreements), and rent increases by requiring that landlords have legally valid reasons for evicting tenants or not renewing their leases. Good cause laws provide tenants with a basis for challenging unjustified evictions. Such laws have been gaining momentum across the country. Since 2019, the states of California, Oregon, Washington, and New York have all adopted good cause eviction statutes (Blount et al. 2023; Legal Aid Society 2024).

accountability. This made it easy and potentially legal to eject Leo from his home with no forewarning. Leo recalled that day vividly and with palpable emotion:

> It was a day before my birthday. . . . You give these people . . . $5,000 to have a roof [over your head] and they just pop up. . . . And [the payment] was in the court records. . . . [The landlord] . . . said, yeah, "I did receive all my money." But you still come for me. That experience, why it was terrible, because . . . it wasn't an eviction, he just came and put us out. . . . He could have just gave us thirty days instead of coming in the rain, and it's hot down South. And you know all of this is going on in the humidity. . . . [It] wasn't a good experience at all. . . . We went to court. Gave him the money. If he wanted the property back, he could just say—it was just on month to month you know—"Hey, I don't want to rent to you no more." Simple. You just give us thirty days to vacate—you see what I'm saying. . . . He could have sent a thirty-day notice. . . . Instead, you got people riding by [during the eviction], they seeing all your everything out [on the street], you know. It's embarrassing. . . . The landlord could have been more considerate in this action.

It is striking that Leo doesn't talk about expectations of better legal protections, more robust support for tenants, greater power in the face of an extractive landlord, or even alternative housing options. His main issue with the eviction was how suddenly and carelessly it was executed—on a rainy, hot, humid day, with Leo's and his partners' possessions humiliatingly strewn on the street in full view of passersby.

What's more is that Leo and his partner went through an eviction—a quintessentially legal process—without legal assistance. When Leo's landlord had initially brought them to court for nonpayment of rent, they were able to get a legal aid attorney (a trained lawyer who advised and represented them at no cost). That attorney helped them to set up a payment arrangement, which Leo followed through on. But just when he completed the payments, Leo's landlord showed up with a sheriff and removed him from the home. When Leo reached out to legal aid a second time in the immediate wake of the eviction, he never received a response. While this made an already difficult circumstance even harder for Leo, it also made sense given the larger context of legal aid in Alabama.

As one of only three states that do not allocate any funding whatsoever for civil legal aid, Alabama legal services attorneys have such limited capacity that they turn away three cases for each case that they take on (Legal Services Alabama 2024). And since almost half the cases at Legal Services Alabama (2023) involve housing, it stands to reason that many of the cases it turns away or cannot respond to, like Leo's, are related to housing. The same year of Leo's eviction, Alabama updated its laws to require landlords to give at least thirty days' notice prior to an eviction—exactly what Leo had desperately needed.[3] But in the absence of legal representation to ensure the fair and appropriate application of that statute, it was not possible for Leo to find remedy in legal reform. While Leo did not seem directly aware of the underfunding that hamstrung Alabama's civil legal infrastructure, he nonetheless observed (without prompting from an interview question) the state and local specificity of eviction processes, lamenting the way things were done in Alabama.

> LEO: They do it different in every state, you know.
> JAMILA: Yeah, they do.
> LEO: *Every state has their own kind of system* the way they like. [In Colorado] they give you . . . a letter of demand if you miss your rent after eight days. The best thing about here, instead of five days' grace, it's like eight days, nine days' grace. Some places is five days; here they'll give you up to eight days, which is nice. Some places it's three. It just depends on what state you're in. Everybody's laws different. And [in Alabama] you go to court, you paying more fees. It's ridiculous, for you to only owe $2,500, but we give you $5,000, and he still came [that day to kick us out]. It sticks with me because I mean, you know, my birthday [was right around then]. . . . He'd taken all of this cash. . . . I just wouldn't do people like that.
> JAMILA: Yeah, I'm with you on that one. . . . How many days did you have between the time that your landlord and the sheriff said they were going to show up to get you out? How many days did you actually have to get out?
> LEO: No days.
> JAMILA: No days? They just showed up and said, "You're leaving now"?
> LEO: Everything out.

Again, though Leo did not formally know the specifics of law or policy, his hunch that "every state has their own kind of system" was correct. And the example he highlighted—tenants being required to pay the cost of legal fees

3. AL Code § 35–9A-441 (2023).

that landlords incur while evicting them—was apt. If Leo had been in New York, California, or Massachusetts, there would have been legal limits on the fees his landlord could charge to cover their own legal expenses. But in Alabama, Leo had no such protections.

After experiencing abrupt dispossession, Leo and his partner went their separate ways. She went to stay with friends, and he found shelter with some of his family. At that point, he began to consider his next steps.

> That's what led to [Boulder] with me thinking, Where do I want my journey to be? . . . I called [Boulder County] and the lady gave me the information. I was like, Where do I want to go? Do I want to go to Raleigh, North Carolina, Charlotte, North Carolina, back to [Michigan]? I don't want to go to Atlanta. So I had this place, Colorado, Boulder. . . . This is what led me here, because I just felt like, Where do I want to go next? . . . That situation kinda amplified me to be where I'm at today. It pushed me.

Leo found a silver lining in the clouds that hovered over him on his rainy eviction day. Yet he didn't find it accidentally; Leo did his research. When deciding where to go, Leo called local county social services offices to evaluate the housing supports he would have access to. He made a constrained but informed choice based on his understanding that social policies were very different across states and localities. When he called Boulder, he spoke to a woman who shared a promising possibility: "We have a voucher program coming up." When Leo heard about Boulders' Housing Choice Voucher (Section 8) lottery, he decided to apply. He applied in October and was notified of his acceptance by November. He moved to Boulder immediately thereafter and has enjoyed a higher standard of living that he attributes to his HUD voucher:

> [The] HUD voucher, it's beautiful. You have to qualify through a lottery, and it gives you an opportunity to have, you know, a diverse lifestyle . . . and to not only just get along with others but even to have the quality of life that you want to have with the living situation. So I look at that as a plus for myself and the quality that it offers.

Even as he expressed appreciation for what he had in Boulder, Leo articulated a recognition of the place-based idiosyncrasies of his experiences. When he discussed receiving legal assistance, for example, he again mentioned that in Alabama, "for some reason I couldn't contact the legal aid for the [eviction]." The reason, as described above, was likely due to Alabama's circumscribed capacity for providing legal services to low-income residents. Importantly, Leo believed that having a lawyer mattered. He thought things would have been much different had he faced eviction in Boulder, where he was more likely to get access to legal counsel:

> Talking to the lawyer, I think, having the lawyer the second time would have worked better. You see what I'm saying. I think anyone should have a lawyer dealing with any legal situation. If that makes sense. . . . Legal counsel is always better. . . . I think the funding [in Boulder] is a great thing. . . . If I was facing eviction, just to use an example for you, I think getting legal aid would be quicker, like quick versus [Alabama]. . . . [In Alabama] I never got a call back [from legal aid]. But I feel like here once you go, if you go to court . . . they probably will say, "OK, well, get legal counseling before you can be evicted." So it's a little, it's a lot different. It's a lot.

Though Leo had not been evicted in Boulder, his suppositions about the city's policy context were reasonably accurate. Boulder voters approved the No Eviction Without Representation (NEWR) ballot initiative in 2020. NEWR provides free legal representation to all Boulder tenants facing eviction. Leo did not have direct knowledge of NEWR, but he intuited the availability of legal representation based on his understanding of Boulder's social policy ecosystem. Crucially, Leo did not limit his comments to discussing legal representation. Rather, he implicated the larger political economy, noting that the (relative) lack of scarcity in Boulder made it possible to receive assistance that would keep you out of court altogether.

> The city of Boulder . . . wants to eliminate homelessness the best they can in their particular county and district. . . . Beautiful thing about being here is they do have lovely assistance . . . to try to help with assisting people that is facing evictions in Boulder. So that's the most beautiful thing I could say that here you don't have to wait months and months and weeks and weeks to get assistance if you're facing eviction. [That assistance] keep you from [having] to get to that point where you have to go to court. They have these programs, a lot of outreach programs that people can go to . . . versus [Alabama]. . . . You're not gonna get any assistance [in Alabama]. You just have to figure it out. . . . It's totally different.[4]

4. Even while Leo's experiences tap into important elements of the Boulder policy context and reflect larger patterns observed in our qualitative data, it is also worth acknowledging that

Leo offered an experiential perspective that was refracted through the lens of federalism—the institutional feature of the US polity that enabled the vast place-based differences he observed (Grumbach 2022; Kousser, Michener, and Tolbert 2024; Michener 2018). Leo's vantage point incorporated his knowledge of what Colorado offered as well as a comparative sense of what other places withheld. Alabama was just one example. Leo also referenced Georgia, where he spent several years. He had applied for the Housing Choice Voucher program in Georgia, but he remained on the waiting list there.

> I did the same thing in Georgia, and I'm still waiting on it. Let me say it again, I signed up for the same type of [housing voucher] program I am on now versus the program there. You know how fast it was for the lottery [in Colorado]. . . . Within days you knew if your name was picked . . . so that was fast. . . . Did you know I'm still on a pending waiting list from Georgia? . . . So *the landscapes in the government* for me, and how they handle money, and how they handle policies and living situations, *it's totally different*. I mean, you select apples and oranges, and apples are different than oranges, and that's just the way it is.

Toward the end of the conversation, Leo talked about what his experiences meant for his views of government and politics. Again, he emphasized the importance of understanding the varied landscape of state and local policy and governance.

> I tell people, if you want to know something about where you're going to live always know the state, local, higher government. That's the most important thing, and how the laws, because of states . . . everybody laws are different. You go to Alaska. It's going to be different. You go to Commonwealth of Boston, Massachusetts, it's going to be different. You go to the Commonwealth . . . Lexington, Louisville, Kentucky. So it's always good to know. Before I came here, I wanted to know, and everybody I came across was like, "Wow, you're very smart how you did it." . . . I just didn't come and

---

his experiences offer a distinct vantage point. June, a Latina woman we interviewed in Boulder, relayed a very different experience with eviction. June was a longtime HUD resident who lost her HUD voucher and was unable to get support in time to fend off her eviction. June and Leo did not have conflicting narratives (some of what she told us about the availability of resources to support tenants aligned with what Leo said), but June did have different experiences and a contrasting vantage point. June, who had only ever lived in Colorado, did not have the comparative perspective that Leo brought to his interpretation of the Boulder context.

say, "I want to be homeless." . . . You have to have a plan wherever you go . . .
So I tell people before moving always research these places, know the
government—the municipal government to your state government. You
see what I'm saying important. You'll know how the laws protect you
against eviction [or] if you lose a job. All sorts of things, you know.

Leo's exhortations underscore the realities and stakes of a political economy
marked by federalism, decentralization, and immense heterogeneity across
states. While scholars have scrutinized such heterogeneity in various realms
of social policy (Michener 2018; Soss, Fording, and Schram 2011; Tani 2016),
the landscape of civil legal policies remains obscured. Like much of the US
"policyscape," civil legal policies and institutions are complex, varied, and dynamic.[5] This chapter describes the diverse and unwieldy panorama of US civil
justice systems, and the correspondingly wide geographic scope of the justice
gap. It charts the state-level structures underlying unequal access to civil legal
representation and the policy patterns that determine such access. By delineat-
ing the institutional components of civil legal systems at the state and national
levels, this chapter lays a crucial foundation for a clear-eyed assessment of the
politics of access to justice.

Access to Civil Justice in the United States

The United States is relatively lackluster in providing access to civil legal justice. The World Justice Project (WJP) *Rule of Law Index* (2024) considers
"civil justice" a key dimension of its systematic cross-national measurement,
defining it in terms of the extent to which "ordinary people can resolve their
grievances peacefully and effectively through the civil justice system." To
measure this, the WJP index gauges seven subfactors, appraising the degree to
which civil justice systems are accessible and affordable, free of discrimination,
free of corruption, free of improper influence by public officials, not subject
to unreasonable delay, effectively enforced, and offer accessible and impartial
alternative dispute mechanisms. Based on these combined factors, the United
States' civil justice score is 0.63 (on a scale from 0 to 1). If civil justice were a
college course, the United States would earn a D grade.

---

5. Suzanne Mettler (2016, 369) defined the "policyscape" as "a landscape densely laden with
policies created in the past that have themselves become established institutions, bearing consequences for governing operations, the policy agenda, and political behavior."

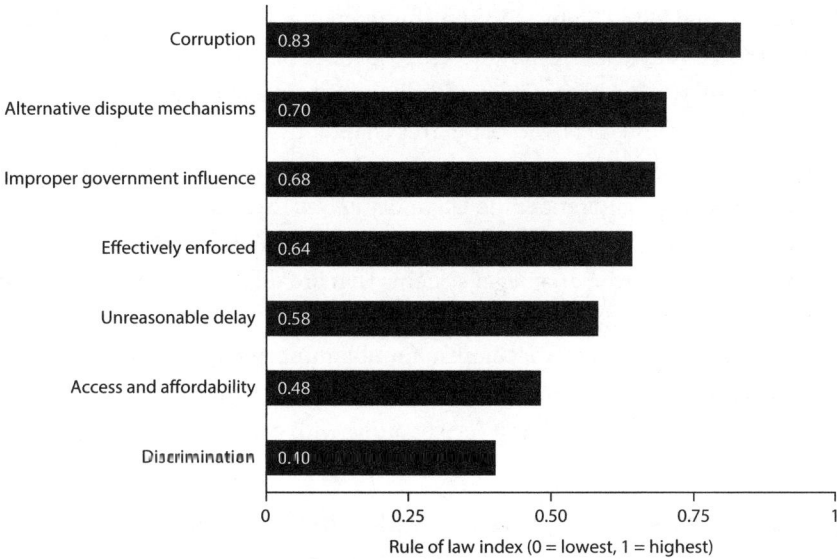

FIGURE 2.1. US civil justice component scores
Source: WJP Rule of Law Index 2024.

Comparatively, the United States ranks 33rd out of 142 countries included in the scoring. For context, this means that access to civil justice in the United States is on par with countries that have vastly fewer resources, like Barbados (0.62), Malaysia (0.62), Kazakhstan (0.62), Cyprus (0.62), Saint Vincent and the Grenadines (0.62), and Portugal (0.63). If we limit our comparison to high-income countries, the United States ranks 31st of 47, falling far behind Denmark (0.87)—the top-ranked country—but also lagging many ostensible peers, including Germany (0.82), Japan (0.77), Singapore (0.79), South Korea (0.76), Australia (0.74), the United Kingdom (0.71), and Hong Kong SAR (0.71).[6]

As figure 2.1 depicts, among the seven factors determining the US civil justice score, the lowest relative scores concern freedom from discrimination (0.40) and access and affordability (0.48). In those categories, the United States ranks last or close to last among its high-income peers (45th and 47th, respectively, of 47), and relatively low globally (115th and 107th, respectively, of 142). These scores and ranks supply cross-national comparative evidence of inadequate access to civil justice for racially and economically marginalized

---

6. The Hong Kong Special Administrative Region of the People's Republic of China.

people in the United States. But they only scratch the surface of the patterns pertinent to understanding how access to justice operates in the United States. Deeper analyses require scrutiny of both the national and state levels.

Turning to these tasks, the rest of this chapter describes the geographically unequal mosaic of civil legal institutions and policies in the United States. The dynamics we expound render the US polity *uncivil* in a most fundamental way. Civil statutes are complex, ever changing, and implemented within a fragmented array of adversarial legal systems that are difficult for nonexperts to navigate (Kagan 1991, 2019). In this context, access to justice through civil legal representation is a pivotal mechanism for obtaining, retaining, and protecting the social and economic benefits, as well as protections that are integral to the welfare state (Michener 2023a). As we (along with coauthor Chloe Thurston) argue,

> Aspects of the civil legal system clearly reflect foundational prerogatives and explicit programmatic efforts of welfare policy. Foremost is the critical role the civil legal system plays in navigating disputes over public benefits, making it a central institution in the implementation of welfare policy. . . . [T]he civil courts also clearly fulfill (or fail to fulfill) a risk protection function. (Michener, SoRelle, and Thurston 2022, 161).

Despite the centrality of civil justice to people's basic well-being, social scientists lack a comprehensive mapping of the policies and institutions that determine civil legal representation. As we sketch the structure of US civil legal institutions as well as examine the emergence, distribution, and substance of civil legal policies, we focus here on the state level because—as Leo makes powerfully clear—states are a crucial pathway through which access to justice flows and a core part of how civil (in)justice is experienced. Federalism and state politics are primary mechanisms of racial, economic, and political stratification in the United States (Grumbach 2022; Grumbach and Michener 2022; Michener 2018, 2024; Miller 2008; Riker 1964). By constructing a state-level picture of access to justice, we clarify essential institutional realities.

Federalism and the Structure of US Civil Legal Institutions

Like many US institutions, civil legal institutions and processes are extensively fragmented across states and localities (Michener 2018). Nothing reveals the sprawling nature of those institutions more acutely than what we heard from our research participants and what we saw with our own eyes observing

```
                    ┌─────────────────┐
                    │ Landlord gives tenant │
                    │  notice of possible   │
                    │      eviction         │
                    └─────────────────┘
```

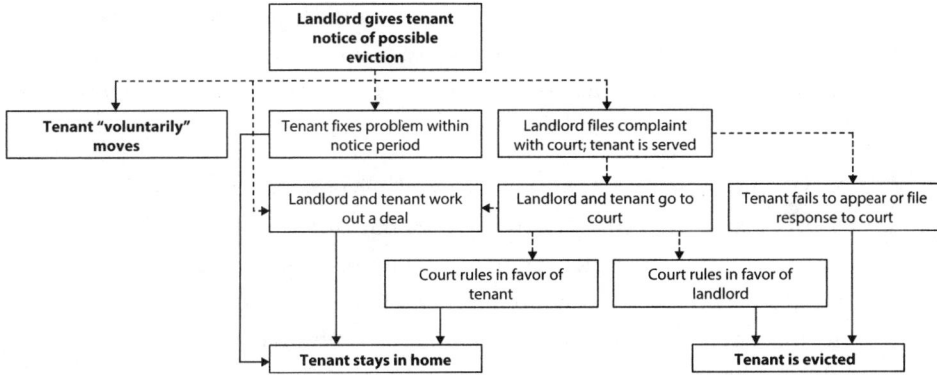

FIGURE 2.2. Basic eviction process and outcomes

housing courts across the country. When it comes to evictions, for example, the most basic elements of the legal process are similar nearly everywhere (see figure 2.2).

In every state, legal evictions require that tenants receive some form of notice specifying a timeline to vacate the property and giving details on the opportunity to appear in court. Whether tenants actually receive such notice, however, and what happens when they do not, varies markedly across states. In Detroit, for example, a systemic failure to deliver the mail means that many tenants were never receiving notices from the court after their landlords' filed evictions. Tyler, a lead attorney who had spent decades providing free legal representation to Detroit tenants, described the problem this way:

> One big issue in Detroit is mail service. . . . [Legally] proper service can be two attempts at physically serving the tenant, followed by tacking [the notice] on their door. . . . And we are about a mile and a half from the court, maybe not even quite that far. And it very often takes us three and four weeks to get a notice from the court. I mean, if we relied on the notices for the motions we file to tell us when our hearing is, we would miss three-quarters of our hearings or more. We don't. We don't. We check online to see what's happening with that case we filed a motion on. "Oh, it's up next week." So, you know, we know that. But we also know from that, that mail service doesn't work in Detroit. And even when you fail to show up at the first hearing, what do you get? You get a mail notice at the second hearing. So, you know, that continues to be a huge problem. And I believe that that's affecting a lot of cases.

These delayed or missing notices primarily affect the legal process by causing tenants to miss hearings. In Detroit, this frequently leads to a "default judgment": a ruling in favor of the plaintiff (landlord) when the defendant (tenant) fails to appear in court. In Tyler's estimation,

> Defaults in Detroit are huge. I don't know what they're like elsewhere, it'd be interesting to know at some point, but in Detroit it's right about 25 percent. And of the [default judgment] cases where [an order of writ to evict] is signed for the bailiff to evict somebody, . . . of those writs that are signed, about 70 percent of the writs signed are from default cases, so defaults are a huge, huge, huge factor here.

Tyler's curiosity about whether Detroit was different is especially germane. Though there is little consistently collected evidence, data from other major cities suggest heterogeneous patterns. A recent study looking at eviction outcomes in New York City between 2016 and 2022 found that 16 percent of all eviction filings there result in a default judgment (Brenner et al., 2023). In Philadelphia, 36 percent of cases end in default judgments (Chiappetta and Howell 2022). In Milwaukee, the default judgment rate was between 29 and 38 percent, depending on whether the tenant appeared in court (Borsuk and Kertscher 2023).

By all appearances, the problem of default judgments is acute in many places, but much worse in some than others. Moreover, the causes of the problem vary considerably. Some studies suggest that racism is a factor, as default judgments are more common among Black and Latinx tenants (Dowdall et al. 2021). Others find that geography is the culprit, with tenants who live farther away from courts more likely to be issued default judgments (Hoffman and Strezhnev 2023). But Detroit's mail problem is distinct. In Philadelphia, for instance, if a landlord or their attorneys cannot demonstrate that tenants have been properly notified, an eviction case is automatically dismissed (Chiappetta and Howell 2022). Tyler explained that Detroit officials did not take such an approach:

> We've talked about the defaults and the need to do something about them, and the mail service. And the administration's position is kind of, "Well, it's not my fault there's a bad mail service." Well, not saying it is. But on the other hand, this is a very large city. It's incredibly disrespectful that the post service is still, you know . . . struggling with that. And the other implication is that, well, if you get ahold of more people and they come to court, then there's more that we're going to have to represent. Well, of course there is,

but that's not the reason not to do it. So there is, you know, a lot there. I mean, we try to weigh in as much as we can on sort of policy issues and then do what we can to represent as many as we can.

Detroit's legal infrastructure is uniquely inhibited by political-economic factors including a substandard postal service along with inept responses from elected and legal officials. In this context, the problem of default judgments has continued, even in the wake of recent policies providing more extensive access to counsel for tenants facing eviction.

Default judgments and defective mail are barely the tip of a gargantuan iceberg of disparate policies and practices related to civil courts and legal access across states and cities. The range and substance of these policies is astounding. For instance, some states (Connecticut, Maryland, and Washington) have enacted policies that ensure access to legal counsel for nearly everyone facing eviction (National Coalition for a Civil Right to Counsel 2025). Others only ensure such protections for public housing residents (Minnesota and Nebraska), and others still (Alabama, Arizona, Wisconsin, etc.) do not provide counsel for tenants who face losing their homes (National Coalition for a Civil Right to Counsel 2025).

Considering a different aspect of legal structure, in Texas, eviction cases are adjudicated by elected justices of the peace who do not need to be lawyers or have formal legal training. Anyone over the age of eighteen who has been a Texas resident for at least one year can become a justice of the peace. Correspondingly, tenants can appoint almost anyone to represent them in the legal proceedings, including nonlawyers without formal legal training. As one Texas tenant organizer told us, "The way it works in Texas is you—because it's the justice of the peace side of this and the justice of the peace isn't a lawyer—you don't have to be a lawyer to represent a tenant in an eviction hearing."

Yet another variation in civil legal institutions lies in the structure of the courts themselves. In some states, certain types of civil legal problems are adjudicated in specialized courts where the entire docket is comprised of a single category of cases. For example, several states (e.g., Maryland and Massachusetts) have specialized courts for housing that are dedicated solely to overseeing disputes between landlords and tenants.[7] When these specialized courts emerged in the 1970s—the civil analog to "problem-solving courts" in

---

7. Variation exists even within specialized housing courts, with some housing courts seeing a comprehensive range of issues, while other specialize in areas like code enforcement or evictions.

the criminal context—proponents argued they would allow for judges and court staff to develop expertise on a particular legal issue, facilitating better dispute resolution (Scott 1979; Steinberg 2017). Nonspecialized courts, by contrast, see all manner of civil cases with judges frequently rotating through different types of claims.

These and innumerable other legal details shape the experiences that tenants have in court, their need for legal counsel, and the material outcomes of their civil legal problems. There is no singular experience or uniform system, and there are vanishingly few standard practices when it comes to civil legal institutions. This means that we cannot provide a concise encapsulation of all civil legal processes across the United States. Nor can we offer a comprehensive primer for the uninitiated reader who may not know much about how civil legal systems operate. Instead, as you will see throughout this book, the common thread that runs through US civil legal systems is not their specific policies or practices; it is their embeddedness in a larger political economy that structures their contours. Federalism, racial inequality, economic precarity, and social welfare retrenchment are all core features of that political economy. This chapter zeros in on federalism, the state and local heterogeneity that it generates, and the implications for access to justice.

The Fragmented Provision of Civil Legal Services

Just as civil courts operate in varied ways, civil legal assistance does as well. Legal aid for civil problems is provided by a vast array of separate and largely independent organizations funded by multiple sources. The system is so disjointed that there is no official count of civil legal aid programs in the country. The National Legal Aid and Defender Association (NLADA) estimated that as of 2019, there were 1,147 programs employing 6,783 full-time attorneys to offer civil legal assistance to at least 2 million low-income people (Consortium for the National Equal Justice Library 2019). This was made possible by the approximately $2.2 billion flowing into civil legal systems across the country. Figure 2.3 illustrates the basic organizational configuration of the programs that supply civil legal services from different funding sources.

The largest source of support for civil legal assistance comes through the federally funded LSC, which chapter 4 examines in rich historical detail. The LSC subsidizes 130 nonprofit legal assistance organizations that operate roughly 900 offices scattered across every US state and territory. These programs take many forms—from law clinics and medical-legal partnerships, to integrated social service providers and joint civil-criminal legal aid programs.

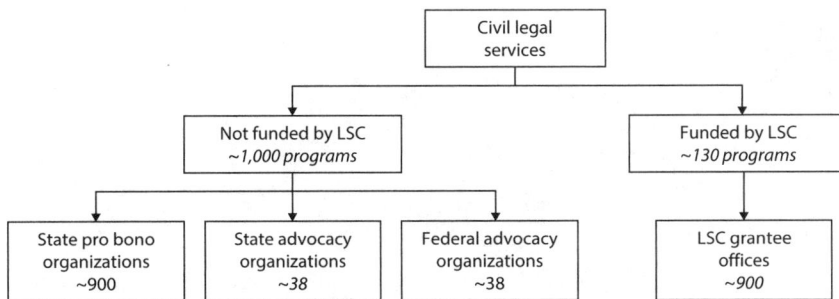

FIGURE 2.3. Configuration of US civil legal assistance programs

Non-LSC-funded programs—dominated by pro bono organizations in the states—are also prevalent across the country. Despite being roughly equal in terms of the raw number of programs/offices, they generally have far lower capacity and serve significantly fewer people than their LSC-funded counterparts (Consortium for the National Equal Justice Library 2019).

Overall, this hodgepodge of legal services programs is extraordinarily uneven across states, both in terms of funding and capacity. For example, Alabama has only one LSC-funded legal assistance program, while New York has seven and California has eleven. These differences are not solely a function of varying state populations or demographic profiles. They reflect the distinct supply (of lawyers) and demand (for legal services) in each state—both of which are a product of larger political-economic dynamics. To further explore the heterogeneity in access to justice, the remainder of this chapter highlights salient metrics of state variation (e.g., the numbers of civil legal attorneys and the sources of funding for civil legal representation) as well as longitudinal patterns of policymaking to address the justice gap.

State Variation in Civil Legal Demand and Supply

The National Center for State Courts recorded more than fifteen million incoming civil cases in state courts in 2023 (roughly one million fewer than the number of criminal cases).[8] The quantity and nature of cases—important indicators of the demand for civil legal assistance—varied widely across states. Florida and Texas led the country, each with more than a million civil cases in state courts in 2023, while Alaska, Maine, and Vermont each had fewer than

8. For details on civil caseloads in state courts, see https://www.courtstatistics.org/court -statistics/interactive-caseload-data-displays/csp-stat-nav-cards-first-row/csp-stat-civil.

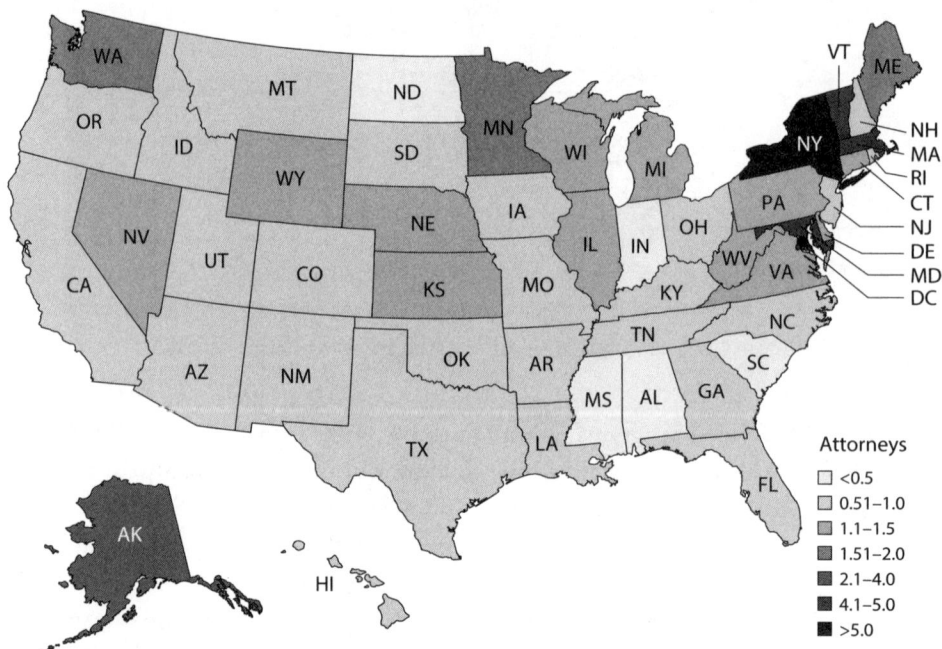

FIGURE 2.4. Civil legal aid attorneys per 10,000 people
under 200 percent poverty level
Source: National Center for Access to Justice 2021.

twenty thousand cases. Even adjusting for population, vast per capita differences persist (Gibson et al. 2024).

Contract cases are the most common category of civil matters in state trial courts. In 2023, 48 percent of incoming civil cases were contract cases, followed by small claims (23 percent), probate/estate cases (12 percent), tort cases (6 percent), mental health cases (4 percent), and a miscellaneous remainder of appeals and other kinds of cases (Gibson et al. 2024). A significant majority (72 percent in 2022) of contract cases involve landlord/tenant disputes (Hamilton 2024).[9] State variation in this metric is substantial. For example, in 2023, Maryland and Nevada had the highest rate of contract cases (with 8,024 and 4,377 cases per 100,000 residents, respectively). Minnesota and South Carolina had the lowest (with 454 and 528 cases per 100,000 residents, respectively) (Gibson et al. 2024). These differences do not map neatly

9. Other examples of contract cases involve debt collection, employment disputes, mortgage foreclosures, and any form of contract fraud.

TABLE 2.1 Civil Legal Funding Sources in 2021

Source	Amount
Other public funds*	$1,031,304,353.87
LSC	$409,293,476.00
State appropriation	$318,682,770.93
Foundation/corporate grants	$272,227,845.38
Other strategies**	$190,136,024.72
IOLTA[†]	$172,288,250.31
Legal community	$152,812,188.00
Cy pres[††]	$77,001,938.00

Source: National Legal Aid Funding Data, abarray.org.

* This includes federal funds (other than those provided via the LSC), state funds (other than those included in state fines and fees or state appropriations), and local funding.

** This includes a wide range of other funding sources like special events, attorney's fees, and nonattorney individual campaigns.

[†] IOLTA accounts are interest-generating trust accounts used to hold money belonging to the clients of legal professionals. Instead of earning interest on the client's behalf, the interest from an IOLTA account is funneled to state bar associations to fund legal assistance for low-income clients and other charitable causes. Over the years, IOLTA programs have funded many beneficial community legal programs, legal aid offices, and pro bono work.

[††] Cy pres, which translates to "as near as possible," is a legal practice that permits a court to award any unallocated, unclaimed, or undeliverable funds—most commonly from class action suits—to a charitable or nonprofit organization that would advance the interests of the class. A cy pres is sometimes allocated to legal services programs.

onto state partisanship or ideology, though they are almost certainly a product of a complex web of political-economic processes that determine whether and how denizens find redress in state courts. We do not attempt to explain the puzzle of state variation in contract cases (that is a different, if important, inquiry than what we take up here). Instead, our main point is to highlight indicators of varied demand for legal representation.

A similar mélange characterizes the supply side of the justice gap. As figure 2.4 shows, the number of available civil legal aid attorneys (relative to the number of people living below 200 percent of the federal poverty line) is abysmally low across the country. Still, the variation is striking. Places like Connecticut, New York, Washington (state), and Washington, DC, boast relatively high numbers of civil legal attorneys (over one per ten thousand people experiencing poverty), while states like Alabama, Colorado, Mississippi, and others lag significantly behind. This is the clearest indication of geographically unequal access to civil legal representation.

TABLE 2.2 Sources of State Funding for Civil Legal Aid

Appropriation only	Court fees/fines only	Both	None
Alaska	Arkansas	California	Alabama
Arizona	Kansas	Colorado	Florida
Delaware	Louisiana	Connecticut	Idaho
Iowa	Mississippi	Georgia	
Massachusetts	Missouri	Hawaii	
Minnesota	Montana	Illinois	
New Hampshire	Nebraska	Indiana	
New Jersey	Nevada	Kentucky	
New York	North Carolina	Maine	
Oklahoma	North Dakota	Maryland	
Utah	South Carolina	Michigan	
Vermont	South Dakota	New Mexico	
Washington	Tennessee	Ohio	
Wisconsin	Wyoming	Oregon	
		Pennsylvania	
		Rhode Island	
		Texas	
		Virginia	
		West Virginia	

Source: American Bar Association Resource Center for Access to Justice Initiatives as of 2018.

Another way to gauge state heterogeneity on the supply side is by considering the sources of funding that states rely on to pay for civil legal services. While national LSC funds are a primary source of support, as shown in table 2.1, states engage an array of sources to finance civil legal assistance including court fines and fees, legislative appropriations from state revenues, other public funds (such as those that come from local governments), and more. Indeed, these state and local funding sources are ever increasing in the face of the ballooning need for legal aid. Between 2003 and 2021, state appropriations for legal aid grew by 343 percent (from $72 to $319 million) while "other public funds" (a large portion of which came from state and local funding) increased by a whopping 426 percent (from $176 million to over $1 billion) (National Legal Aid Funding Data 2024).

Notwithstanding growing state investments, states have taken very different approaches to funding civil legal aid. Table 2.2 illustrates the mix of revenue sources states use to support legal services. For example, Alabama, Florida, and Idaho stand out for having no state appropriations for legal aid. Other states like Arkansas, Louisiana, Nebraska, and North Dakota use the extractive and sometimes predatory practice of levying court fines and fees to pay for legal aid (Page and Soss 2021). Some states rely solely on legislative appropriations for funding. Others still, such as California, Pennsylvania, and Texas, leverage all of these tools to fund their civil legal systems. One consequence of depending on such a variegated amalgam of funding structures is deep geographic inequity among the states. Though the extent of those disparities is hard to track given the loosely coordinated nature of civil legal institutions, some estimates have suggested that the best resourced states—concentrated in the mid-Atlantic, Midwest, Northeast, and West—can garner as much as ten times the funds of their less resourced peers, predominantly the Southern and Mountain West states (see Houseman 2015).

The Descriptive Contours of State Policy on Civil Legal Representation

Funding, of course, is only one piece of the state policy puzzle for governing access to civil justice. With the aim of more systematically mapping the scope and substance of policies addressing civil legal representation in the United States, we collected data on all state bill proposals related to civil legal protections between 1990 and 2016. The data were drawn from Lexis Nexis State Capital, a comprehensive database that provides summary information on state legislative activity beginning in 1990. Together with a team of five research assistants, we identified and coded 823 bill proposals initiated in the states during the specified period. We identified the bills by searching Lexis Nexis (on a state-by-state basis) for six key phrases: legal services, indigent defense, legal assistance, legal aid, indigent services, and Legal Services Corporation. Though we found significant overlap in the results that turned up using various terms, we opted to use all six search terms to identify as many relevant bills as possible. After identifying all the distinct bills, we developed codes based on an initial review of a small sample of bills from a variety of states.[10] The coding process involved collecting data on the following attributes of each bill: the status of the bill

10. Data also include house and senate resolutions. Once the coding scheme was established, each of the research assistants undertook significant training on how to employ it. When it was

(whether it was passed or not), whether the bill was specifically focused on low-income people, if the bill was specifically related to civil legal representation, the main population that the bill targeted, and the primary subject of the bill.

What actions did state policymakers take with respect to civil legal representation between 1990 and 2016? How have those actions varied by state? We consider the following questions: How many bills addressing access to counsel were proposed and enacted, and how did those rates vary by time and place? What aspects of representation did those bills address, what remedies did they employ, and how did those substantive features vary by state?

Civil Legal Representation Bills Proposed and Enacted

Between 1990 and 2016, just over a quarter (28 percent) of the 823 bills addressing civil legal representation considered at the state level were adopted. Figure 2.5 depicts the number of bills that were proposed and passed by year for this period. In general, the number of bills considered and adopted each year has grown over time. In 1990, the states cumulatively considered fewer than twenty bills addressing civil legal representation. By 2016, however, the states combined to propose just over 100 access-to-counsel bills in their legislative chambers. Two notable spikes in bill proposal and passage emerge after 1996 and 2010, respectively. Between 1990 and 1995, an average of 8 bills addressing access to counsel were proposed each year, and 2 were enacted annually. Between 1996 and 2010, the average number of bills proposed across the states rose to 21, with the number of bills enacted in an average year increasing to 5. Between 2011 and 2016, those numbers increase even more dramatically, with 76 bills proposed in an average year and 23 becoming law.

While further investigation is necessary to determine the origin of these spikes, there are two important federal trends that likely inform these shifts. Wave elections in 1994 and 2010 ushered in new Republican and Democratic majorities in Congress, respectively. Following the party's takeover in 1994, the Republican-led Congress enacted major cuts to federal legal services funding in the 1996 appropriations act, while Democratic leaders worked to reverse

---

clear that the coding process was systematic (intercoder reliability > 95 percent), we proceeded to code the full set of bills.

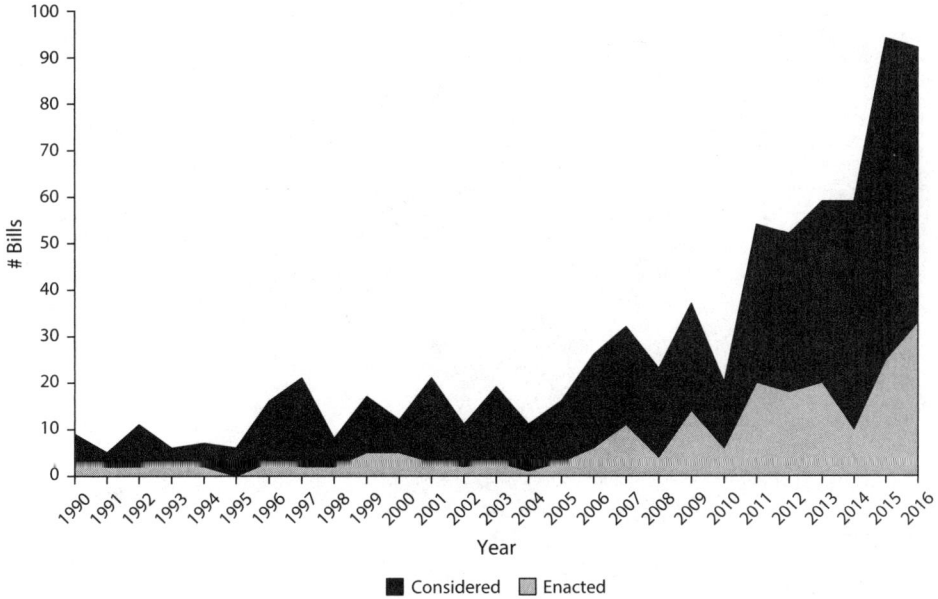

FIGURE 2.5. State bills considered and adopted, 1990–2016

those cuts after resuming control in 2010. It would be reasonable to expect state legislatures to respond to both considerable shifts in access to federal support. Similarly, federal policy changes like welfare reform in 1996 and health care reform in 2010—both of which enacted changes to benefits that affected issues central to the civil legal process—may be driving state attention to access to justice measures as well.

Of course, not all states contribute equally to the number of bills proposed and enacted. As figure 2.6 demonstrates, states have varied dramatically in terms of legislative activity on legal services. New Jersey and New York proposed more than fifty access-to-counsel bills between 1990 and 2016, while eighteen states proposed fewer than ten laws in the same twenty-six-year period. Interestingly, however, the amount of legislative action in a particular state does not correlate with the rate of successful passage.

Figure 2.7 presents the number of successful statutes enacted and the rate of bill passage between 1990 and 2016 by state. While New Jersey and New York lead the pack in bill proposals, they have lower rates of enactment, with each state passing fewer than five access-to-justice laws, respectively, between

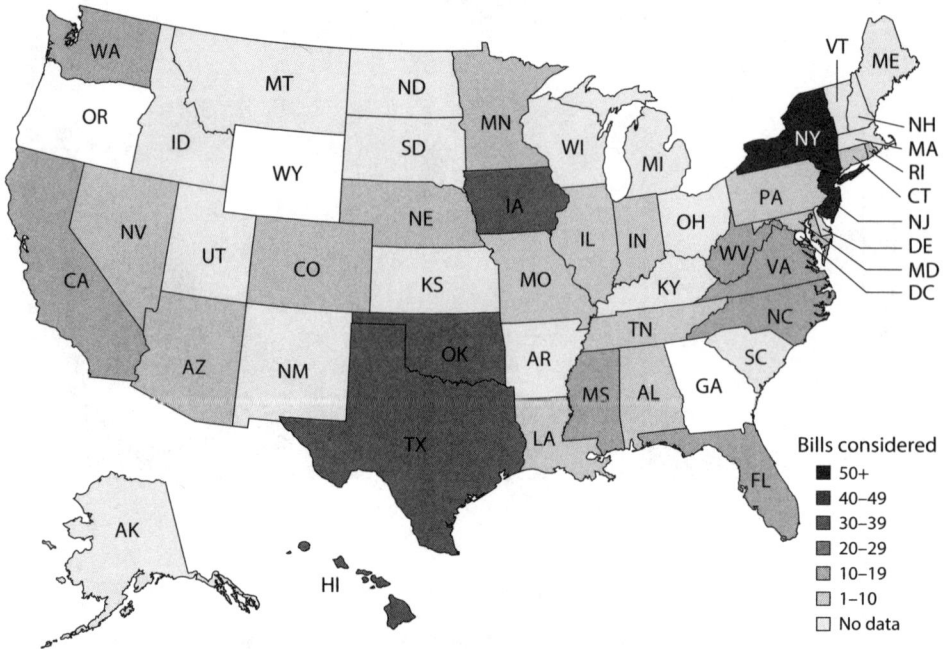

FIGURE 2.6. Civil legal representation bills proposed by state

1990 and 2016. By contrast, California, Colorado, Iowa, Louisiana, Texas, and Virginia have enacted the most statutes for this period. These states represent a diverse group with respect to region, partisan governance, and the demographics of their citizenry. Another group of states, predominantly in the Mountain states and Northern Plains, are notable for relatively high rates of passage on a more limited number of bills.

Policymaking with respect to civil legal representation varies dramatically by state. Some states have been quite active in proposing legislation to address civil legal representation, but limited in their ability to enact those statutes. Other states have proposed and enacted a relatively high number of bills. Finally, a handful of states, including Alabama, Alaska, Connecticut, Indiana, Kentucky, Massachusetts, Minnesota, Missouri, Montana, New Hampshire, New Mexico, and South Carolina, remain laggards, falling behind in both proposing and enacting bills related to civil legal representation. It is possible, of course, that some of these states may have strong statutes in place that predate our data, but they certainly were not active in the more than quarter century we examine here.

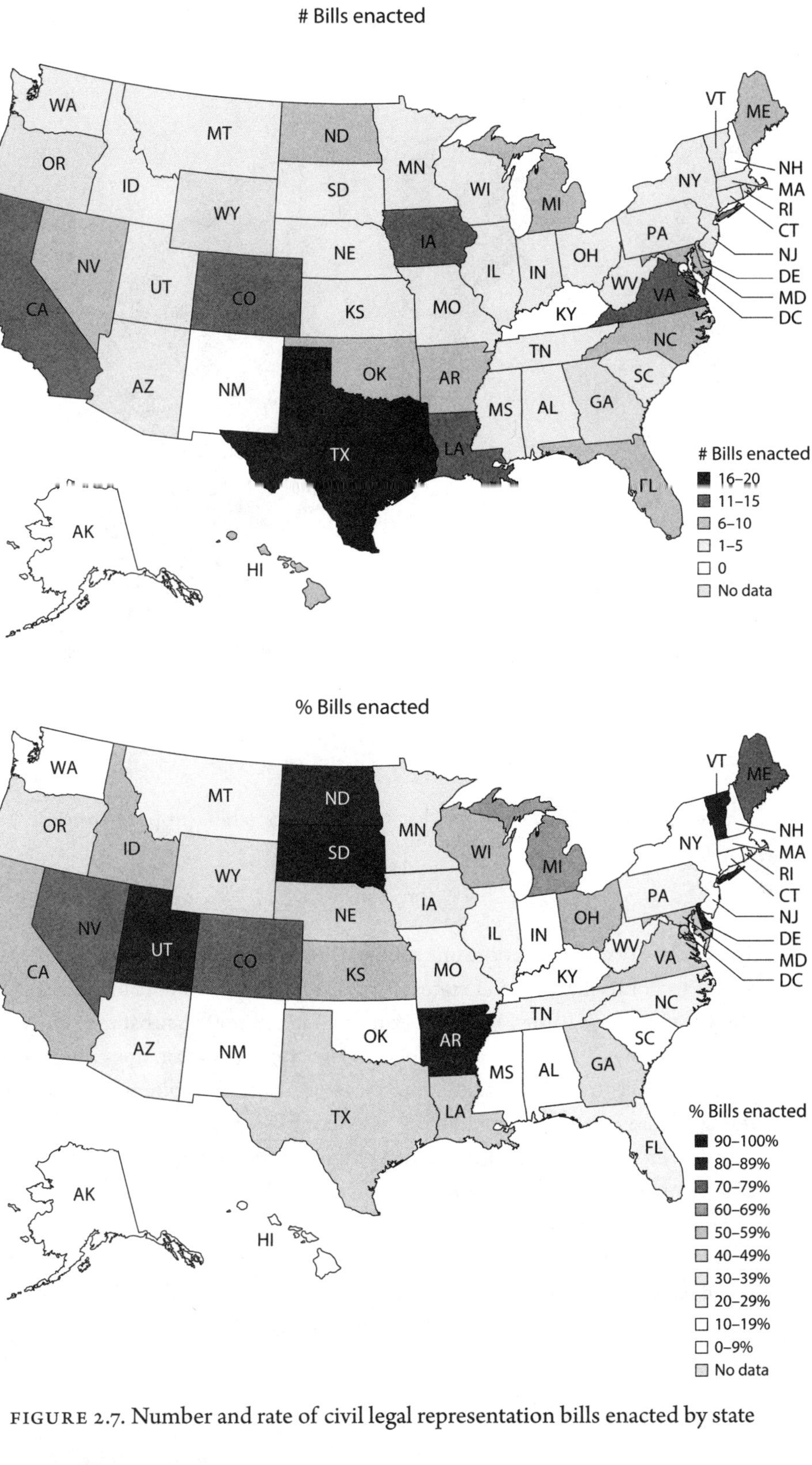

Bills enacted

# Bills enacted	
■	16–20
▨	11–15
▨	6–10
□	1–5
□	0
□	No data

% Bills enacted

% Bills enacted	
■	90–100%
■	80–89%
▨	70–79%
▨	60–69%
▨	50–59%
▨	40–49%
□	30–39%
□	20–29%
□	10–19%
□	0–9%
□	No data

FIGURE 2.7. Number and rate of civil legal representation bills enacted by state

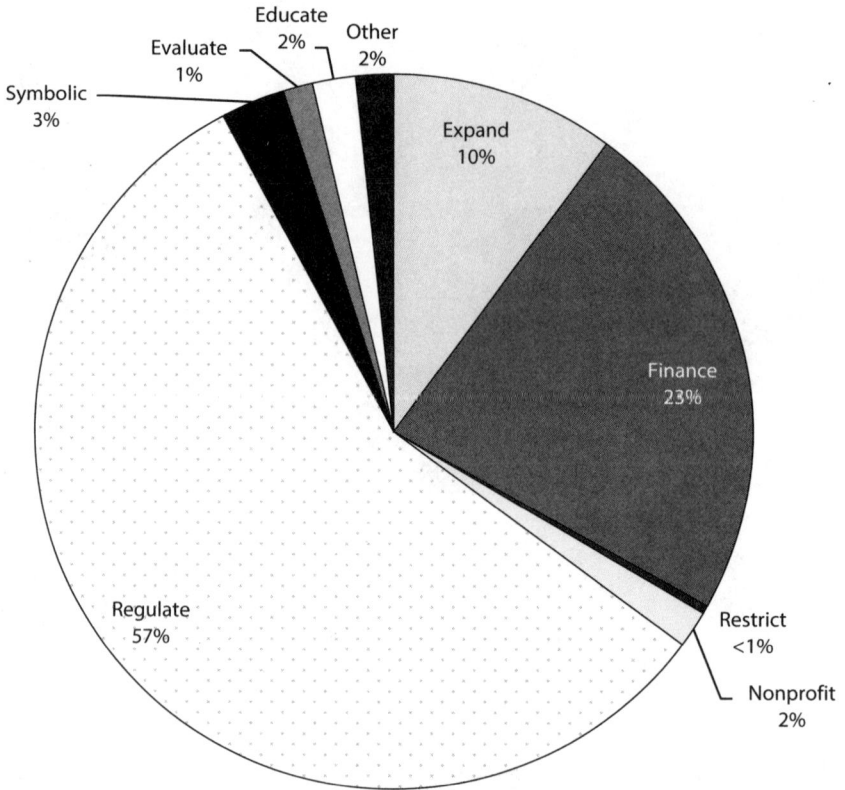

FIGURE 2.8. Substance of civil legal representation bills proposed by state

Substance of Civil Legal Representation Bills

The volume of statutes is only one salient measure of policymaking to address access to counsel across the states. It is also necessary to consider the substance of these statutes. We have conceptualized policy substance in two important ways. First, what aspect of civil legal representation does the policy address? We established eight subject categories to describe what bills are doing: expanding services, financing, restricting services, providing nonprofit support, enacting regulations, taking symbolic actions, requiring evaluation, and creating educational incentives. As figure 2.8 illustrates, the most common feature of proposed statutes is regulation.

More than half of all bills (57 percent) proposed between 1990 and 2016 regulated civil legal service provision in the states. These bills focused on setting rules for everything from the types of attorneys who can benefit from state

TABLE 2.3 Rate of Passage and Percent of All Bills Passed by Type

Type of bill	Rate of passage	All bills passed
Regulate	30%	60%
Finance	20%	16%
Expand	25%	9%
Restrict	67%	1%
Symbolic	63%	6%
Evaluate	45%	2%
Nonprofit support	21%	1%
Educational incentive	25%	2%
Other	46%	3%

funding for representation to policies regulating the services clients can access. About another quarter of the bills (23 percent) specified financing arrangements for civil legal representation, such as directing revenue from court filing fees to support civil legal services. One of every ten bills proposed was designed to expand access to legal representation through, for example, expanding appropriations or extending service to new beneficiaries. The remaining bills covered a range of functions from providing support for nonprofits engaged in civil legal representation and offering educational incentives for law students to participate in legal aid to evaluating existing programs.

Table 2.3 presents both the rate of passage for each type of bill and percent of all passed bills each type accounts for between 1990 and 2016. These results suggest that on average, only slight disparities exist between rates of bill proposal and passage. Laws to regulate access to counsel are slightly overrepresented, with 60 percent of all enacted bills focusing on regulation (compared to 57 percent of bills proposed). By contrast, laws to finance and expand civil legal representation are both slightly underrepresented (respectively, 16 percent enacted versus 23 percent proposed, and 9 percent enacted versus 10 percent proposed). It is notable how different the rates of passage are among bill types. While they represent a much smaller number of the bills considered, bills that restricted or evaluated access to counsel, or made only symbolic contributions, had the highest rates of passage (67, 45, and 63 percent, respectively). Bills that expanded access, or provided support or incentives to promote civil legal representation, passed at significantly lower rates.

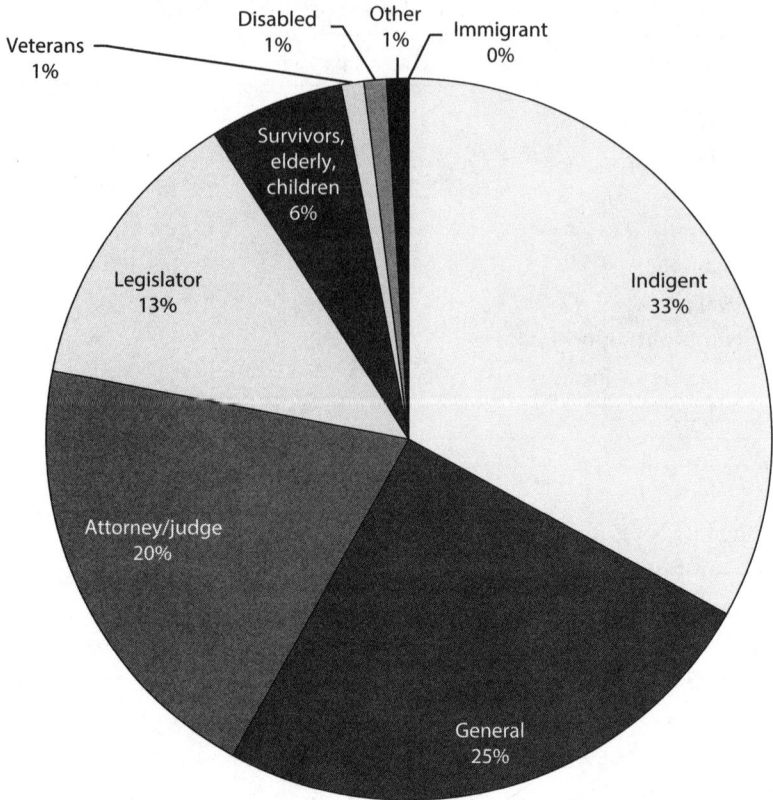

FIGURE 2.9. Target populations of civil legal representation bills proposed

Another way to measure the substance of these policies is to consider what, if any, specific populations they are designed to affect. Each bill was coded for the mention of several common target populations. Target populations refer to the "persons or groups whose behavior and well-being are affected by a policy" (Schneider and Ingram 1993). We established twelve categories of target populations defined by each bill: general litigants, low-income litigants, attorneys/judges, legislators, elderly, survivors of domestic violence, children, parents, immigrants, veterans, students, and people with disabilities. As figure 2.9 shows, indigent people comprised the largest target population addressed by these bills. About one in every three bills proposed was specific to the indigent—a finding that is perhaps unsurprising given the goals of civil legal service provision. There is, however, significant variation across states with respect to bills targeting the indigent.

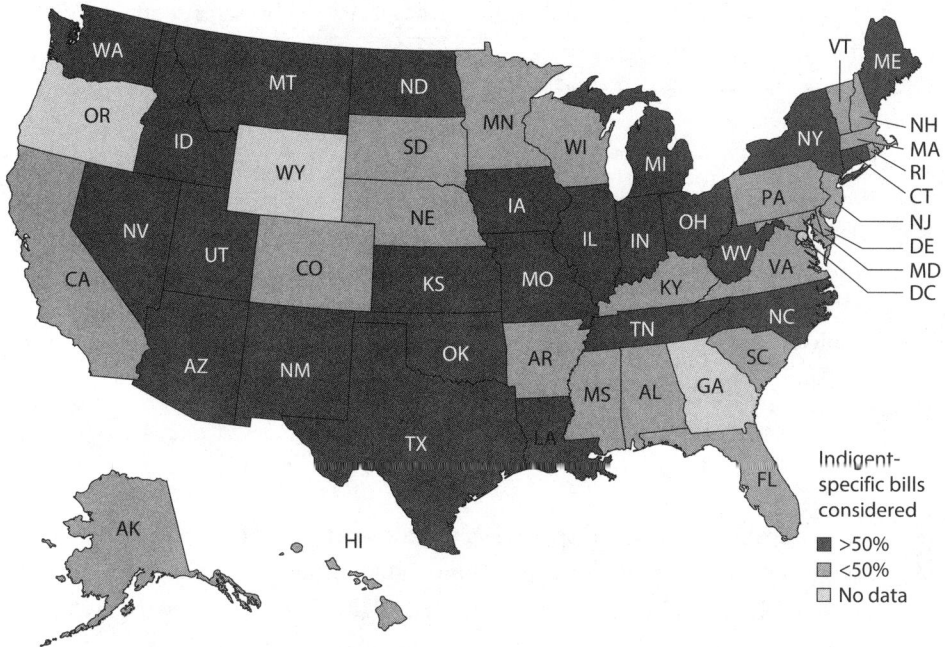

FIGURE 2.10. Percent of indigent-specific bills proposed by state

As figure 2.10 shows, indigent-specific legislation comprised more than half of all civil legal representation bills considered in about half the states. In Indiana, Iowa, Kansas, Louisiana, Maine, Michigan, New Mexico, North Carolina, North Dakota, Oklahoma, Tennessee, and West Virginia, more than 75 percent of all bills considered were targeted specifically toward indigent people. By contrast, in Alabama, Alaska, Arkansas, California, Colorado, Delaware, Florida, Maryland, Minnesota, Mississippi, South Carolina, South Dakota, Vermont, and Wisconsin, indigent-specific legislation accounted for less than 20 percent of all civil legal representation bills considered.

As figure 2.9 portrays, the next most common type of legislation was general in its application. A quarter of all bills proposed (25 percent) specified no target population. Interestingly, the next two most common target populations were attorneys or judges and legislators. In combination, these types of bills represent another third (33 percent) of all access-to-counsel legislation considered by states between 1990 and 2016. While we identified other target populations subject to legislation, they comprised a much smaller number of bills.

TABLE 2.4 Rate of Passage and Percent of All Bills Passed by Target Population

Type of bill	Rate of passage	All bills passed
General	32%	28%
Attorney/judge	25%	18%
Legislator	21%	9%
Indigent	31%	36%
Survivors, children, and elderly	27%	5%
Veterans	22%	1%
Disabled	0%	0%
Immigrants	25%	<1%
Other	36%	2%

Once again, only slight disparities exist between rates of bill proposal and passage with respect to target populations. Table 2.4 suggests that laws targeting general and indigent populations are slightly overrepresented, with 28 percent of all enacted bills targeting no specific group (compared to 25 percent of bills proposed) and 36 percent of all enacted bills focusing on indigent people (compared to 33 percent proposed). By contrast, laws targeting attorneys, judges, and legislators are slightly underrepresented compared to the number of bills proposed. With respect to target population, bills concerning the indigent and general populations have the highest rates of passage, at 31 and 32 percent, respectively. Interestingly, the major outlier in these results are bills designed to target disabled people. While they represent a small number of laws overall, only eleven are proposed in our data, disability-focused access-to-counsel bills are the only type with a 0 percent success rate.

Finally, we consider whether overlapping patterns emerge between the type and target population of bills. For example, we might expect that bills speaking to attorneys, judges, and legislators are more likely to take the form of regulations, placing restrictions on who can participate in civil legal representation or might benefit from state subsidies for representation. By contrast, we might expect that expanding access or providing finance would be a more prevalent strategy among bills that target a specific population of beneficiaries. Figure 2.11 depicts the overlap of bill substance by target population for all bills considered in our data.

Regulation is the most common type of bill for every category except legislation targeting veterans. As predicted, they are especially common among

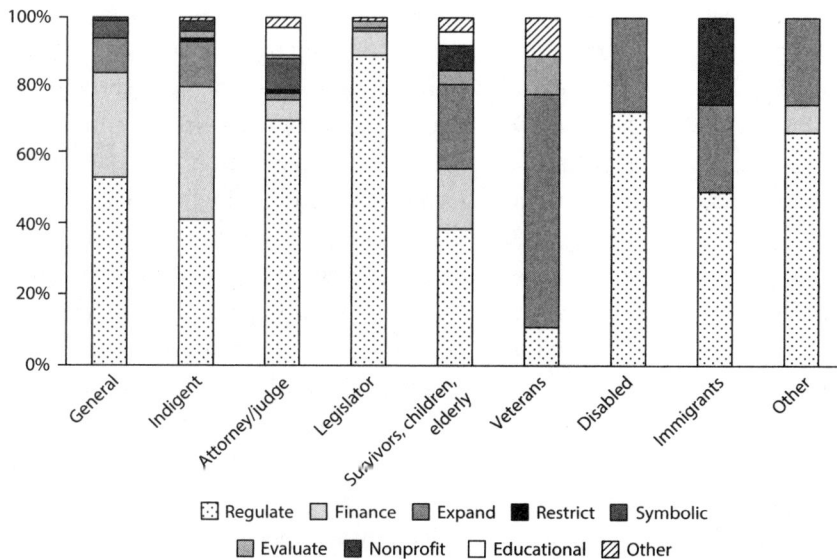

FIGURE 2.11. Civil legal representation bills proposed by target population and type

bills addressing attorneys, judges, and legislators. Yet regulations also comprise most bills addressing the general population, immigrants, disabled people, and other nonspecified groups. In addition, regulations make up about four out of every ten bills proposed for the indigent as well as survivors of domestic violence, children, and the elderly. Perhaps unsurprisingly given the generally positive orientation toward veterans in the United States (Schneider and Ingram 1993), bills to expand access to counsel are most prominent for this target population.

From Access to Justice to Democratic Citizenship

One of the major arguments we make in this book is that access to civil legal representation is a key component of democratic citizenship and crucial part of the experience that marginalized denizens have with the state. The civil legal institutions that determine such access reflect enduring and dynamic political-economic relationships. Nevertheless, scholars have paid insufficient attention to the politics and policy of access to justice. Delving into a core element of such politics, this chapter describes how fragmented civil legal institutions embedded within a federated polity operate a profoundly unequal patchwork of legal assistance programs. Leo concretizes the stakes of this: his experience painfully taught him that his prospects for being treated in a fair, humane way during a time of acute need were much brighter in Boulder (with its well-implemented housing lottery, higher-capacity social service infrastructure, and municipal resources ensuring that tenants facing eviction were represented in court) than in Alabama (where not a single dollar of state-appropriated funds supported civil legal aid provision). By mapping state variation in numerous aspects of civil legal systems and charting civil legal policies in US states over a twenty-six-year period, we place Leo's insights in a much broader context, illuminating the policy and institutional dynamics that undergird a racialized political economy of civil justice in the United States. The bird's-eye view we offer in this chapter illustrates the basic landscape of civil legal institutions and policies across the United States. In the next chapter, we consider the material consequences of such facts for the people who live daily with their upshots and the implications for political life.

3

"We're Not Being Heard"

HOW CIVIL JUSTICE PROBLEMS ERODE DEMOCRATIC CITIZENSHIP

ARIA, A forty-one-year-old Black woman living in western New York, came to housing court to contest her landlord's eviction attempt. She did not have a lawyer. When her landlord's attorney claimed that she did not pay rent in July, August, or September, Aria produced an official record from the local Department of Social Services indicating that the department had directly paid for these months. When her landlord's lawyer then pivoted to assert that she did not pay for December and January (a claim not reflected in the papers filed with the court, according to the judge), Aria admitted that she had stopped paying because "we have no heat." For the second year in a row, Aria and three of her children had been living through a harsh northeastern winter without heat. The judge nonchalantly instructed her landlord to fix the heat and then adjourned the eviction proceedings until the following week, but he warned Aria that she would need to pay all of her rental arrears at her next court visit to avoid being evicted within thirty days.

On the way out of the courtroom, Jamila asked Aria if she was willing to talk about her experiences. They then sat and spoke in a nearby cubicle for the next forty minutes. After Aria meticulously described her dilapidated living conditions—corroborating her claims with pictures and a video that she presented right then and there—she confessed, "I'm very honest. I didn't pay December and January because of the issues, [but] I pay my rent. Let me live nice. . . . The way you enter your house, I want to be able to enter my house. It might not be as beautiful, but I want heat." It was a simple, fair—and legally required—expectation. Aria did not ask for very much. Nonetheless, her pleas were ignored. When Jamila asked Aria whether she felt she had power over her circumstances, Aria's response was pointed: "No. I feel like I'm nothing. I'm in charge of paying this [rent]. But my word is nothing. My kids' health and the way we live is nothing. They don't care. They don't care."

Aria had been in the courtroom for over two hours before her case was called. Her landlord refused to adhere to the habitability standards mandated by state law. Jamila sat in the aisle across from her for that entire time witnessing a procession of Black women, most with the same landlord, describing atrocious housing conditions. The judge Aria encountered in court, an amicable Black man who spoke calmly and respectfully to everyone around him, ignored the fact that nearly every case that day featured a Black woman being evicted by the same landlord. Like Aria, the other women in the court detailed a host of flagrant habitability violations: leaks, mold, lack of heat, and multiplying rodents. Though the judge lightly rebuked the landlord's attorney, he did not halt any of the eviction proceedings, reduce the rent owed due to the harms incurred by the landlord's infractions, or take any other steps to help the women being evicted. He handled each case individually, never acknowledging the larger pattern of neglect. Aria viewed this as an unfair double standard:

> Why doesn't the judge recognize how many people this [landlord] has at court? . . . It's impossible for all of us to be the problem. None of us live in the same neighborhood, same street, don't know nothing about each other, but got all the same issues. That's wrong for the judge not to recognize, that alone should be a problem. . . . Why isn't [the landlord] being subpoenaed or took into court? Why [are] they able to take us to court, and they're slumlords? And for the judge to hear everything and still address it the way he addressed it, that's wrong. . . . That forces us to where, basically, I'm sitting here fighting to take care of my kids.

Later, when Jamila again asked Aria if there was anything that could be done about her housing situation, Aria was unequivocal in her declaration: "no." She remained steadfast in her insistence that

> they don't care. It's just—it drives me crazy because it's just like I'm left without really, the right support and help. And for [the landlord] to say I got to be out in thirty days. Now me and my kids got to pack all of this stuff up and find somewhere to go because these people don't want me to live right? Because he would have got his rent in December if he did his job. When I had the money, he would have got it.

Aria's experiences with civil justice problems (eviction and substandard housing), civil legal institutions (housing court), and civil legal actors (her landlord's attorney and the judge) left her deflated and defeated. She understood these experiences in distinctly racialized terms.

I'm not being funny, if a Caucasian goes into DSS [Department of Social Services] with an eviction notice or say they need somewhere to go, it seems like it's just always easier for a Caucasian. And I'm not prejudiced. I have Caucasian friends. I have a Caucasian sister-in-law, I have a Caucasian daughter-in-law. I have [biracial] grandkids. You know, it's the facts and the truth. And people don't never look at it like that. But these are facts and truth. Now, prime example, I goes in front of the judge. I have all of my proof. I have pictures, videos. I got to get an attorney. Why do I have to get an attorney? Why I got to take another day off? Now, what if I want to take extra [work] hours? I can't, because guess what? I got to come to court.

Toward the end of the interview, Aria confessed that she did not "know which way to go now." Aria did not land at this impasse because of weakness on her part. To the contrary, she displayed a fierce strength in court as she spoke out assertively against her landlord's attorney. Aria's predicament was also not due to ineptitude; she had the acuity and wherewithal to equip herself with documents, pictures, and a video to prove her case. She had the forethought to take time off from her nursing job—risking a promotion she was hoping could move her from a temporary to a permanent role—so she could show up punctually and prepared. Even further, Aria's dilemma was not a function of passivity or apathy; when the judge sent her into the hallway to "negotiate" with her landlord's attorney, she held her own, calling out inaccuracies in the documentation and refusing to sign an "offer" that would have had her paying rental arrears she did not owe. Notwithstanding her strength, resourcefulness, and courage, Aria began and ended our interview in tears. She was convinced that no one with the power to help her cared enough to do so and that she had no power to protect her family from impending houselessness.

Aria's experiences highlight how low-income people's civil legal problems and their corresponding encounters with the civil legal system can undermine their material well-being. Going further, Aria's experience points to how civil legal inequalities can erode expectations of redress and undercut political efficacy. In the remainder of this chapter, we examine how civil justice problems come to bear on people's senses of efficacy and democratic standing.

Drawing from theories of political behavior and policy feedback, we hypothesize that civil justice problems can diminish feelings of political efficacy and democratic belonging. Given the racialized political economy of civil justice, we also consider whether these processes differ across racialized groups. To explore these questions, we draw from two key data sources. First, an original set of questions collected as part of the 2020 Collaborative Multiracial Post-Election Survey (CMPS), which surveyed 14,988 US respondents from April 2 to August 25, 2021, and allows for racial group analysis.[1] After charting the breadth and type of civil legal problems experienced by members of different racialized groups in the United States, we then employ statistical matching techniques to examine the associations between civil justice problems and political outcomes.

To provide deeper insight into the processes underlying these statistical patterns, we next turn to qualitative data. Through in-depth interviews and observation of people navigating housing courts in multiple jurisdictions across the United States, we detail the perspectives of people with civil legal problems, document experiential pathways that connect civil legal problems to political outcomes, and describe the ways that civil legal processes are racialized. We show how civil justice struggles can corrode faith in legal and political institutions, and undermine people's sense of their own political efficacy. Moreover, we highlight that these patterns are differential across racial groups, with Black and Latinx denizens experiencing the negative political consequences of civil legal problems more acutely. The evidence presented in this chapter sheds light on critical experiences that race-class-subjugated communities have with the state, revealing an underexplored facet of inequality in American political economy.

The Political Repercussions of Civil Legal Experiences

Notwithstanding the scope and reach of the civil legal system, social scientists know relatively little about the ramifications of civil legal processes and institutions for *democratic* life within race-class-subjugated communities. Because

---

1. The survey was administered by Pacific Market Research. Respondents received a gift card for up to forty dollars for their participation. The survey was available in multiple languages to accommodate the diverse respondent pool. The data are weighted within racial groups to be representative of the US population (using 2019 American Community Survey estimates) with respect to age, gender, education, nativity, and ancestry.

legal processes mediate access to housing, medical care, government benefits, consumer protections, and more, unaddressed civil justice problems often threaten basic material security. Scholars of political participation have demonstrated how economic insecurity and constrained financial resources can reduce political efficacy and engagement (e.g., Brady, Verba, and Schlozman 1995; Burden and Wichowsky 2014; Leighley and Nagler 2014; Pacheco and Plutzer 2008; Rosenstone 1982; Shaub 2021). Moreover, negative life events like eviction, loss of health insurance, and job loss can dampen political engagement by reducing access to resources, reshaping demand for resources, or heightening stress (e.g., Estrada-Correa and Johnson 2012; Haselswerdt and Michener 2019; Ojeda, Michener, and Haselswerdt 2024; Shah and Wichowsky 2019; Shaub 2021). Based on this literature, we surmise that when civil legal problems deepen economic precarity, we should expect them to inhibit political life too, thereby undermining political efficacy and stifling democratic citizenship.

Civil legal problems also implicate critical citizen-state interactions. Many civil legal issues emerge because of difficulties accessing social policy benefits (Michener 2023a). Furthermore, even when civil legal problems stem from other causes (e.g., a predatory landlord or an inability to pay consumer debt), they can spark interactions with government officials (e.g., judges and court officers) and a reliance on publicly funded institutions (e.g., legal services organizations and courts). In these and other ways, civil legal problems spur encounters with public policies and institutions. As scholars of legal mobilization theory note, "The legal system . . . provides a uniquely democratic . . . mechanism for individual citizens to invoke public authority on their own and for their benefit. . . . [They] employ the power of the state and so become state actors themselves" (Zemans 1983, 692).

A deep and growing literature on "policy feedback" demonstrates that such encounters have repercussions for political life. The core logic of policy feedback lies in the observation that "new policies create new politics" in ways that durably remake political landscapes (Schattschneider 1935; Skocpol 1992). This happens (in part) because interactions with state actors and institutions can structure the contours of political attitudes and engagement. Evidence of such feedback abounds (Béland, Campbell, and Weaver 2022). Scholars have charted the political effects of the GI Bill, cash assistance programs, Medicaid, the Affordable Care Act, Social Security, after-school programs, immigration enforcement, criminal legal policy, consumer finance, education policy, and more (Barnes 2020; Brown 2021; Campbell 2003; Cruz Nichols, LeBrón, and

Pedraza 2018; Hertel-Fernandez 2018; Johnson, Meier, and Carroll 2017; Lerman and Weaver 2014; Martinez 2024; Mettler 2005; Michener 2018; Rocha, Knoll, and Wrinkle 2015; SoRelle 2020; SoRelle and Laws 2023; Soss 2000).

Feedback effects typically take one of two pathways (Mettler and SoRelle 2023; Mettler and Soss 2004; Pierson 1993): First, they can generate resource effects that shape the incentives for or capacity of people to engage in politics by providing (or taking away) monetary or other types of resources. Second, they can generate interpretive effects that shape the norms, values, and attitudes people hold about their own efficacy and citizenship. When policies diminish resources, or when experiences navigating state institutions are negative, political efficacy and trust are frequently undermined (e.g., Lerman and Weaver 2014; Michener 2018; Soss 2000).

Both processes could be at work in the case of civil justice issues. Beyond the resource constraints imposed by civil justice problems, the outcome of civil legal processes can increase or diminish access to resources in the form of public benefits, housing, debt, child support, and so on. Furthermore, for those who pursue legal action (or are compelled into it) because of their civil justice problems, how they experience the legal process may generate interpretive effects that influence perceptions of their value as citizens as well as feelings of governmental efficacy. Scholars have established that legal processes can actively construct categories of citizenship in ways that structure who gains access to particular rights and protections (e.g., Brown 1995; Burbank and Farhang 2017; Law 2010; Novkov 2001, 2002; Smith 1997; Spade 2015; Yoshino 2007). But beyond these legal constructions of citizenship, we contend that the quality of interactions with civil legal institutions and actors have meaning for people's perceptions of their value as citizens and civic participants—as they do in the case of social policy implementation (e.g., Barnes 2020; Mettler 2005; Michener 2018; Soss 1999) and contact with the carceral state (e.g., Lerman and Weaver 2014; Walker 2020).

When people feel respected and treated fairly by the legal process, they may come to understand that their voices matter, they have the power to affect legal outcomes, and government actors are receptive to their voices and concerns. By contrast, negative interactions, like Aria's, may leave people feeling undervalued, ignored, and powerless to successfully exercise their rights and protections vis-à-vis the courts. Echoes of this policy feedback logic can be found in research on procedural justice. Working at the intersection of law and social psychology, scholars of procedural justice explore how people's perceptions of the fairness of their legal experience shape a variety of outcomes from preferences for types of dispute resolution (e.g., arbitration versus jury trials) to legal compliance and many others (see MacCoun 2005). For example, when people feel they can "tell their side of the story" or meaningfully influence the outcome of a decision through their participation in the legal process, they are more likely to be satisfied with both legal procedures and outcomes (e.g., Lind and Tyler 1988; MacCoun 2005; Thibaut and Walker 1975, 1978). The adversarial nature of many legal proceedings has been shown to further shape evaluations of citizenship by rendering some parties "villains" and others "victims" (Barnes and Burke 2015), which has consequences for how people interpret their value vis-à-vis the state.

Of course, such feedback loops are neither automatic nor inexorable (Jacobs and Mettler 2018; Michener 2019a, 2023b; Patashnik and Zelizer 2013). Instead, they are contingent and complex. Systematic analysis of the sort we present in this book is necessary for tracing feedback processes within and across policy domains. Like other scholars of policy feedback, we deploy a range of methods to do this (SoRelle and Michener 2022). We also pay particularly close attention to racial dynamics, which fundamentally structure policy feedback processes in the United States (Garcia-Rios et al. 2023; Michener 2019b).

Taken together, insights from scholars of political participation and policy feedback alongside work on procedural justice inform our expectations that people who experience civil legal problems will display signs of attenuated political efficacy as well as a less sanguine sense of democratic citizenship. We anticipate that such patterns will be heterogeneous across racial groupings, reflecting the reality that Black and Latinx denizens are more frequently exposed to deleterious civil legal problems, and more likely to experience more punitive institutional encounters while navigating them (Brito et al. 2022; Rosenthal 2021; Soss and Weaver 2017).

A Quantitative Assessment

To investigate whether civil legal problems correspond to diminished democratic citizenship, we first turn to survey data collected as part of the 2020 CMPS. Designed to provide oversamples by racial groupings, the CMPS core sample used here includes 3,002 White respondents, 4,005 Black respondents, 4,006 Latinx respondents, and 3,975 AAPI respondents. In addition to a standard battery of demographic questions, respondents were asked to report whether they or any member of their household experienced specific civil justice problems in the past two years. Respondents were randomly assigned to receive one of three lists of civil justice problems derived from a battery used in the 2017 LSC survey of civil legal need. The first list included six questions spanning multiple dimensions of civil legal need; the second repeated those questions for nonrenters, while directing renters to a separate battery of five housing-specific questions; and the third focused on seven financial problems.[2] Responses to these questions allow us to gauge whether people are experiencing civil legal problems and with what frequency. We constructed a binary variable to capture anyone reporting yes to at least one problem, and we created a count variable to capture the number of problems people noted.

We draw on two measures to assess political attitudes toward the civil legal system. The first gauges *internal efficacy*: how able people feel navigating a particular political institution (Craig 1979; Craig, Niemi, and Silver 1990). We ask respondents, "To what extent do you think people like you have the ability to use the courts to protect yourself and your family or enforce your rights?" The second gauges *external efficacy*: whether a person believes a system will be responsive to their needs and engagement (Craig 1979; Craig, Niemi, and Silver 1990). We inquire, "To what extent do you think people like you are treated fairly in the civil legal system?"[3]

Next, we use several measures to grasp how people with civil legal problems perceive democratic inclusion and external efficacy more broadly (i.e., not only in relation to the civil legal system). First, we ask how much respondents agree with the statement "I feel like a full and equal citizen in this country with all the rights and protections that other people have" as a means of assessing their sense of democratic inclusion.[4] Second, we query whether respondents think politicians listen to their concerns as a way of appraising external political efficacy: the sense that their actions can affect the political system.[5] Finally, to account for people like Aria who observe racial inequalities in civil legal

2. A full list can be found in the quantitative appendix. Notably, we did not include questions about divorce, custody, or other family civil justice issues.

3. Answer choices included "not at all," "rarely," "some of the time," "most of the time," and "all the time."

4. This is measured on a seven-point scale, where one equals strong disagreement and seven equals strong agreement.

5. Specifically, they were asked whether they agree with the statement "Politicians don't listen to people like me" on a four-point scale, where one equals strong agreement (and low efficacy) and four equals strong disagreement (and high efficacy).

processes, we ask respondents to report how often they think politicians helped people from their racial group.[6]

Analytic Strategy

Exposure to civil justice problems is likely shaped by a range of characteristics such as race, income, age, gender, and more. In this context of complex multi-causal processes, precise identification of the causal relationships between civil legal problems and the political outcomes described above is not feasible in the absence of experimental or quasiexperimental sources of variation. For this reason, we cannot make dispositive claims. As noted in chapter 1, causal explanation is not a core aim of this research. The processes and patterns we explore here are too important to give up on better understanding. So while we refrain from making strong causal claims, we nevertheless assess relationships between civil legal problems and political outcomes to produce descriptive analyses that corroborate relevant patterns and point to potential causal pathways.

To address obvious confounders when analyzing statistical associations, we employ coarsened exact matching techniques to create comparison groups among those who are "treated" by experiencing civil justice problems and those who are not (Iacus, King, and Porro 2012).[7] By matching along five key demographic characteristics—race, gender, education, income, and age—coarsened exact matching reduces imbalance along these covariates, pruning the sample to exclude those observations without a valid match in the treatment or control. The resulting samples of those who have and have not experienced at least one civil legal problem in the past two years are alike on all covariates, and each treated unit is randomly paired with an untreated unit of the same covariate values (Iacus, King, and Porro 2012).[8] This process addresses some, but not all, of the bias that would likely emerge in a simple regression context. Put most simply, matching gives us a less biased sense of the

6. This was measured on a five-point scale ranging from "never" to "all the time."

7. We call this limitation different things—correlated causes, endogeneity, spurious correlations—but the underlying thread centers on risks of identifying misleading associations.

8. The results for the matching algorithm and tests of imbalance can be found in the quantitative appendix along with a description of the binning process for each of the matched covariates. Note that the matching process employed here did not require pruning a significant number of observations, with the matched sample incorporating 99 percent of participants.

statistical associations we are studying, but it does not resolve the fundamental challenges of using cross-sectional observational (survey) data (as opposed to longitudinal or experimental data). Nevertheless, this analysis offers instructive, if imperfect, evidence on the politics of civil justice.[9]

Who Has Civil Legal Problems?

We begin by exploring the prevalence of civil legal problems among our sample. Table 3.1 reports the percent of people who experienced each of nineteen civil legal issues for the full sample as well as broken down by respondents' racial and income classifications. About one-third of survey takers (34 percent) reported that they or someone in their household experienced at least one civil legal problem in the previous two years. Among those in the sample who made less than $30,000 annually—the federal poverty level for a family of four—that rate increased to 45 percent.[10]

But there is notable racial heterogeneity. White and AAPI respondents reported problems at considerably lower rates, with roughly a quarter of each group experiencing a civil legal problem. By contrast, 38 percent of Latinx respondents and 44 percent of Black respondents experienced at least one civil legal problem. While not depicted in table 3.1, these patterns persist when looking at lower-income participants across racialized groups. Racially disparate experiences of civil legal problems occur across all the issues we survey—a finding consistent with existing scholarship (Brito et al. 2022). Perhaps the most dramatic differences emerge in the context of financial problems, for which Black borrowers in particular report issues at twice or in some cases three times the rate of their White counterparts. For example, Black respondents were twice as likely to experience foreclosure and bankruptcy and three times as likely to report being subjected to unfair credit terms or deceptive practices.

9. In the analyses to follow, descriptive results are presented for the full sample, while regression results are conducted with the coarsened exact matching pruned samples. The estimated predictors for the following models represent the local sample average treatment effect, which is the treatment effect averaged over only those treated units for which matches were available along the specified covariates.

10. Because this number does not reflect the full range of civil justice problems, including any family-related issues (e.g., child support and divorce), it is lower than the rates typically found from more comprehensive measures.

TABLE 3.1 Percent of Respondents with Civil Justice Problems by Race

	Full	White	Black	Latinx	AAPI	Lower income
Any problem	34%	27%	44%	38%	25%	45%
General problems						
Bank or lender	15%	12%	22%	17%	9%	22%
Other financing	13%	10%	19%	15%	9%	20%
Medical care	17%	14%	21%	19%	13%	22%
Government benefits	13%	11%	17%	16%	9%	20%
Employers	13%	10%	17%	16%	10%	18%
Renter problems						
Deposit	13%	12%	14%	13%	11%	14%
Property destruction	11%	5%	13%	13%	10%	13%
Accommodation	9%	6%	12%	9%	7%	10%
Services	18%	13%	20%	19%	15%	22%
Eviction	14%	11%	18%	14%	8%	17%
Tenants' rights	12%	8%	14%	12%	9%	13%
Financing problems						
Deceptive practices	15%	7%	22%	16%	13%	20%
Access to credit	17%	12%	25%	20%	11%	24%
Identity theft	18%	12%	24%	17%	16%	21%
Credit terms	12%	6%	19%	13%	9%	17%
Collection Harassment	15%	9%	24%	18%	9%	21%
Foreclosure	7%	4%	10%	7%	6%	10%
Bankruptcy	10%	6%	15%	11%	7%	14%

In addition to the types of civil legal problems people encounter, we might want to know how many problems the average person experiences. Figure 3.1 illustrates the number of civil legal problems people in our survey faced over the past two years, examining those patterns by racialized groups for those who experienced at least one problem. As figure 3.1 highlights, about 40 percent of White and AAPI respondents who have experienced a civil justice problem had only one in the past two years. While experiencing a single problem remains the most common outcome for Black and Latinx respondents as well, they were more likely to report multiple problems than their White or AAPI peers. But does that pattern hold when we account for other demographic characteristics? And what characteristics are correlated with whether and how many civil legal problems people report?

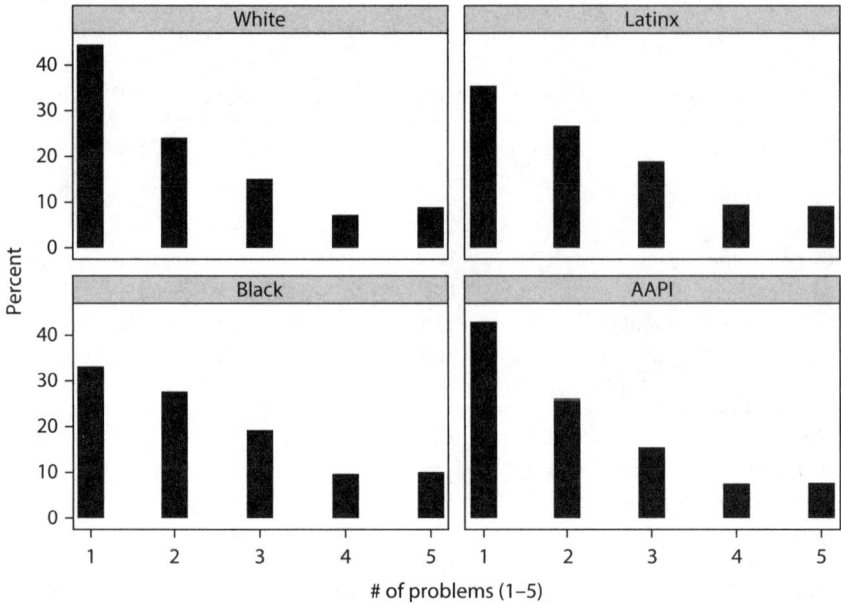

FIGURE 3.1. Number of civil justice problems by racial group

Figure 3.2 provides more information about how demographic traits are associated with the likelihood of having civil justice problems. As shown, both the prevalence and frequency of civil legal problems varies across racial groupings, even after controlling for characteristics including income, education, age, gender, and nativity. Relative to White respondents, Black and Latinx survey takers were statistically more likely to experience at least one civil legal problem by nearly 6 and 14 percentage points, respectively. They also report having a slightly higher number of civil legal problems, although it is only a small difference of between one-tenth and one-quarter of a point (on a scale from zero to five). By contrast, AAPI respondents note slightly fewer civil legal problems relative to their White peers.

Income, education, gender, and age are also correlated with whether someone has civil legal problems as well as how many problems they experience. Every $10,000 increase in annual income is associated with a 1 percentage point reduction in the chance of experiencing a civil legal problem. So, for example, someone who reports making $100,000 each year is 7 percentage points less likely to report having had a civil legal problem compared to someone making $30,000 annually. Similarly, as education and age increase, people are less likely

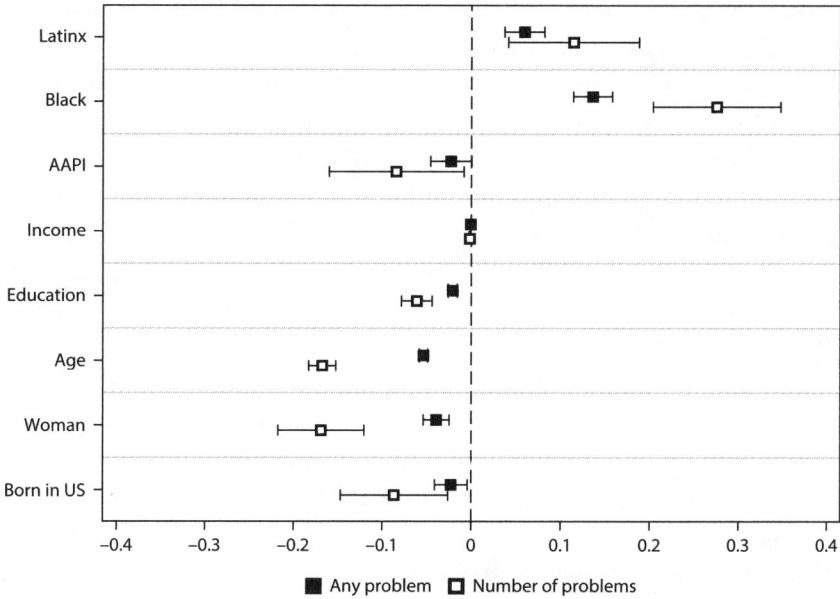

FIGURE 3.2. Correlates of experiencing civil justice problems
Note: Points represent coefficients from ordinary least squares (OLS) regression, with confidence intervals in bars.

to have civil legal problems.[11] Finally and perhaps unsurprisingly, native-born participants experienced fewer civil legal problems than their immigrant peers.

Civil Legal Problems and Democratic Citizenship

Following the logic of policy feedback, we expect economic and racial dispari-ties in experiences of civil legal problems to be politically meaningful. More precisely, we anticipate that experiencing a civil legal problem may undermine political efficacy, reducing people's expectation of assistance by governmental institutions. This could be particularly true for evaluations of the civil courts because they are the political institution most closely tied to the relevant

---

11. Interestingly, women in our sample also report slightly fewer problems than men, which contrasts with findings from the LSC. It may be the case that the types of problems we ask about are more frequently experienced by men. In particular, the exclusion of domestic violence and family-related issues may shape this outcome. More broadly, the gendered politics of civil justice bear further exploration.

experience. Figure 3.3 depicts whether people with civil justice problems feel a diminished sense of internal and external efficacy vis-à-vis the civil courts. It also considers whether those patterns are different across racialized groups.

The top panel of figure 3.3 considers the association between experiencing civil legal problems and *internal political efficacy*: a person's perception of whether they can successfully use the civil courts to protect their rights.[12] Experiencing civil legal problems corresponds with a reduced sense of internal efficacy as it pertains to the courts. People with civil justice issues were more than a quarter point (0.29) less likely to say they could use the courts to protect their rights. This is substantively meaningful: having a civil legal problem is significantly associated with people believing that they are rarely able to use the courts to protect their rights. When it comes to external efficacy (the bottom panel of figure 3.3), respondents are about one-fifth of a point (0.19) less likely to say they expect fair treatment from the courts when compared with demographically similar respondents who don't have civil legal problems. These results are consistent with our expectation.

Notably, the observed patterns between civil legal problems and political efficacy manifest for people from all racialized groups: everyone who experiences at least one civil legal problem feels attenuated efficacy relative to the courts. White respondents, however, evince a higher starting evaluation of their capacity to use the courts and their expectation for fair treatment relative to all other cohorts. Put simply, Black, Latinx, and AAPI respondents begin with a lower sense of efficacy, and experiencing civil legal problems is associated with that being significantly worse.

Importantly, these patterns of political efficacy extend beyond the realm of the courts. Figure 3.4 shows how experiencing a civil justice problem relates to feeling like a full and equal citizen when compared to demographically similar peers who have not had civil legal problems. Across all groups, having a civil legal problem is correlated with a slightly less positive evaluation of citizenship. As with the previous analyses, these patterns are consistent across racialized groups, but White respondents start with the most robust sense of full citizenship, while Black respondents express the lowest. This means that the lower feelings of efficacy expressed by those with civil legal problems are most substantively deleterious for Black respondents, whose baseline is considerably lower.

---

12. The following analyses focus on "any problem" and not the number of problems people experience. The patterns are consistent across both measures, but the sample of people with multiple problems is sufficiently small to make that analysis less robust.

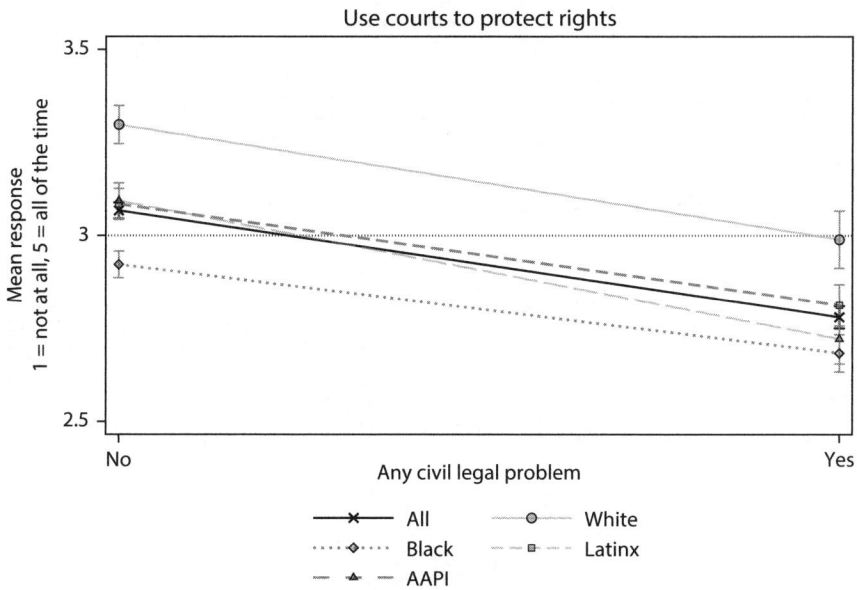

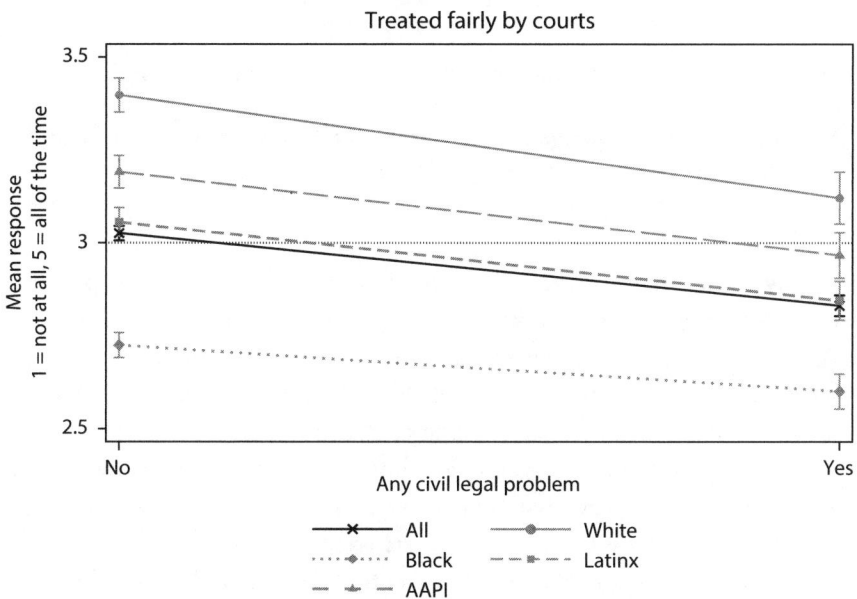

FIGURE 3.3. Civil justice problems and civil legal efficacy by racial group
Note: Points represent marginal effects from OLS regression with coarsened exact matching weights; confidence intervals in bars.*

*Because the different outcomes we explore in the book's quantitative analyses rely on different measurement scales (ranging between 4 and 7 points), we do not standardize the axes across all figures as doing so would make the results difficult to view. Instead, we standardize the axes for figures reporting analyses for like outcomes. So, for example, both graphs in figure 3.3 report results for outcomes measured on a 5-point scale. Thus we use a standard axis range for each as well as the corresponding figures in chapter 5. Moreover, the slope and intercept of the analyses can be compared for similar outcome measures across and within chapters.

Feel like full and equal citizen

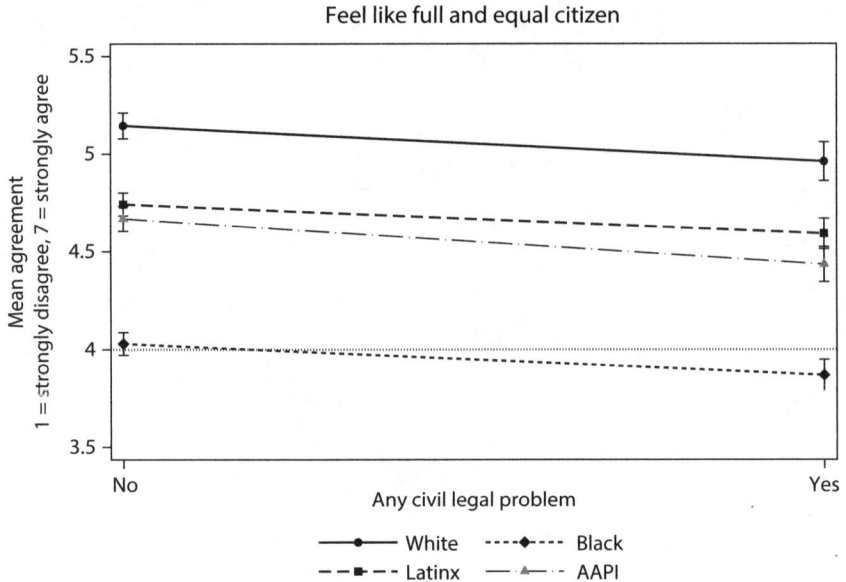

FIGURE 3.4. Civil justice problems and perception of citizenship by racial group
Note: Points represent marginal effects from OLS regression with coarsened exact matching weights; confidence intervals in bars.

One common way people evaluate how efficacious they are as political actors is by considering whether they feel politicians listen to their concerns. Those who feel more heard likely have a greater sense of external political efficacy. Figure 3.5 examines this type of efficacy along two dimensions. First, it considers whether individuals feel like politicians respond to their concerns. In general, the average respondent does not believe politicians are responsive to their needs—irrespective of whether they have experienced civil legal problems. But those with such problems do report a lower evaluation of their efficacy with respect to policymakers' attention. This pattern is (again) consistent across racial groups. Interestingly, though, White respondents are less likely to say that politicians listen to people like them when compared with their differently racialized peers—a reverse of the trends we have identified for previous questions.

A different picture emerges when we ask people to evaluate efficacy based on racial group classification. While the average person who has experienced a civil legal problem reports a slight decrease in whether they believe public

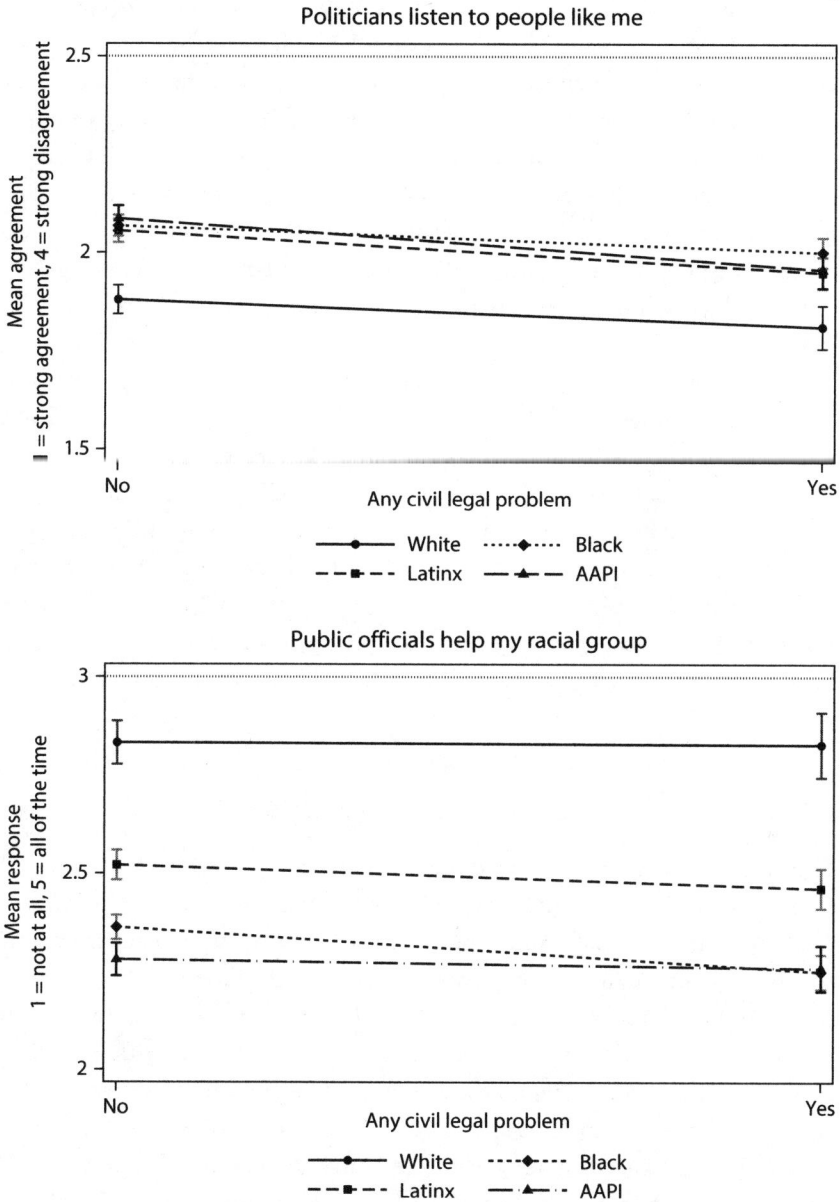

Politicians listen to people like me

Mean agreement
1 = strong agreement, 4 = strong disagreement

2.5

2

1.5

No — Any civil legal problem — Yes

White ———•———   Black ·····•·····
Latinx — –■– –   AAPI — –▲– —

Public officials help my racial group

Mean response
1 = not at all, 5 = all of the time

3

2.5

2

No — Any civil legal problem — Yes

White ———•———   Black ·····•·····
Latinx — –■– –   AAPI — –▲– ·

FIGURE 3.5. Civil justice problems and political efficacy by racial group
Note: Points represent marginal effects from OLS regression with coarsened exact matching weights; confidence intervals in bars.

officials help their racial group, the overall decline is driven primarily by Black and Latinx respondents. White and AAPI people who report experiencing civil legal problems are no more or less likely to view public officials as willing to help their racial group. By contrast, Black and Latinx people who report a civil legal problem are less likely to believe that policymakers are accountable to their group. This distinction is consistent with the assessment Aria made at the beginning of this chapter—that government officials are treating people like her differently than White people who are navigating the civil legal system—suggesting that Aria's view may be more broadly shared.

The survey results are largely aligned with our expectations: people who experience civil legal problems exhibit diminished political efficacy both specific to court institutions and extending to broader political contexts. Civil justice problems are also associated with feeling less included within the democratic polity. These broad statistical associations underscore the potential consequence of civil legal problems for democracy. Yet quantitative observations can only go so far in explaining, contextualizing, and making sense of the political world. To more deeply understand how and why civil legal problems come to bear on political life, we turn to the people who experience them.

A Qualitative Perspective

Our qualitative analysis is based on participant observations and in-depth interviews—some of which have already been featured. We collected this qualitative data (virtually and in person) over a period of six years, from 2018 to 2024.[13] Because the civil legal realm is vast, we decided to focus on housing. As we describe in the first chapter, housing is an appropriate case for numerous reasons. It is the largest expense for most people, with prevailing market conditions causing many people to struggle finding affordable options. In 2019, for example, 46 percent of renter households (over 20 million people in the United States) were cost burdened, expending upward of 30 percent of their incomes on rent (Joint Center for Housing Studies of

---

13. The qualitative appendix contains detailed descriptions of our qualitative methods. To maximize clarity and transparency, we also include some of this in the text and some in footnotes. Nonetheless, readers with interest in our qualitative approach should read the appendix, which is both robust and substantive.

Harvard University 2024). People living in or near poverty bore the heftiest burden: more than 80 percent of renters making below $25,000 were cost burdened in 2019 (Joint Center for Housing Studies of Harvard University 2024). Racial and ethnic inequities were also striking: 54 percent of Black renters and 52 percent of Latinx renters were cost burdened in 2019, compared to 42 percent of White renters (Joint Center for Housing Studies of Harvard University 2024).

The politics of housing is a deeply racialized element of the broader American political economy (Feldman and Stall 2004; Rodriguez 2021; Taylor 2013; Thurston 2023; Williams 2004). While there is nothing innate about housing that links it to the construct of race, long-standing policies and practices—for example, the use of redlining, racial covenants, and other exclusionary zoning practices have rendered racism a fundamental factor structuring the design and implementation of housing policies (Freund 2007; Massey and Denton 1993; Michener 2023c; Rothstein 2017; Satter 2009; Seligman 2005; Taylor 2013, 2019; Thurston 2018; Trounstine 2018).

Housing is "a pivotal site of power," which is mitigated as well as contested via political institutions like courts and political actors, including judges, lawyers, tenants' organizations, and more (Michener 2022, 2023c; Michener and SoRelle 2022). Racialized patterns in civil legal problems and the associated political outcomes become more legible when we pay close attention to the domains that represent key pain points in US political life. Housing is just such a pain point. It is the source of many civil justice problems. Recall that between 2018 and 2022, contract cases accounted for more civil cases nationwide than any other civil legal problem, and most contract cases involve housing. Overall, housing problems draw millions of people into the US civil legal system each year, catalyzing and exacerbating racialized experiences that have political implications. We elaborate the content and nature of these implications in the remainder of this chapter.

Data and Analysis

Given the focus on housing, participant observations for this research took place in housing courts, tenant meetings, and tenants' rights workshops. Observations occurred over six years, beginning with court observations in 2018. Before and after the most intense periods of the pandemic, ethnographic observations happened mostly in courts. During the pandemic, observations primarily occurred in (virtual) tenant organizing meetings and tenants' rights workshops. When the pandemic subsided, they took place via in-person field visits across the country.[14]

Altogether, across these spaces, we conducted nearly 100 hours of ethnographic observations.[15] As a critical complement to these ethnographic observations, we conducted in-depth interviews with people facing civil legal problems related to housing (n = 104). Some interviewees had lawyers, and some did not (and some had lawyers at various points or for some issues, but did not at other points or for other issues). Finally, we interviewed lawyers who represented low-income clients with housing problems (n = 20).[16]

In total, we interviewed 124 people. We stopped when we reached the point of saturation: when we were no longer hearing significant new information related to the focus of this book. Each category of interviewee offered a distinct and informative outlook on civil legal systems. People facing civil legal problems without lawyers recounted experiences that underscored the confusion, alienation, and harm that came with being unsupported while traversing complex, adversarial legal proceedings that privilege expertise. People with civil legal problems who had lawyers afforded a view of that same system under the quite different condition of having support (even if legal aid was limited and contingent). Lawyers described the operation of civil legal processes from their vantage point as experts whose job it was to help clients engage the legal system.

Finally, members of tenant organizations emerged as pivotal (and unexpected) sources of information. Tenants who joined such groups sought to act collectively, and they often did so directly in relation to civil legal processes, which we concentrate on in chapter 6. Tenant organizations contested civil

14. We conducted in-person ethnographic observations in Georgia, Kentucky, New Jersey, and New York.

15. Most of these observations were conducted by Jamila. To ensure multiple perspectives on civil legal problems, some of the observations were conducted by two trained research assistants (a graduate student and an undergraduate student). All researchers took detailed field notes during observations, and we draw on those notes to provide context and texture when we discuss the qualitative work throughout this book.

16. There was substantial overlap between these interviewee categories. Most members of tenant organizations were also tenants who were themselves facing or had faced legal problems (that is what brought them to those organizations). The lawyers interviewed for this study often did not overlap with other interviewee categories, though in two instances we interviewed civil legal attorneys who were members of a tenant organization (we count them as lawyers for the purposes of categorizing, mostly due to their emphases in our research interviews).

legal systems in numerous ways: facilitating tenants' rights trainings, offering court support (e.g., standing with fellow tenants to court proceedings), staging courthouse protests, physically blocking legal eviction processes from proceeding, helping tenants identify alternatives when legal systems failed, and much more (Michener 2022, 2023c; Michener and SoRelle 2022). Altogether, culling perspectives from these various interviewee groups enabled complementary evidence on how civil legal institutions affect the people most vulnerable within them.

The empirical logic of the qualitative strategy used in this book orients around a case study approach (Small 2009; Yin 2009). Our goal was not to interview a "representative sample" of people with civil legal problems to make claims about frequency or generalizability. The survey data serve some of those functions. Our aim for the qualitative aspect of this research was to identify a range of diverse cases that could reflect heterogeneous perspectives in informative ways. The point was to learn things we did not know and garner insights we could not have predicted (and thus never could have included on a survey instrument). This is exactly what happened. For example, when we first started this project, tenant organizations were not on our radar at all. It was through ethnographic fieldwork and interviews that we came to learn that such organizations were important civil legal actors (Michener 2022; Michener and SoRelle 2022). There are many other ways that our qualitative work illuminated processes and realities that we simply had not thought of. Even beyond this, the qualitative work made the civil legal phenomena we sought to understand concrete in ways that allowed us to make better sense of the meaning of civil legal institutions for political life.

Though we did not "randomly" select interview cases, we did so purposively and with sound rationale. To guide our case selection, we focused on geography as a core axis of variation.[17] As chapter 2 demonstrates, civil legal systems are distinct in different places. For instance, in some locations, tenants navigating eviction proceedings have a right to counsel, nominally guaranteeing them access to an attorney (Benfer et al. 2025; Michener 2020). In others, they do not. To account for this kind of contextual variation,

---

17. We also selected interviewees who were in different places along a spectrum of legal experiences. This allowed us to achieve range in relation to the core phenomena of interest: civil legal experiences. The civil justice problems that interviewees faced included eviction, substandard housing, landlord refusal to accommodate disabilities, exposure to lead and other health-threatening housing conditions, challenges with illegal squatting, and more.

we recruited interviewees from twenty-five states and forty localities, spanning regions (e.g., Northeast, Southeast, and Midwest) and ranging from major urban centers (e.g., Los Angeles and New York City) to midsize cities (Louisville and Milwaukee) to rural counties.[18]

Interview participants were recruited through numerous channels including outreach to tenant organizations, code enforcement agencies, legal aid organizations, and housing organizations; interactions in housing courts; and social networks / snowball techniques. Having many streams of recruitment ensured that participants were from a wide range of backgrounds and were not reflecting any systematic biases from a particular organizational or social network. The interviews were conducted online via Zoom, on the phone, and in person depending on what was most convenient for participants. Interviews generally lasted an hour, but they ran longer or shorter based on how conversations organically progressed.

Interviews were intentionally loosely structured, with different protocols for each interviewee group (tenants with civil legal problems, members of tenant organizations, and lawyers). All interviewees were asked to share about themselves. If interviewees were not associated with tenant organizations, we asked them to share their experiences with housing, civil legal problems, experiences in court, interactions with lawyers, and general attitudes toward civil legal actors and processes. If they were members of tenant organizations, we asked all of those things in addition to inquiring about organizational structure and activities. Interview participants were given leeway so that conversations could go in whatever direction the discussion dictated. This enabled people to share things that we did not anticipate. Our research process was iterative, sequential, and inductive. We learned from interviewees as the project progressed and made decisions about who else to interview based on those learnings. Sometimes we interviewed people twice, if they indicated wanting to speak again or reached out later with more to say. All interviews were recorded and transcribed. The transcripts were analyzed via Dedoose, a web-based qualitative software program that facilitates systematic coding.[19]

18. One county was so rural as well as so White that an interviewee suggested that Jamila end her interviewing and drive back to the nearest city before dark for fear that it wasn't safe for [Black] people in the area after dark. Jamila heeded the advice.

19. Our approach to coding—the process of classifying and methodically analyzing qualitative data—was initially open, with a focus on surfacing very broad patterns. In progressive

In the remainder of this chapter, we highlight the words and experiences of the people we interviewed to expand on the themes underscored in the first part of the chapter. Though some of the narratives we share may seem striking or dramatic, we have not cherry-picked the most appalling or compelling situations. To the contrary, so many of the tenants we spoke to had arresting experiences that we struggled to decide who to include and found it difficult to stop writing.

The qualitative narratives relayed below will revolve around how interviewees understand civil justice problems. The details we recount matter because they are the actual phenomena of political interest, and specifics help to illustrate why they are politically significant. After elaborating on the nature of civil legal problems, we relay interviewees' interpretations of what their experiences meant in relationship to democratic citizenship (broadly construed). To be clear, interviewees do not refer directly to concepts like political efficacy, democratic citizenship, or sometimes even politics. These are academic terms that we apply as a matter of interpretive inference. Such application reveals that the learnings from the quantitative and qualitative aspects of this research are distinct but self-reinforcing.

The Substance of Civil Legal Problems

Sheila, a low-income Black woman in her forties who had lived in Upstate New York for her entire life, had confronted an onslaught of hazardous living conditions including insect infestation, mold, flooding, inadequate heating, a malfunctioning stove, a broken front window, a house fire, and more. Though these circumstances patently endangered her family, Sheila's landlord refused to make legally required repairs (Michener 2023c). Worse still is that Sheila was stuck. She described her dilemma this way:

> [My landlord] knows that he has me because [of] my three-year-old; she was born during the pandemic. And she was a micropreemie. And she spent a very, very long time in the [neonatal intensive care unit]. When we brought her home, she was on ventilators. . . . And we lost our jobs through the pandemic. And then there was a nursing shortage. So her dad and I had to provide the twenty-four-hour nursing care ourselves, changing out her

---

iterations of analysis, coding became more thematic, identifying precise categories connected to key emergent ideas in the research.

trach, doing her [gastrostomy] tube, all of that. So we have no money to move. So I guess I'll just bite the bullet. Stop complaining.

When "the bathroom was . . . leaking into [the] dining room" and widespread mold caused her children to fall ill with respiratory infections, Sheila bit the bullet. But her forbearance became unsustainable when her family was nearly killed in a house fire: "We woke up to a small explosion in my basement. . . . And we open the basement door, and there's flames. So we had to get all the kids out." After the fire, Sheila could not continue to suffer "the issues in the house . . . presenting a risk to our baby." So she reported her landlord to code enforcement. Her landlord responded by "going down to code enforcement and threatening them with a gun." Sheila was appalled that he seemed to get away with this without legal repercussions, and she perceived a racial dimension to the circumstances:

I don't know how he managed to not get arrested, but—I'm not saying it's White privilege, but it kind of looks like White privilege. . . . Mind you, he did it while on probation. . . . I'm talking to the code directors. He's threatening the lives of the code directors [with a gun] while on probation from a gun charge.

Code enforcement ultimately did nothing in response, and Sheila's landlord "downright refused to do repairs." With nowhere to go, she remained locked in a bitter battle to survive. She mostly fended for herself—a skill she had honed over many years of dealing with predatory landlords who seemed immune from legal reproach. At one point in the interview, Sheila recounted this startling array of experiences that began at the cusp of her adulthood:

I've had landlords before try to screw me over. And I've been screwed over so many times that I now know all the tricks that they use. . . . Let me tell you this story. I was eighteen years old. This is my first apartment. It was a dive. It was a dive, but it was mine. It was my first little situation. . . . One day I wake up to boom, boom, boom, boom, boom. The marshal's at my door. I'm like, "What is y'all here for? I didn't do nothing wrong. Don't know why y'all here." I'm already like, "You got to talk to my lawyer, don't talk to me . . ." I know for a fact I didn't do nothing wrong. They told me I had to get out immediately. Excuse me? Apparently for three and a half, four months, I was living in a house that was condemned. He wasn't supposed to be renting it at all. It had power and everything, but he had illegally reconnected the power.

Sadly for Sheila, this was only the start of her journey as a tenant facing legal problems related to housing. Years later, Sheila had another nightmare landlord, whom she described in excruciating detail:

> I had this one landlord—and he's still a landlord to this day. I will never rent from him because I am terrified of this guy. But he'll let you move in with $20, right? As in a security deposit, first month. . . . As long as you pay your rent, he's fine. But if you're a female, he manages to always find a reason to come into your little crappy apartment to "fix things" and flirt with you and ask who's all in your house. And if he sees too many men, he gets jealous. He tries to hit on you. He frequently tells women that they can pay their rent in alternative ways. And he does it with all women, but especially Black women, especially ones with kids, because they're the ones that need the apartment the most. That's why we moved in with $20. I mean, that was all we could spare. I lived in one of his apartments. And I used to have my brothers and my cousin—my male cousins, everybody over—there was always dudes in my house, so I was never alone. . . . Whether he thought I was the whore of Babylon or what—it didn't matter. There was always a male presence in my house so he couldn't come at me crazy.

Sheila went on to relay other harrowing experiences. Along the way, she consistently noted the ineptitude of government actors including police, code enforcement officials, and lawyers. Sheila had endured, but despite her resilience, she had not emerged victorious. By the time we spoke, after decades of battling predatory landlords, she was bereft of options and close to hopeless about finding relief via governmental institutions. Her cynicism was broadly informed by an understanding of how race and class operated within the American political economy:

> I don't think [tenants] have any power because the system in place to check these private landlords, which is code enforcement—they don't do a good job . . . [and] these politicians that are in charge of doing the laws . . . they don't care. Because it's not affecting them. It's not affecting people like them. It's people like me, *people who look like me, people who are in the same income bracket.*

It was Sheila's assessment of her positioning (vis-à-vis race and class) that drove her negative assessment of the power of tenants like herself.

Sentiments such as this emerged again and again among interviewees. And though the political ramifications were sometimes subtle, more often they were direct and clearly spelled out by the people we interviewed. Delilah, a White woman from Upstate New York who had gone through the same court-room and judge as Aria (from the opening of this chapter), offered an instruc-tive example. Facing eviction for reasons she did not understand, Delilah practically scoffed at me when I asked her about whether she engaged in politics and if that might be a route of redress for people like her. A closer look at Delilah's experiences is illuminating. These snippets of our exchange pro-vide useful context:

> DELILAH: My landlord's trying to evict me. For what reason? I don't know. Like my rent's paid. He has no reason to evict me. He doesn't communicate with me at all. . . . I have so many violations on this house. He's not supposed to be renting. . . . My fourteen-year-old just went through her bedroom floor.
>
> JAMILA: Went through, like, fell?
>
> DELILAH: Through like her whole leg. There's a hole in the middle of her bedroom floor. And I text him because he don't answer the phone. I text him when it happened. I think it happened Thursday or Friday. I still haven't gotten a response. I mean, thank God it wasn't broken. It was just badly bruised.

After talking through her housing situation, complete with extensive details about everything that was broken in the home she rented, Delilah confessed her state of mind:

> I'm going crazy because I don't know how to do this. I don't even know why I'm [in court]. And then I call [a lawyer], and they told me, legally, you don't have to leave until he takes you to court. But I'm like, Why is he evict-ing me? There's no reason, my rent is paid. I should be taking him to court. . . . [You don't want to get in trouble for the violations], that's all you have to tell me. That's all you have to tell me. You don't have to evict me. Don't this [eviction] stay on your record? I mean, when you go look at houses, they ask you, Have you ever been evicted? . . . I got to find spots for my two daughters that got the hole in the floor to put like, man, it's stressful. Like it really is. And I'm not in the best of health at nighttime. I be in so much pain as I cry myself to sleep because I don't know what to do, like I try to do what I'm supposed to do and it don't work out. . . . When [the court officer] called everybody [in the courtroom] to see who was here, they said, If you don't have a lawyer, go out there to legal aid, but [legal aid] said they can't do it. For what reason? I don't know.

Delilah's experiences were mostly marked by confusion. She did not understand why she was being evicted despite her rent being paid. She also did not understand why she did not qualify for legal aid despite being a low-income mother of four. Toward the end of our conversation, when asked about whether she engaged in politics or ever would, she clearly explained why she did not:

> I never signed up for voting. I don't. I don't. I think it's a headache. Like, I go through enough stress. I got enough health problems. You know, it's too much drama. I hate drama. Every politician has drama. They say what you want to hear. And then they don't follow. They don't follow through. . . . I understand the point of voting to get your voice heard. But why vote for someone who's just going to lie?

This negligible faith in political actors—including but not limited to civil legal actors—aligns with the eroded political efficacy suggested by the quantitative data described in the first part of this chapter. Civil legal problems bring people into contact with state institutions at acutely vulnerable points in their lives. Often, though not always, the resulting experiences leave people feeling alone and unprotected. Civil legal processes infrequently provide redress, as we assert in chapter 1, because they are neither equipped nor designed to do so. Instead, civil justice problems bring people into encounters with a wide range of actors who are not positioned to fix the fundamental causes of their problems—and in many cases, make them worse through punitive judgments. This is a structural feature of the civil legal system, and it predictably undermines political efficacy and perceptions of democratic inclusion.

As suggested by Sheila, the negative experiences with state actors that stem from civil legal problems are often perceived as racialized. This was a common observation among Black interviewees. Even if subtle, Black women understood the racial stereotypes that people associated them with and interpreted their treatment through the lens of that knowledge. This is consistent with legal consciousness reasoning in which people's conceptions of their own identity shape how they experience and interpret legal interactions (Chua and Engel 2019).

For instance, Deanna was an older Black woman who suffered a tragic loss when her adult son contracted COVID and died during the pandemic. While she was grieving, Deanna took several days off from work. This unpaid time combined with the loss of her deceased son's income (he had lived with her and helped with bills) caused her to fall behind on rent. When her property manager noticed this, she asked Deanna about receiving Section 8:

[The property manager] said she thought that I had a government subsidy to pay part of my rent. And I told her, I said, "I don't know what about me that you think or classify me as being on Section 8." And I'm not saying anything about Section 8 at all. But what about me that you thought that I received government assistance? I said, "Is it the way I talk or my family size? What exactly is it?" And after that, it was done. . . . It was always a power struggle, even with paying my rent. It was always that she had to have the last word. . . . She told me if I didn't like the way she spoke to me, that I could just move. I don't have to stay there. . . . And so she was very secure in just doing what she wanted to do and talking and treating me in a very poor, poor manner.

When Deanna was struggling in the wake of a devastating tragedy, her property manager approached her with inaccurate and (per Deanna's implication) racialized assumptions. And when Deanna called her out for it, their relationship deteriorated. Even though Deanna soon caught up with her rent, her housing was never safe again. Before long, her landlord attempted to evict her. Deanna described what happened in this exchange:

DEANNA: I ended up in court. The court thing was a real shocker to me . . . when they filed a retainer and eviction.
JAMILA: And what was the reason they stated for that?
DEANNA: That I owed money in the amount of two thousand plus dollars.
JAMILA: Even though the checks had cleared?
DEANNA: Correct.
JAMILA: So you didn't owe anything even when they filed?
DEANNA: That's correct. . . . I was served the papers by a process server. . . . When I came home from work . . . the papers were laying by my back door. . . . They were laying by my back door, and so I picked them up, and that's when I learned about the eviction. . . . [So] I [immediately] went to legal services. . . . I went to their website, and I did an application and just explained this packet of [eviction] papers I received [on December 4]. . . . I immediately got a call from legal services. . . . The lady on the phone told me, "I'm going to help you as much as I can . . . but you have a return to court date. You have a court

date on December 8." And so December 8, I went to court [without a lawyer because it was too quick for legal services to get me one for that]. . . . I went before the judge and she said, "We're going to set a trial or hearing." . . . With it being nearer to the holidays, someone in the court said, "Well, you know, we break [soon], so are we going to hold this over?" And the judge responded, "No." And [my landlord's attorney] requested that it be expedited.

Deanna was astonished at the pace of the proceedings. Despite it being the holidays, the eviction moved forward swiftly. And though she was eventually assigned a legal services attorney, Deanna never spoke to that person until a single brief conversation two days before the hearing. Deanna wanted to pursue mediation, but she was never able to arrange that process with her lawyer:

> I knew about mediation . . . to have a conversation and to come to an agreement [because] I did not want an eviction on my record. I had been doing very well for the last three years . . . and I wanted to continue to improve, not go backward, but [my attorney] was not invested [in] or connected to my case at all because he didn't have the time to be. . . . His representation, it didn't get me anywhere. And when I say that, I don't say that to criticize, I just say that it was not beneficial in any manner.

Ultimately, Deanna was evicted and forced out of her home just before Christmas. Her first Christmas without her son was also without a place to live. Upset about how things turned out, she went to the supervising attorney at the legal services organization that assigned her a lawyer. It did not go well.

> What the supervising attorney told me as I made a complaint about my representation, he said, "Well, we're going to close your case because I don't think there's anything further that can be done." . . . He bragged to me about how he's been in this position for the last twenty-seven plus years. So I thought, wow. If anyone has been treated in the manner that I have over the last twenty-seven years, there's no wonder people have evictions on their record and they're having a difficult time finding housing and that they move from the area because they can't; you don't get a second chance here.

The spiral of events that unfolded in Deanna's life over the span of less than a year began with her experience of racialized stereotyping, escalated when she tried to push back against that, and was exacerbated by ineffective legal counsel. Like Sheila and Delilah, she came to believe that courts, lawyers, and government officials could not help her. But unlike Sheila and Delilah, she knew where she could find help: Deanna became involved with her local tenant union. It supported her throughout her legal debacle, showed up in court when she was there, raised funds to help her find a new home, and helped her to channel her frustration toward larger efforts for change in her local area. In chapter 6, we delve into what happens when tenant organizations intervene in the lives of people experiencing civil legal problems—and what it means for democracy. The broader point of this chapter, however, is that in the absence of such nongovernmental involvement, civil legal problems, institutions, and processes can create negative feedback loops that attenuate political efficacy and democratic citizenship.

The Political Consequences of Civil (In)justice

Ray, a Black man in his late thirties who faced eviction in an Atlanta housing court, was given seven days to vacate the home that he had lived in with his wife and children for the last seven years. The judge at Ray's eviction hearing allowed him time to speak in court, but Ray did not have formal legal representation. In the end, Ray's arguments did not prevail. The judge told Ray that though he was "very passionate," her hands were tied. She insisted that seven days was the "most the law allows." Ray left the eviction proceedings with a decidedly cynical view of the legal process:

> I didn't have a chance for a fair trial today. . . . No matter what I did today, the judge already knew what she was going to do. . . . The judge represents the bankers. . . . I don't understand why there aren't lawyers here representing us. . . . It's about the pockets. . . . These folks, it's a game they playing.

As this chapter has made clear, Ray is not alone in his experiences or the political inferences he draws from them. Millions of people in the United States—disproportionately those living in or near poverty, women, and people of color—face circumstances like this each year. They move through civil courts, engage (or are unable to engage) civil legal attorneys, seek help from local organizations, and find manifold ways to confront their civil legal problems (Michener 2022). As Ray intimates ("The judge represents the bankers. . . . It's about the pockets"), civil legal predicaments are not isolated or arbitrary troubles. Instead, they stem from policy choices connected to a racialized political economy of scarcity and inequality (Michener 2023c; Shanahan et al. 2022; Brito et al. 2022). Such political-economic circumstances are ultimately a function of power relations. This observation underscores the importance of studying the political repercussions of civil legal systems. In this chapter, we examined relationships between civil legal experiences and political life. Given the racial disproportionalities endemic to civil legal processes, we paid particular attention to racial heterogeneity in such relationships.

As expected, we found negative correlations between civil justice problems and political efficacy, with especially acute patterns among Black and Latinx denizens. We also found associations between civil legal problems and perceptions of democratic inclusion. Turning to extensive qualitative evidence, we considered the experiences of people like Sheila, Delilah, and Deanna. The details of these women's lives are not just morally disconcerting, they are politically meaningful. The actors and institutions that each woman encounters map to political sensibilities like those we find in the quantitative data.

Altogether, these findings point to the significance of civil legal processes for US democracy. In the context of continued underinvestment in social welfare policies and growing economic inequality, civil justice problems are both plentiful and racialized. Civil legal systems are crucial to managing these problems, particularly within race-class-subjugated communities. Along the way, civil legal institutions shape the political lives of the people who engage them. Civil justice thus plays a pivotal role in structuring democratic governance in the United States. While this chapter has focused primarily on the political upshots of the demand side of the justice gap, the stories of people like Delilah, Deanna, and Ray also bring into focus the importance that the supply of legal representation plays in how people navigate civil legal problems. In the next two chapters, we turn our attention to the politics of supply in the political economy of civil justice.

4

"I Feel Like They Should Be Doing More"

RISE AND RETRENCHMENT IN THE POLICY FOUNDATIONS OF THE JUSTICE GAP

QUIANA, A Black woman from Upstate New York, didn't think that she should pay to be poisoned. Shortly after a local code enforcement official observed lead paint in Quiana's home, her children's doctor informed her that three of her four kids had borderline high levels of lead. Her fourth and youngest—a three-year-old boy—had dangerously high levels. Public health officials told her to move, but Quiana could not afford to leave her current apartment. She was on a long waiting list of people eligible to receive Section 8 vouchers. Moreover, there was a massive shortage of affordable rental units in her city. The local department of health fined her landlord and directed him to abate the lead, but more than a year went by without him taking any action to do so. While Quiana and her children continued to be exposed to dangerous levels of lead, her landlord suffered little punishment beyond relatively modest fines.

Quiana sought a lawyer to help her address the lead issue, but she could not find one. Her local civil legal services office focused mostly on eviction cases and did not have the bandwidth to take on lead cases in a city with a rampant lead problem. Federal guidelines limiting the ability of civil legal services programs to engage in class actions for issues like lead abatement precluded a more efficient legal approach to helping people like Quiana. After a frustrating year of hoping and waiting for help, Quiana decided to stop paying rent.

Though her landlord was unresponsive to the lead situation, he swiftly initiated eviction proceedings once Quiana withheld her rent. She went back to legal services when she was served eviction papers. This time, she got an attorney to represent her in housing court. Eviction proceedings were within the ambit of what legal services in her city could take on. With the help of a lawyer, Quiana opposed her eviction. She managed to ward off displacement from her home, yet Quiana remains in unsafe housing with an unaccountable landlord who is complicit in harming her family. It may only be a matter of time, given the circumstances, before further legal problems arise. When Quiana described the needs of tenants like her, she focused on their lack of voice:

> When it comes to the judges and even code enforcement, I feel like they should be doing more. Because I'm quite sure this is not the only house that's going through situations. So for [the landlord] to still be out here collecting his rent and half-ass doing his job, I feel like that's where the higher-ups should come in . . . but it doesn't seem like they're doing anything about it really, and what can we do? Like me, for example, I'm trying. I been trying to contact these people and that people, and it's like, I'm not getting nowhere. . . . Tenants like me, we need a voice because we're not being heard.

Quiana lacked the power and resources to change the circumstances that produced her legal problems. The primary reasons for Quiana's predicament emerge at the intersection of political and economic power: inadequate regulation of predatory landlords, insufficient availability of affordable housing, and an underfunded housing voucher program. These are the types of problems described in the previous chapters that generate demand for the civil legal system. But Quiana's experience was also shaped by the dynamics of supply. While having legal representation in her eviction case helped Quiana to avert further disaster, it did nothing to address the situation generating her legal need in the first place. And her inability to retain legal counsel to tackle the underlying problem she faced—the presence of unsafe levels of lead in her housing—was not the result of chance or solely the consequence of underfunded legal services. As this chapter will detail, the resource and regulatory limitations that make it so people such as Quiana cannot rely on access to counsel in certain types of civil legal proceedings are the result of intentional policy choices about how to structure markets as well as distribute resources to preserve a fundamentally unequal political economy.

———

In 1964, US president Lyndon Baines Johnson signed into law the Economic Opportunity Act—a central pillar of his War on Poverty. The act allowed for the creation of a federal program to provide funding for civil legal aid to people living in and near poverty. While the Office of Economic Opportunity's (OEO) Legal Services Program (LSP) was not the best known of the War on Poverty policies, Senator Walter Mondale described it, as cited earlier, as "the most effective poverty program, dollar for dollar," and argued that it "probably caused more hope and trust in the system and more basic legal reform per dollar than has any other program" (US Senate Hearings 1970). It was also an initiative that garnered considerable bipartisan support among legislators. Although elements of the program attracted critics—most prominent among them California governor Ronald Reagan—the goal of using the civil courts to help lift people out of poverty was initially popular among members of both parties. In 1974, Congress passed legislation to create a new federal entity—the LSC—to oversee the continued provision of federal grants to support civil legal representation for low-income people.

One of the LSC's major goals was to secure enough funding to support "minimum access" to low-cost civil legal representation across the country. Minimum access is defined as sufficient funding for each local legal services provider to support two attorneys for every ten thousand low-income people in its jurisdiction. By 1981, the LSC annual budget topped $321 million—more than quadrupling the agency's initial allocation in 1975. Minimum access had been achieved. Reaching that target marked a major victory for policymakers and advocates who saw civil legal services as a key tool for combating poverty in the United States. But this early success was not a harbinger of things to come.

With the presidential election of Reagan in 1980, the LSC's chief antagonist was now in a position of power to oversee the fledgling agency. While bipartisan support in Congress remained, efforts to reauthorize the LSC continually failed throughout the Reagan presidency, leaving the agency's funding subject to the whims of each annual appropriations process. Figure 4.1 depicts the amount of funding necessary to achieve minimum access compared to the budget allocated to the LSC by appropriation year. As it illustrates, funding to support the LSC remained relatively stagnant for forty years after hitting the target of minimum access in 1981.

While Reagan's departure offered a spark of hope for revitalizing the LSC, the Republican House majority that swept into office in the 104th Congress ushered in a wave of conservative legislators who embraced Reagan's hostility toward the agency, further eroding support for federal civil legal aid. The LSC budget was slashed, and a slew of new restrictions were enacted to limit the types of cases and activities grantees could undertake. Even though the LSC

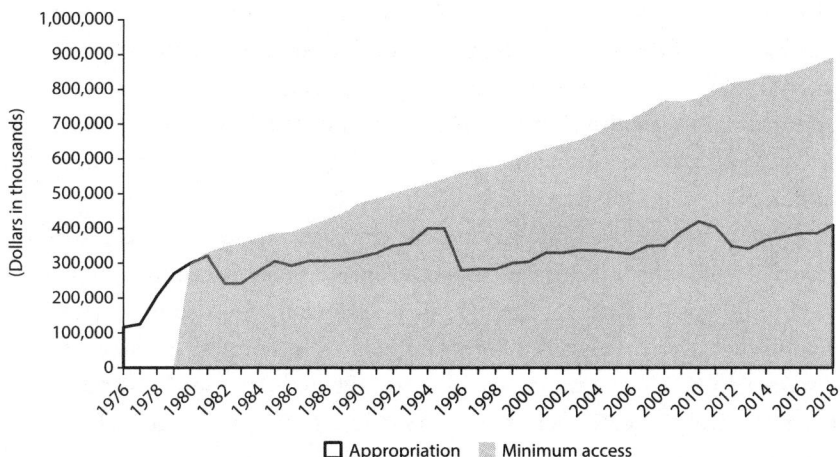

FIGURE 4.1. LSC annual appropriations versus necessary funding for minimum access
Source: Congressional appropriations 1976–2018 (LSC 2024).
Note: Appropriations not adjusted for inflation. For inflation adjusted numbers, see Reich 2021.

budget reached a high-water mark of $420 million under unified Democratic control of the government in 2010, the Trump administration subsequently tried to eliminate the agency in each of its four annual budget proposals. The result of this political tug-of-war was an annual appropriation of $385 million in 2018—an increase of only $60 million from the agency's 1981 budget without accounting for inflation. Thus by 2017, LSC funding secured only half the necessary amount to help meet the baseline need for civil legal representation for low-income people.

How did federal efforts to support access to civil legal representation go from a bipartisan measure hailed as one of the most effective tools to combat poverty to a target for elimination by conservative groups and politicians? This chapter tracks the rise and retrenchment of federal efforts to provide access to civil legal representation for low-income people. Drawing from archival and legislative records as well as an original dataset of all federal bills proposed to address access to civil justice from 1966 through 2020, we explain how the politics of civil legal representation became entangled in a larger debate over who deserves power in the American political economy.

Specifically, we demonstrate how three main approaches emerged in deliberations over access to civil legal representation, each with a distinct vision for its relationship to the distribution of economic and political power in the United States. Proponents of what we call a *structural transformation approach* to civil justice saw the federal funding of civil legal representation as an opportunity to use the courts to fundamentally restructure power relations, acting to give greater influence to people living in poverty in the absence of sufficient legislative will to do so.

Proponents of a second alternative, what we call a *procedural justice approach*, envisioned civil legal representation as a means to address individual legal problems through the "civilizing" mechanism of the courts. While this tactic sought to provide aid to low-income people, many adherents did so to improve compliance among race-class-subjugated communities and thwart what adherents perceived as the threat to existing power relations that collective political action might spark. For these proponents of procedural justice, civil legal representation was a conservative policy tool to individualize collective problems to preserve existing power arrangements.

Finally, a third approach—one that came to dominate among a growing cohort of Republican lawmakers over time—sought to eliminate federal legal services funding altogether. This view encompassed what we call a *welfare retrenchment approach* whereby legal services were emblematic of a larger welfare regime deemed to be a waste of public money directed to the "undeserving poor," who were often construed in racialized terms. It was also part of a larger movement of judicial retrenchment that sought to weaken the US civil rights infrastructure (Burbank and Farhang 2017; Staszak 2015). We show how the push and pull among these three approaches corresponds with larger ebbs and flows in support for the welfare state, ultimately limiting the prospects for a thriving program of access to justice along with its potential to combat poverty and reshape power relations.

The Scope and Consequences of the Justice Gap

E. Clinton Bamberger Jr., who would become the first director of the OEO's LSP, recognized a fundamental truth about inequality in the US civil justice system: "A search for truth and justice which depends upon an adversary system gropes half-blind when there is no advocate for one side of the proposition" (LSP 1966b). In a polity increasingly characterized by adversarial legalism, access to civil legal representation is a basic aspect of a free and fair society (Kagan 1991, 2019). Civil statutes protect vital economic, social, and political rights, such as preventing unfair evictions, securing proper access to public benefits, representing borrowers in disputes with lenders and debt collectors, safeguarding women from abusive relationships, resolving family-related disputes (e.g., child support and custody), and adjudicating deportation proceedings. Hence the ability of people to navigate the civil legal system is central to realizing their full citizenship.

Despite the profound importance of the protections provided by civil law, recall that there is no constitutionally guaranteed right to civil legal counsel. As a result, a pervasive "justice gap"—the chasm between low-income people's civil legal needs and their ability to get legal representation—exists in the United States. This gap is especially critical because low-income, racially marginalized people are most liable to fall between its cracks.

The consequences of lacking representation are severe: unrepresented or self-represented litigants are at a dramatic disadvantage in the complex, highly specialized US court system. For example, a randomized experimental study of the effects of legal assistance for low-income tenants in New York City housing court found that tenants with legal assistance were 32 percent less likely to have final judgments against them relative to pro se tenants (Seron et al. 2001). A preponderance of available evidence indicates that when low-income people secure legal representation, the courts are more likely to work in their favor. Quite often, however, litigants who are denied access to legal representation have negative experiences of the courts (Tyler and McGraw 1986; Zimmerman and Tyler 2009). This perpetuates a troubling cycle of economic inequality wherein the ability of a person to successfully petition the courts to receive or maintain resources that bolster their economic position depends not purely on the merits of a case but instead on a person's capacity to afford or obtain representation. As the previous chapter demonstrates, inadequate access to counsel not only can threaten people's health and well-being but also undermines people's feelings of political efficacy and ultimately their trust in governing institutions.

Given the extraordinary stakes, why do policymakers consistently fail to address this gap? Historians, legal scholars, and former government officials have offered rich descriptive accounts of waxing and waning federal government support for civil legal aid (Eakeley 1997; Houseman 2001; Houseman and Perle 2007; Johnson 1974; Rhode 2004) along with the changing approach to legal services within the LSC (Houseman 2001; Quigley 1997; Vivero 2001). Others have explored the broader patterns of judicial retrenchment by which conservatives sought to roll back private enforcement actions for a bevy of federal protections (Burbank and Farhang 2017; Staszak 2015, 2024). But such work scratches the surface of the politics of civil legal access (Michener 2018; Michener, SoRelle, and Thurston 2022). Indeed, there is little evidence to show how political processes systematically structure the development of federal policymaking to address access to civil justice for marginalized communities. We offer such evidence here.

Explaining the Politics of Federal Support
for Civil Legal Representation

We contend that policymakers' preferences for how best to address the justice gap can be understood as the intersection of their positions on two key questions about the goal and scope of civil legal representation. First, should the government fund a program designed to address the individual legal needs of low-income litigants? Second, should the government fund a program designed to address poverty in a more systemic or transformative way? The primary vehicle to achieve this second vision was called "law reform": leveraging legal tools like class action lawsuits, test cases, and lobbying to "change [the] legal, political, social, and economic system to the advantage of [indigent] clients" (Quigley 1997, 242). Law reform was, in essence, an effort to use civil legal institutions to enact wholesale change to what was deemed a structurally unfair political and economic system that disadvantaged poor and minoritized people (see Lawrence 2014). Figure 4.2 shows how these dimensions overlapped to create three major approaches to federal policy innovation to address inadequacies in civil legal representation.

In the 1960s, a group of progressive reformers and philanthropists began to consider the possibility that the civil courts could be used to challenge the social policies—and larger social structures—they deemed to be regressive. Shaped by the efforts of a variety of civil rights organizations, like the National Association for the Advancement of Colored People's (NAACP) Legal Defense Fund, the idea to employ subsidized civil legal representation for low-income people to not only assist individuals but also change existing laws in service of broader constituencies became known as law reform (Houseman and Perle 2007; Lawrence 2014). The litigators who led this work—spearheaded initially by Edward Sparer, who oversaw the legal efforts of the transformative Mobilization for Youth program in New York City—"envisioned a constitutional 'right to live' that would require the federal government to guarantee a minimum standard of living to all citizens. They also

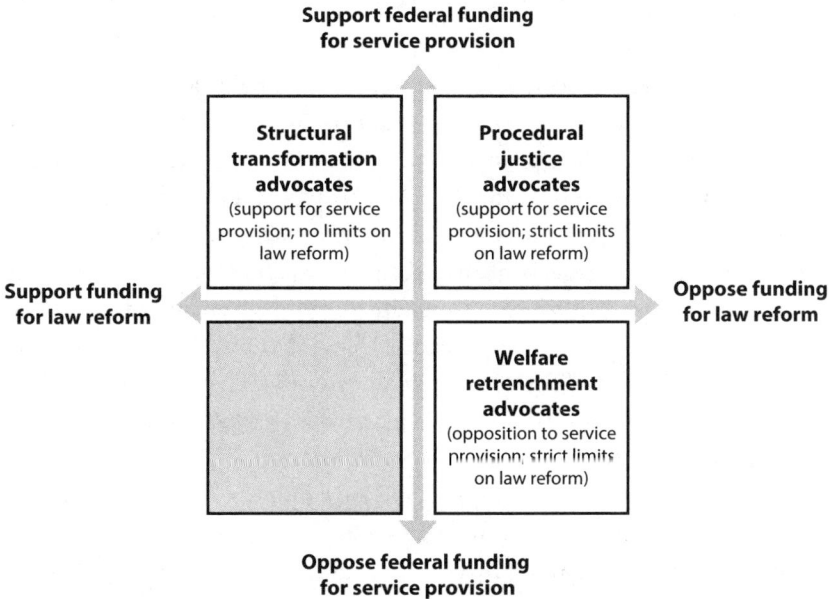

FIGURE 4.2. Political coalitions and support for federal legal services program

intended to bring welfare administration . . . within the general legal confines of the federal constitution" (Davis 1993, 2).

Policymakers who embraced this vision, supporting funding for both individual service provision and robust law reform efforts, represent what we call a structural transformation approach to addressing the justice gap. As we will show, proponents of this approach supported a federal program of civil legal services that could help to fundamentally remake the American political economy into a system that more equitably served structurally disadvantaged communities. They viewed the courts as an arena in which a range of issues from welfare policy to civil rights could be expanded in the absence of a political will to do so through legislative means.

Moreover, political elites who set their sights on structural change envisioned law reform as part of a broader effort to build collective political power among marginalized communities (Davis 1993; Loffredo 2001). They imagined that law reform might spark a broader collective movement for social change that would exert simultaneous pressure on the political system to enact policies to address poverty. This logic is consistent with the theory of policy feedback, in which the expansion of policy benefits can mobilize constituents to exert political pressure to maintain those benefits. Policymakers who embraced this scheme sought not only to deal with the supply of legal representation but to ameliorate the demand necessitating it too.

A second approach, which we refer to as procedural justice, embraced the provision of individual legal services, but opposed using federal funds to engage in law reform. The primary goal, as we will demonstrate, was to "civilize" marginalized groups through the legal system. For procedural justice proponents, civil legal representation and its capacity to address individual legal needs served as a mechanism to curb efforts, especially among less affluent, urban communities of color, to agitate for systemic change to the existing political-economic order. As legal scholar Deborah Rhode (2004, 59) explains of these policymakers, "Their objective was not to reform the law but to enhance its credibility and ensure its acceptance in the eyes of the lower classes, who might otherwise be led astray by 'social agitators.'"

The idea that a robust program of civil legal representation could be used as a mechanism for social control came into sharp focus during the upheaval of the 1960s. Sparked by concerns over so-called race riots that ignited tensions in urban centers across the country, policymakers began to consider whether programs like government-funded civil legal representation might not only boost the economic conditions of marginalized communities in cities throughout the United States but tamp down on civil disorder as well. Legal leaders emphasized this rationale in their entreaties to Congress:

> Lawyers serving the poor help them to develop self-confidence and a new respect for themselves when they realize that they need not be afraid to lawfully express themselves against governmental authority or welfare agents or unscrupulous landlords or lenders. Through appropriate legal help, an impoverished person may . . . come to learn that the law is intended for his protection, not his degradation. (ABA 1966, 7)

This approach is consistent with the neoliberal, paternalist trend in the welfare state more broadly (Soss, Fording, and Schram 2011). It was designed to individualize what were ostensibly structurally rooted, collective problems that disproportionately affected marginalized communities. And it put the onus on individuals, rather than policymakers, to pursue recourse. Thus procedural justice advocates opposed efforts that might seek to fundamentally change existing political-economic power arrangements through law reform activities. Instead, their goal was to individualize collective problems and preserve the existing social order. Despite an approach that took responsibility for solving structural socioeconomic problems out of the hands of public agents, procedural justice advocates nonetheless spoke directly to how the provision of legal assistance could restore faith in public institutions, increasing people's trust and efficacy in the legal system:

> The law—known in the ghetto as "the man"—seems to the poor man always to be on the other side. . . . The disasters that are visited upon the poor are compounded by their ignorance, lack of education, poverty and helplessness. Put a lawyer by their side and the whole outlook changes in almost every particular. (ABA 1966, 6–7)

In practice, the procedural justice approach mirrored what many of the existing legal aid providers operating piecemeal across the country were already doing to tackle individual client needs. It sought to address the question of supply without altering the conditions of demand for civil legal justice. By contrast, the foundation-backed structural transformation approach emphasizing law reform represented a new style of poverty lawyering that focused on not only individual client needs but also the larger policy landscape that shaped those needs (Lawrence 2014).

Finally, a third approach emerged that, as we will demonstrate, linked federally funded legal services to what conservative Republicans perceived to be the worst elements of the welfare state. For these advocates of welfare retrenchment, neither individual service provision nor law reform were desirable programs for federal policymakers to purse. Instead, opponents of welfare campaigned to weaken or outright eliminate any federal funding for civil legal service provision. They fought against addressing both supply and demand problems.[1]

We contend that the political development of federal policy to address the justice gap reflects the evolving relationships among these three primary approaches and their distinctive goals. In the following pages, we detail those relationships along with their correspondence to the emergence, growth, and retrenchment of a federal program of civil legal assistance for people living in poverty. We draw from historical accounts as well as legislative records and archival material from the Johnson and Clinton Presidential Archives and the

---

1. Theoretically, a fourth group could have emerged seeking transformational shifts in power relations while not actively supporting individual legal service provision. In practice, however, such a group did not manifest among policymakers during the period we observe.

Consumer Movements Archives.[2] We then explore an original dataset of all bills proposed in Congress from 1966 to 2020 that address civil legal assistance, paying careful attention to the frequency, substance, and beneficiaries of that legislation. Ultimately, the story that unfolds shows how these three approaches were shaped by as well as responsive to broader patterns of the racialized discourse on welfare policymaking and political economy in the United States, with consequences for the fate of "the most successful poverty program" to emerge from the War on Poverty.

The Political Development of US Civil Legal Services

As we describe in chapter 2, US civil legal institutions are extensively fragmented, as are the sources of financial support for civil legal representation. Hence federal funding is perhaps the most crucial tool for ensuring that low-income people have sufficient access to justice within the civil court system. The availability of federal support for low-income civil legal assistance is the result of a near century-long process of political development.

Civil Legal Aid before Federal Intervention

As with many forms of social assistance in the United States, support for low-income civil legal aid was initially a private affair. Apart from a short-lived program of civil legal assistance provided to newly emancipated Black Americans by the Freedmen's Bureau between 1865 and 1868, the federal government—and indeed most state and local governments—was largely absent from the provision of civil legal representation at the beginning of the twentieth century (Westwood 1971). Instead, local self-help and charitable organizations began to fill the gap.

A group of wealthy German immigrants founded what is widely accepted as the first organized private program of civil legal assistance in New York City in 1876; it would later become the Legal Aid Society of New York (Rhode 2004). Other cities followed suit, with legal aid programs often initiated by women's organizations (Batlan 2015). By 1965, most large urban areas had some form of civil legal aid program in place (Houseman and Perle 2007), and many of them were designed to facilitate immigrant assimilation (Davis 1993).

2. The qualitative appendix contains further detail on the historical archival methods used in this chapter.

Several were offered by private businesses with full-time staff, while others were housed in law schools, local government agencies, or even local bar associations supported by pro bono work.

The effort to provide more extensive low-cost or free civil legal assistance was initially championed by two major national organizations. The first was the American Bar Association (ABA). In 1920, Reginald Heber Smith, the director of the Boston Legal Aid Society, addressed the ABA's annual meeting to urge its members to take up the cause of civil legal aid to the poor (ABA 1966). The year prior to his speech, Smith (1919, 9) published a book, *Justice and the Poor*, in which he argued that "without equal access to the law the system not only robs the poor of their only protection, but it places in the hands of their oppressors the most powerful and ruthless weapon ever invented." Smith's assessment highlights the link between legal power and a more equitable political economy. The ABA (1966) responded to Smith's call, establishing the Committee on Legal Aid Work, which formed the foundation of the group's expanding efforts in the realm of access to civil legal representation. The second major organization to emerge in support of low-income civil legal representation was NLADA. Established in 1911 as the National Alliance of Legal Aid Societies, NLADA incorporated in 1949, and it became the only national organization dedicated solely to coordinating and assisting with the provision of civil legal aid (ABA 1965).

By the early 1960s, and with encouragement from the ABA and NLADA lobbying efforts, federal policymakers espoused a growing interest in the potential for civil legal aid to improve the conditions of low-income communities across the country. As leaders of the major legal associations articulated about the link between poverty alleviation and access to justice, "It will be impossible to . . . completely eradicate poverty wherever it is found in this country—if the poor man does not have a lawyer to speak for him and guide him in solving his problems" (ABA 1966, 5).

Legal Aid in the War on Poverty

The opportunity to create the first federal program of civil legal assistance ultimately emerged as part of President Johnson's War on Poverty. In 1964, the central policy plank of Johnson's effort—the Economic Opportunity Act—was signed into law. While the act did not explicitly allocate funding for civil legal aid, Title II-A authorized the creation of local community action agencies empowered to "mobilize all resources within the locality to combat poverty"

(LSP 1966b). In 1965, Congress amended the Economic Opportunity Act to clarify that funds could be used for programs not explicitly enumerated by the law. As the Senate Committee on Labor and Public Welfare explained, "The listing of activities in Section 205(a), of course, is not intended to exclude other types of activities . . . such as legal services to the poor" (Senate Report 599 1965).

At the 1965 ABA convention in Miami, Sargent Shriver, director of the OEO, underscored his desire to see the agency develop a program of legal services for low-income people: "There is growing awareness across the country that the poor have, in fact, been deprived of their rights under the law. With this awareness, there is a new appreciation of the contributions the law and lawyers can make to get poor people out of poverty" (LSP 1966b). Thus the OEO established the LSP in 1965. Much of the early program leadership came, however, not from the ranks of legal services providers but instead from private law. The new initiative was led by Bamberger, and in its first year, the LSP (1966b) distributed over $27 million in grants to more than 160 local programs representing forty-three states. In 1966, amendments to the Economic Opportunity Act formally authorized the LSP.

The new federal program represented a fairly radical departure from efforts to provide similar services in other countries. Most existing programs employed a system known as judicare, wherein private attorneys were paid a fee-for-service to represent low-income clients. While the Association of Trial Lawyers of America preferred a judicare approach, the ABA and NLADA backed the OEO's plan to fund full-service legal aid providers.[3] Bamberger and other key actors in the LSP's development preferred this model because they both felt it would be less expensive, and critically, believed dedicated legal services attorneys would be more likely to advocate for the needs of their low-income clients (Houseman and Perle 2007).

The result was a federal program with three main approaches to combating poverty. First and most prominently, the LSP sought to assist low-income individuals with their specific civil legal problems. The LSP issued grants to

---

3. Notably, however, NLADA was initially reticent about the LSP because, first, the organization was not adequately consulted about the LSP's design, and second, the LSP was modeled on the foundation-backed civil legal programs of the 1960s that emphasized policy change in addition to the more traditional modes of client service, which were most common among NLADA members (Lawrence 2014). For a more thorough overview of the competing visions of a federal legal services program, see Davis 1993; Lawrence 2014.

support a web of existing civil legal service providers across the country. Most of the decision-making power about client eligibility and service provision was left to these local providers, but the LSP issued clear guidance that "all areas of the civil law should be included, and a full spectrum of legal work should be provided: advice, representation, litigation, and appeal" (LSP 1966a). Federal funds were thus used to support a variety of different programs across the country. For example, grants funded a program in Washington, DC, that maintained twenty-five attorneys across eight neighborhood offices, a program in Indianapolis launched jointly by the Indiana University Law School and School for Social Work, a combined criminal-civil program run by the Houston Legal Foundation, and direct support to small law offices in towns like Lynn, Massachusetts, and Fort Pierce, Florida (LSP 1966b). After only three years in operation, the LSP supported over 260 operations, covering every state except North Dakota (Houseman and Perle 2007).

While these programs helped expand access to civil legal representation for low-income communities across the country, the LSP funds were nowhere near sufficient to meet the demand. Recognizing the limitations of direct service provision, the LSP leadership encouraged grantees to expand their focus to a second plank: law reform.[4] The goal in doing so was not only to offer individual service provision to clients in need but also to tackle the underlying structural issues that generated the conditions of poverty in the first place. As Bamberger clearly articulated in a 1965 address at NLADA's annual meeting,

> "Lawyers must be activists to leave a contribution to society. The law is more than a control; it is an instrument for social change. The role of [the] OEO program is to provide the means within the democratic process for the law and lawyers to release the bonds which imprison people in poverty, to marshal the forces of law to combat the causes and effects of poverty." (Houseman 2017)

This approach was championed by so-called poverty lawyers like Sparer, many of whom had roots in labor organizing and operated within a broader network of activists involved in collective mobilization around welfare rights,

---

4. Leaders at the LSP considered several options to supplement direct service provision. For instance, the "whole person" coordinated programs piloted by Grey Areas sites funded by the Ford Foundation like New Haven that integrated social workers to address economic, social, and legal needs in a one-stop-shop model (Davis 1993; Lawrence 2014).

such as the National Welfare Rights Organization and the Poor People's Campaign (Davis 1993).

The LSP's second director, Earl Johnson—an outlier in relation to other LSP administrators for his considerable experience in the legal aid community—issued a managerial directive that would put law reform efforts at the top of the agency's priorities (Lawrence 2014). In its 1969 report to Congress, the LSP explained this choice: "One of the principal missions of the LSP is to . . . challenge the statutory, regulatory, and administrative base of the existing order considered to discriminate against the poor" (General Accounting Office 1969). The goal was to utilize class action suits, test cases, and legislative and administrative advocacy to expand the reach of civil legal representation to those who were not personally involved in cases (LSP 1966a). In essence, Johnson encouraged a dual focus on increasing the supply of lawyers while using law reform as a mechanism for system-level change that would ultimately decrease the demand for legal services.

Much of the law reform work took shape in appellate advocacy, which extended from individual client cases. Although the number of funded providers determined to be engaging in effective law reform activities was relatively low—only 18 percent according to a sample studied by the General Accounting Office in 1968—LSP-funded law reform efforts nonetheless had considerable reach. Of the 1 million cases litigated by LSP grantees between 1966 and 1974, 164 made their way to the US Supreme Court (Lawrence 2014). As public law scholar Susan Lawrence notes, this represented a watershed moment for legal doctrine on poverty law, which languished prior to the LSP's law reform efforts due in large part to the unavailability of legal counsel to represent poor people's claims. As she puts it, "The dearth of case law was not the result of a lack of legal problems among the poor, but rather, it was the result of their inability to retain counsel and their resulting de facto exclusion from the appellate courts" (Lawrence 2014, 10).

LSP attorneys won landmark decisions that fundamentally reshaped the provision of welfare both nationally and in the states. At the federal level, for example, LSP lawyers brought cases that overturned residency requirements for welfare benefits and struck down the "man-in-the-house rule."[5] At the state level, LSP lawyers helped to outlaw retaliatory evictions, protect against

---

5. The man-in-the-house rule stripped welfare benefits from eligible children if their mother lived with or was in a relationship with a single or married man, even if he did not financially support the child.

wage garnishment, and support migrant farmworkers (General Accounting Office 1969).[6] The OEO estimated that law reform efforts benefited more than 1.5 million low-income people in the United States between 1966 and 1968 alone—far beyond the reach of LSP-funded individual client services.

To support both its legal aid and law reform efforts, the LSP embraced a third initiative: legal education. It funded the Reginald Heber Smith Fellowship, which was created to recruit "the best and the brightest" law graduates to legal services. Recipients of the fellowship were known as "Reggies," many of whom would become leaders not only within the legal services community but in the wider progressive movement too.[7] The LSP also funded the creation of backup centers, frequently housed in law schools, to provide technical assistance and support for legal services attorneys. Backup centers were a critical tool, as LSP program director Theodore Tetzlaff told Congress, because they supplied expertise in "specialized areas of the law so that every poverty lawyer need not be an expert in all areas of the law affecting the poor" (US House 1973, 46).[8]

The LSP gained momentum, but as it grew in scope and impact, cracks began to emerge in its support. A contingent of conservative lawmakers from both parties started to push back against the program when the LSP attorneys continued to win the law reform battle in opposition to some local, state, and federal policymakers' efforts to curb or dismantle programs. As Senator Mondale articulated during US Senate (1970, 135) hearings for the program:

> This remarkable organization has brought an awful lot of important lawsuits that have stepped on some very big toes. Consequently, for a long time, people have been trying to figure out some way of getting their hands on the program and civilizing it. The thought that the poor could actually come in and bring a lawsuit was deeply offensive to some people.

6. The LSP's litigation in support of migrant farmworkers created one of the most powerful and persistent enemies of federal funding to support civil legal representation: the American Farm Bureau Federation (General Accounting Office 1969).

7. Deputy director of advocacy organization, personal interview with authors, November 20, 2014.

8. For example, Mallory worked for the National Consumer Law Center (NCLC), which was originally created as a backup center to help attorneys supporting low-income clients with consumer law problems (e.g., debt collection). While no longer a backup center, the NCLC still publishes a series of reference texts to support attorneys representing low-income clients in different areas of consumer law.

Indeed, the possibility that law reform efforts, and in particular the use of class actions and test cases, might serve to reshape power dynamics in favor of economically and racially marginalized communities frequently emerged in congressional debates over the future of the LSP. Opponents of the LSP started to construct a narrative suggesting that legal services attorneys were pursuing political objectives at the expense of client needs. But supporters pushed back against this as a false dichotomy. As William Wagner, president of the National Clients' Council representing the interests of individual litigants, explained, "The general view [among opponents in the Nixon administration] . . . is that legal services attorneys spend all of their time pushing test cases—putting causes ahead of cases—at the expense of individual clients." Wagner challenged that assessment, noting that

> an objective examination of legal services cases which have turned out to be landmark law reform cases supports the view that, just as the civil rights movement of the 1960's began with one tired lady, Rosa Parks, refusing to give up her seat on a bus, so did these cases begin with one individual client or group of clients coming to a legal services attorney for help. And, even more importantly, the record shows that individual legal problems were dealt with effectively, even though the vision achieved had wider impact. (US House 1973, 78)

William Klaus, director of the Philadelphia Urban Coalition, went one step further, contesting the notion that there was a clear delineation between law reform, or politically motivated cases, and politically neutral legal representation. He offered the following example about a real class action suit—the type that LSP opponents viewed as inherently political and sought to curtail. Describing a case that legal services attorneys in Philadelphia brought against the Department of Housing and Urban Development (HUD) to enjoin it from selling reconditioned homes without addressing the presence of unsafe lead paint, Klaus opined,

> I submit to you that any person with a family of small children in a poverty condition in a major city is an adequate member of that class. There are over 5,000 houses in the city of Philadelphia which have been certified to contain lead-based paint in their interiors. They are all in the urban inner city and people with small children are living in them at this moment, and I am sure children are eating that paint today. . . . [Has] the case that I described been a politicization? Have these been cases which lawyers bring on the

theory that they should change the social order and put forward their political concepts and their social ideas ahead of the rights of the individual client? . . . If this is politicization, then I submit that politicization is good. The entire concept of the lawyer in our society is a political concept. . . . [H]e is involved in a political process to some degree. (US House 1973, 81–82)

Scholarly accounts of the LSP similarly suggest that the division between individual client services and law reform was murky. While the intention of law reform to use policy as a poverty alleviation tool was not hidden by the LSP administrators, the appellate casework at the foundation of the agency's law reform efforts did stem relatively organically from client needs (Kessler 1987; Lawrence 2014; Marks, Leswig, and Fortinsky 1972). As Lawrence (2014) notes, it was this very commitment to serving specific client needs that preempted a more explicit political strategy with clear aims vis-à-vis the welfare state. Instead, the limited but impactful law reform efforts from LSP grantees emerged as an extension of their core client services mission.

Law reform efforts like the case Klaus describes also introduced the uncomfortable juxtaposition of government funds being used to support lawsuits brought against government agencies—and frequently over politically sensitive topics (Marks, Leswig, and Fortinsky 1972). As President Richard Nixon (1971) worried in a speech before the 92nd Congress, "Much of the litigation has placed [the LSP] in direct conflict with local and state governments. The program is concerned with social issues and is thus subject to unusually strong political pressures." As law reform detractors in Congress and the White House began to consider policies to curtail what they viewed as undesirable political activity among LSP grantees, attorneys resisted, contending that such limitations were an incursion on professional ethics. Robert Meserve, ABA president at the time, explained during congressional hearings on the program that

> the lawyer-client relationship does not change just because the Federal Government is paying the fee. There is only one code of professional responsibility. Its provisions are equally applicable to private lawyers and legal services lawyers. That is the way it should be. If we are serious about providing counsel to the poor, I think we should offer the same service as we give to our paying clients. (US House 1973, 33)

Debates over who ought to control local programs also emerged. The ABA and NLADA forcefully argued that legal professionals, and not politicians, ought to be in charge of strategic plans for the LSP. But others sought to place the LSP under the auspices of regional or state control. Donald Rumsfeld, the Nixon-appointed OEO director, testified before Congress about his concerns over local legal professionals making decisions about, for example, client eligibility for services, which had long been within the purview of LSP grantees (see LSP 1966a). As Rumsfeld pronounced,

> We have some problems which are giving me a great deal of distress . . . where the local board of directors or the local executive director or the local attorney gets involved in representing a person who is voluntarily poor as opposed to a person who is poor without any assistance from himself, if you will. I think there is a good deal of question about the desirability of the limited resources variable in the legal services program going for the defense . . . of an individual who is voluntarily poor. (US Senate 1970, 126)

These remarks are notable not only because they contradict the idea that legal professionals receiving funds ought to be able to make decisions about how best to use them but also because they demonstrate how some conservative policymakers started to extend the logic of deservingness used to attack welfare beneficiaries to the provision of civil legal assistance. But supporters of the program resisted the idea that political appointees should control local service decisions. In a back and forth with Rumsfeld, Senator Mondale raised this concern:

> If we are going to have a program for the poor, it ought to be a program that permits these lawyers to bring lawsuits that the poor most need brought, and not what some regional bureaucrat character—who probably has his political career tied up with some local politician—feels to be the best type of lawsuit. (US Senate 1970, 136)

Each of these emerging critiques center issues of political power: who has it, who is able to wield it, and whether government ought to support programs that change its allocation. They highlight how evolving debates over the future of federal support for civil legal representation ultimately represented a clash over who deserved power in the American political economy.

Despite the emergence of opposition to the LSP, bipartisan support persisted among federal policymakers in both Congress and the Nixon administration for some type of program to fund the civil legal representation of people living in poverty. As Republican senator Jacob Javits declared, "I consider the legal services program to be the most essential priority element of the war against poverty" (US Senate 1970, 120). And despite concerns over law reform, conservative supporters of civil legal aid, like Javits, who hoped it would act as a deterrent to social unrest, also had reasons to be pleased with the program. The National Advisory Commission on Civil Disorders, known colloquially as the Kerner Commission (1968, summary), singled out civil legal assistance as a key element in the limitation of civil disorder:

> Our investigation . . . establishes that virtually every major episode of violence was foreshadowed by an accumulation of unresolved grievances and by wide-spread dissatisfaction among Negroes with the unwillingness or inability of local government to respond. Overcoming these conditions is essential for community support of law enforcement and civil order. . . . Expand opportunities for ghetto residents to participate in the formulation of public policy and the implementation of programs affecting them through . . . expansion of legal services.

Indeed, the Kerner Commission (1968, 293) report noted that "the Legal Services Program . . . has made a good beginning. . . . Its present level of effort should be substantially expanded through increased private and public funding." Recently, scholars have marshaled empirical evidence to support this position, finding that cities with greater investment in Neighborhood Legal Services programs between 1965 and 1975 experienced a reduction in civil disorders (Cunningham and Gillezeau 2018). The result, as Tetzlaff conveyed to Congress, was that

> no domestic program has been more fundamentally conservative and thoroughly American than legal services. It extends the centuries-old Anglo-American notion that disputes must be settled peacefully in courts, not violently in the streets. . . . [T]hese are not the notions of class or revolution. Rather they are age-old principles which protect and elevate the individual. (US House 1973, 44)

But clear divides continued to grow between the two main blocks of LSP supporters. Structural transformation advocates, bolstered by the success of law reform, increasingly embraced more expansive policy designs that sought to reshape existing power relations between marginalized and privileged political actors. To do so, they hoped to preserve service providers' authority to take on cases with limited restriction. By contrast, conservative proponents like Tetzlaff were less interested in transforming the social order. Quite the opposite. These supporters focused on using legal services to maintain the status quo. Employing a procedural justice model, they sought to preserve or even increase program funding while restricting its use to individual-level service provision in lieu of more transformative initiatives.

Launching the LSC

To preserve the program while addressing the concerns of its detractors (and increasingly, its conservative proponents), proposals began to emerge to remove legal services from OEO control, decoupling the LSP to a degree from its origins as a poverty-reduction program. As Senator Alan Cranston floated during hearings over the future of the LSP, "I think we might better preserve the viability and integrity of a nonpartisan legal service of this type if it were totally independent" (US Senate 1970, 133). The idea to create an independent legal services agency garnered the support of the ABA, the legal services community, members of Congress, and critically, the Nixon administration. While the legal community initially imagined a private, nonprofit organization that would distribute federal funds, policymakers proposed plans for an independent government corporation to do the job. In 1971, separate proposals to create such an entity were presented by the White House and a bipartisan group of congresspeople, respectively. Describing his goals to Congress, President Nixon (1971) stated,

> Even though surrounded by controversy, this program can provide a most effective mechanism for settling differences and securing justice within the system and not on the streets. . . . It is important that the lawyers on the receiving end be able to use the money . . . without unnecessary or encumbering restrictions.

Despite his rhetoric, however, Nixon's proposal for a new LSC introduced several "encumbering restrictions" on how grantees could use federal funds. His position represented the goals of procedural justice advocates: a program with a narrow scope of authority designed to help individual clients navigate politically palatable civil claims. Most notably, Nixon sought to eliminate all lobbying and political efforts by legal services attorneys. Attorneys active in the provision of legal services fought against this effort, noting that limitations on attorneys' abilities to appear before administrative or legislative bodies to represent their clients was anathema to the legal code of professional ethics adopted by most states. As Klaus explained,

> Those rules are very explicit. They say you must, not you may, but you must zealously represent your client and utilize every tool within the bag of skills which is available to a lawyer in order to represent him properly. . . . The code then goes on to . . . specifically state that representation before municipal, State, and National legislative bodies is part of the obligation of the lawyer. (US House 1973, 86–87)

Nixon's proposal also made attempts to exempt cases that would address politically sensitive topics like abortion and desegregation, which had particularly salient material and political consequences for racially marginalized communities. In response to many of these concerns with the initial Nixon proposal, the bill that ultimately passed did not include most of the president's preferred restrictions, nor did it give Nixon his desired amount of control over the LSC board of directors. As a result, Nixon vetoed the bill (Houseman and Perle 2007).

Shortly thereafter, the president appointed Howard Phillips, an outspoken opponent of the LSP, as the acting director of the OEO, where the LSP was still housed. Phillips, who once argued that "legal services is rotten and it will be destroyed," sought to hobble the program from within (see Houseman and Perle 2007). His motivations for doing so were explicitly political, noting publicly that he blamed the LSP for a series of liberal policy victories and conservative policy defeats (Kessler 1987). Phillips tried to defund the activities most despised by the program's opponents as well as some derided by procedural justice advocates, including support for migrant labor, law reform activities, and legal training and backup centers. Phillips's actions were so extreme that even more conservative procedural justice supporters like Tetzlaff expressed concern and dissatisfaction with his leadership (US House 1973). While the courts in the end prevented the bulk of these actions from coming to fruition due to Phillips's status as an acting and not Senate-confirmed director, the writing was on the wall.

Both the Nixon administration and Congress came back to the table with new legislation. The House version of the bill reflected more of the wishes of procedural justice proponents, placing limits on the types of cases that grantees could take, and prohibiting a variety of lobbying and administrative actions. It also eliminated resources for backup centers. The Senate version, by contrast, preserved much more freedom for grantees to represent clients, including the more transformative elements espoused by law reform advocates. The bipartisan Senate bill did grant the president the ability to appoint the LSC board with Senate confirmation, ceding to Nixon's desire for presidential control over the new agency. After a raft of amendments were dealt with, a conference committee bill was finally adopted. The ability of attorneys to represent clients in a variety of suits as well as before legislative and administrative bodies was largely preserved. But restrictions were put in place to prevent grantees from pursuing cases about abortion access, school desegregation, and selective service. Limits were placed on the political advocacy efforts of legal service providers too, placating procedural justice supporters.

The conference bill ultimately passed both chambers with bipartisan support (and opposition). In the House, 86 Republicans joined 178 Democrats to support the bill for a final passing vote of 265–136. The bill passed the Senate on a vote of 79–19, with 28 Republicans joining 49 Democrats in support of the proposal. President Nixon signed the Legal Services Corporation Act into law on July 25, 1974, shortly before his resignation. The act authorized the creation of the LSC and four years of funding to support it.

From Fighting Poverty to Fighting Welfare

The newly minted LSC largely took off where the old LSP ended. It blended federal grants to support civil legal assistance for low-income individuals with continued coordinated efforts to pursue law reform. The agency began to flourish under the leadership of its second board chair, a young Arkansas-based attorney appointed by President Jimmy Carter: Hillary Rodham Clinton. In her three-year tenure leading the LSC from 1977 to 1980, Clinton successfully advocated to triple the LSC budget and placed considerable emphasis on expanding the organization's ability to improve the lives of low-income people through successful law reform efforts.

In response to the increasing success of law reform, the late 1970s and 1980s saw expanded energy to curtail the agency's activities from policymakers opposed to this more transformative vision of the LSC. With LSC authorization expiring in 1981, Congress began to undertake the reauthorization process. But a growing contingent of conservative Republicans, upset by many of the LSC's successful legal challenges, sought to limit LSC representation for undocumented immigrants, prohibit LSC grantees from bringing cases against government agencies, and further restrict their lobbying activities. While several of these attempted amendments initially failed, the fortunes of the LSC took a turn with the election of President Reagan in 1980.

Reagan's opposition to government-funded legal services was deeply rooted in his experiences as governor after California Rural Legal Assistance, an LSP grantee, won several high-profile cases that both overturned his preferred welfare restrictions and successfully represented migrant workers in California. President Reagan sought to eliminate the LSC entirely, and when he was unable to do so, he pushed Congress to enact dramatic budget cuts to the agency. His threat of a veto also helped to foreclose any efforts to reauthorize the Legal Services Corporation Act, instead leaving the agency to rely on annual appropriations for its continued existence. The president also worked to install board members who were overtly hostile to the agency.

During debates over the future of the agency under the Reagan administration, LSC opponents ramped up their attacks on the idea that the program was too political at the expense of serving individual clients. William Clark Durant, appointed by Reagan as interim chair of the LSC board of directors, testified about efforts to reauthorize the program:

> The legislation must attempt to bring an end to the variety of abuses committed by legal service attorneys, primarily in the area of lobbying. . . . The reauthorization should insure that the public's tax dollars are spent on the provision of legal assistance to individuals in need—not on a political movement or someone's personal ideological agenda. . . . We cannot allow our ideological desires to overshadow the immediate needs of the poor person. (US House 1985, 10–13)

When it came to offering evidence to support these claims of political abuse, however, opponents relied primarily on referencing an exceedingly small number of cases they argued were outside the scope of permissible activities. Indeed, when sufficient evidence of the much-maligned political violations failed to materialize, Reagan-appointed board members were reported to conspire with Senators Orin Hatch and Jeremiah Denton—both outspoken opponents of the LSC—to conduct "illegal" raids on local legal services offices in search of any exculpatory material they could find to paint grant recipients in an unfavorable light. As the *New York Times* reported, the results only amounted to a few statements from staff attorneys "rallying defense against the Reagan administration's assault on the corporation" ("Illegal Raids on Legal Services" 1983).

Durant also attempted to undermine the program—and its law reform efforts in particular—by suggesting it was counterproductive. Citing political scientist Charles Murray's controversial book *Losing Ground*, which argued that welfare policy was responsible for worsening rather than alleviating poverty, Durant testified that "some of the [LSC] activities, however well intended, may be, in fact, injuring poor people because of a whole series of economic policies that are being fostered" (US House 1985, 14). In congressional questioning, though, Durant struggled to pinpoint specific actions for legal services attorneys to take that were not anathema to constitutional rights or legal professional ethics, such as refusing to undertake an eviction case because the tenant was undesirable to other residents.

While Reagan and his supporters in Congress were ultimately able to thwart reauthorization of the LSC, reduce LSC appropriations, and enact some new restrictions on support for undocumented litigants, their goal of eliminating the agency was stymied by a bipartisan group of senators and representatives who worked together to protect the procedural justice elements of the program. Thus as outright opposition to the LSC grew, procedural justice advocates became the political fulcrum in debates over legal services provision, and it was their preferences that manifested most obviously in subsequent compromise appropriations. As a result, federal funding came to more fully embody the approach articulated by procedural justice proponents like Republican representative Carlos Morehead, who asserted,

> This shouldn't be partisan. It shouldn't be one side against the other, one group against the other, because most of us believe that everyone should have legal counsel if they have a personal, legal problem. But it certainly becomes controversial when you find Government money being used . . . in trying to change society. (US House 1985, 99)

President George H. W. Bush proved much less adversarial to the LSC, restocking the board with actual advocates of civil legal services and embracing more of a procedural justice approach in contrast with the outright opposition of his predecessor. But the successful law reform efforts that were a hallmark of the LSP and early LSC withered in the face of new limitations, significantly curtailing the potential of the LSC to combat poverty on a larger scale (Lawrence 2014). With the election of President Bill Clinton in 1992, LSC advocates hoped they could finally reauthorize the act and begin to improve its funding. Recall from figure 4.1 that the annual appropriation for the LSC increased considerably during the first two years of the Clinton administration, hitting $400 million in 1994.

But as Congress prepared to address reauthorization, supporters' efforts were struck a devastating blow. Republicans swept the midterm elections in 1994, returning a GOP majority to the House of Representatives for the first time in nearly half a century. And the new House Republican majority looked much more like Reagan than the procedural justice conservatives who prevailed in the previous decades. Led by Speaker Newt Gingrich, the Republican "Contract for America" called specifically for the elimination of federal support for legal services.

The new Republican majority's hostility to the LSC appeared to revolve around three main issues. The first was its connection to former LSC board chair Clinton, who was now the First Lady. Indeed, on Bill Clinton's initial elevation to the White House, noted conservative columnist Cal Thomas (1992) wrote of the new First Lady,

> Hillary Rodham's coming of political age occurred during her tenure as a member of the board of the LSC, a government-funded agency originally conceived to help poor people with their legal needs, but quickly transformed into a radical organization that has used government money to promote a liberal social agenda.

Thomas's effort to link the LSC to Clinton wasn't an exception; a variety of conservative commentators criticized the program for its ties to the First Lady. As activist Phyllis Schlafly (1995), an opponent of the Equal Rights Amendment, wrote after the 1994 midterm elections, "The ideological incompatibility of the LSC with the new Republican regime is indicated by the fact that Hillary Rodham Clinton used to be its chairman of the board." But the program's connection to Clinton wasn't its most significant flaw in the eyes of the new conservative majority. As Schlafly's (1995) article demonstrates, Republicans saw the LSP as an enabler of the welfare state that they were determined to eradicate:

> The Legal Services Corp. is the acid test to demonstrate whether the new Republican majority really intends to reform and reduce big government. . . . [The] LSC has spent $5 billion since 1974. If the left-wing lawyers had merely torched the money that wouldn't have been nearly as destructive. . . . [The] LSC's litigation deserves a large share of the blame for the out-of-control, failed welfare crisis we have today.

They viewed the activities of the LSC as benefiting the so-called undeserving poor, echoing implicitly (and sometimes explicitly) racialized arguments that Rumsfeld had begun to perpetuate decades before:

> When most people think of legal aid services for the poor, they think of victims. Instead, [the] LSC works for such causes as preventing the eviction of drug dealers from public housing, shielding violent offenders' criminal records from the public, getting perks for prison inmates, and releasing mental patients (who often then join the ranks of the homeless). When LSC lawyers talk about conducting "research" and facilitating "training," they are using euphemisms for political organizing and lobbying for pro-abortion, pro-gay rights, pro welfare entitlement, pro-drug, and pro-illegal alien causes. (Schlafly 1995)

Antiwelfare sentiment came to dominate conservative critiques about the LSC's so-called political activity. For example, in hearings to once again attempt to reauthorize the agency, conservative Republican representative Bob Barr was explicit in his disapproval:

> I have long disagreed with a number of cases that legal services programs, which receive LSC monies, have chosen to take on. . . . [I]n Georgia . . . an LSC recipient represented a transsexual against the Georgia Department of Health to overturn a Georgia prohibition on Medicaid reimbursement for sex change operations. . . . [The LSC brought] together large groups of people in class action law suits to stop certain states from imposing restrictions on welfare benefits or strong-arming small farmers who hire much needed migrant labor to "settle out of court, or face the expense of federal litigation" for an onslaught of minute charges for being in violation of the Migrant and Seasonal Farm Workers Protection Act. While the plaintiffs may have a right to bring these cases forward, they should not be doing it with the taxpayers' money. (US House 1995, 14–15)

As Barr's words lay bare, opponents' accusations that legal services attorneys were politicizing the program increasingly meant rendering services on behalf of marginalized clients who policymakers didn't wish to support in pursuit of the legally guaranteed benefits and protections they didn't wish to confer.

And this opposition wasn't simply about individual policy preferences. It represented a broader concern among opponents that federally funded legal services, once again, might empower marginalized communities. As David

Keene, chair of the American Conservative Union, accused in congressional testimony about the LSC,

> The LSC has spent millions of dollars on quasi-legal political activity designed to organize and empower the poor as a group or a class. . . . The mission, as those running this Corporation has seen it, is to transform American society by changing laws and government policies. . . . The simple fact is that the Legal Services Corporation's major impact has not been in serving these clients but in funding a network of activists dedicated not to helping clients function better within the framework of our society but to changing that society. (US House 1995, 256)

Perhaps for no issue did this concern over power building manifest more clearly among conservative detractors as well as many procedural justice advocates than in the case of LSC-funded organizations taking on voting rights litigation that would directly expand the political power of racially marginalized communities. The most visible of these battles unfolded in response to work in Val Verde, Texas, in 1996. Attorneys from Texas Rural Legal Aid filed suit in *Josita Casarez v. Val Verde County* challenging on Fourteenth Amendment grounds the absentee ballot participation of military voters who were once stationed at the local Laughlin Air Force Base, but were transferred elsewhere in the United States or abroad.[9] The suit alleged that the military absentee votes from nonresidents, who were estimated to be over 95 percent White, deprived the 70 percent Hispanic community of local representation (LSC 1997). The effects were particularly noteworthy, as the *New York Times* reported, because the wave of late arriving military ballots "turned the tide, giving Val Verde a Republican, all-white county government for the first time in more than a century" (Milloy 1997). Making the outcome even more newsworthy, it came to light that one of the Republican officials elected was a member of the Ku Klux Klan—having been pictured in national news coverage sporting full Klan regalia as recently as 1981 (Milloy 1997).

The new Republican majority was furious at what it saw as Texas Rural Legal Aid flouting the restriction on LSC funds being used for partisan political purposes. While the agency's investigation found that the case did

---

9. Of the eight hundred absentee military votes cast, estimates found that the majority were from voters who had not lived in the county in the past six years (including more than one hundred who had not resided in the county for a decade or more). A further one hundred ballots were cast by military personnel registered elsewhere (Milloy 1997).

not violate these regulations, it was sufficient fuel for the GOP to usher in the most significant set of restrictions on LSC (1997) funding to date.[10] These new regulations took shape in the 1996 appropriations act. First, the legislation slashed the annual LSC budget from $400 to $278 million. Next, it finally managed to adopt long-sought prohibitions on LSC grantees' abilities to challenge welfare laws or represent prisoners, most undocumented immigrants, and public housing residents being evicted on drug-related charges. It also removed LSC recipients' ability to engage in class action suits, like the Philadelphia suit regarding lead paint—exactly the type of resource that would have benefited a client like Quiana decades later. Furthermore, LSC attorneys were prevented from engaging in almost all forms of lobbying and administrative rule making on behalf of their clients. The new appropriation eliminated all remaining funds for national and state backup centers. And perhaps most controversial, the new regulations extended not just to activities undertaken with LSC funds. Instead, grantees were bound by these restrictions for all activities no matter the source of their revenue—a measure that supporters argued was designed to starve programs of other sources of funding (LSC 1997; US House 1995). The intent was to prevent any grant recipient from engaging in activities that could be construed as law reform or that conservative opponents found politically unappealing, rather than focusing the newly limited funds only on support for narrowly defined individual legal problems for those deemed by the Republican majority as deserving of assistance.

Thus while the remaining bipartisan congressional support for the procedural justice elements of legal services, combined with a divided government, prevented the new Republican House majority from eliminating the LSC altogether, it could only do so in exchange for severe funding cuts and new restrictions designed to once and for all eliminate the agency's transformational policy efforts. The regime put in place by the 1996 law is still largely intact today, with a few minor exceptions that have rolled back some restrictions under Democratic leadership. As such, the LSC's capacity to bring about systemic change to support marginalized communities remains curtailed, and procedural justice advocates remain—sometimes by a narrow margin—the pivotal members in votes on legal service provision.

10. Texas Rural Legal Aid was found to have been in violation of a different regulation prohibiting receipt of legal fees for services on the case (LSC 1997).

Exploring the Evolution of Federal Policy Proposals

While the historical record illustrates how contestation among these distinct approaches promulgated the ebb and flow of federal policymakers' efforts broadly construed, how does that translate to the universe of legislation enacted to address civil legal assistance? With the aim of more systematically mapping federal civil legal policies in the United States—as we did in chapter 2 with state policies—we collected data on all federal bill proposals related to civil legal protections between 1966 and 2020.[11] Bills were identified from GovTrack, a comprehensive database that provides summary information on federal legislative activity.[12] After identifying 520 distinct bills initiated in Congress during the time period in question, we coded each bill to identify the Congress and year in which it was proposed, the name, party, and district of the sponsor; the number of cosponsors and whether they were bipartisan; the final status of the bill; and the year that enacted bills became law.[13]

We also developed codes based on our evaluation of bills at the state level to identify the substance and target population for each bill that was subsequently enacted. We established ten subject categories to describe what the laws do: expanding funding for services, restricting funding for services, expanding service to groups, restricting service to groups, regulating grant recipient activities, providing nonprofit support, mandating program evaluation, creating educational incentives, symbolic actions, and other. With respect to the amount of funding, we looked to see, first, whether a law creates a new source of funding for a particular type of activity. Moreover, because much of the legislation addressing legal services happens through the appropriations process, we capture expansions and restrictions in funding based on the change in appropriations from one year to the next. A similar logic is used to describe whether new groups are being served or denied service relative to the time-specific status quo. Regulations report whether the law requires

---

11. The coding was conducted with the help of four research assistants.

12. We identified the bills by searching GovTrack for six key phrases: legal services, Legal Services Corporation, legal aid, legal assistance, indigent defense, and indigent services. Though we found significant overlap in the results using these terms, we opted to use all six search terms to identify as many relevant bills as possible.

13. The party measure includes Democrats and Republicans. Senator Bernie Sanders is the only independent to sponsor a civil legal representation bill (he sponsored two). He has been coded as a Democrat since that is the party he caucuses with.

funding to be used in a particular way, such as by restricting the types of cases grantees can pursue. Education captures whether a law provides funding to support related training—typically legal education to develop legal services attorneys. And codes are included to identify any laws that have specific programs for nonprofit providers or require programmatic evaluation. Finally, we note any language that offers symbolic remedies, like honoring a particular legal figure.

The second major element we code identifies the specific target populations implicated by a particular law. They are important to understand not only to know who benefits from a particular program but also because policies—through their language and remedies—socially construct how policymakers and the public come to think about the deservingness of beneficiary groups over time (Schneider and Ingram 1993). In the context of legal services provision, identifying the target populations tells us which groups were viewed as deserving of help or not over time, and by differing political factions—a critical point of debate with respect to civil legal service provision. We use the same categories employed in our chapter 2 analysis of state bills with the addition of Native Americans, who feature more prominently in federal legislation.[14] Each substantive area and target population was coded as a bivariate measure, where the presence in a law equaled 1. Policies could address multiple substantive issues and populations. The average law contained 2.4 substantive codes and specified 1.4 target populations.

In the following pages, we describe the specific legislative actions that federal policymakers have taken with respect to civil legal representation since the creation of the OEO's LSP in the 1960s, how those actions have varied over time, and what that variation indicates about the relative power of each of the three policy approaches explored above.

Civil Legal Representation Bills Proposed and Enacted

Between 1966 and 2020, members of Congress proposed 520 bills addressing civil legal representation, about 20 percent of which were ultimately signed into law. Figure 4.3 depicts the number of bills that were proposed and passed by each Congress during this period. As a reference point, it also illustrates

14. While each of these populations are well represented in bills at the state level, legislators and parents were targeted in fewer than 2 percent of all federal bills. As such, they are not represented in the following analysis.

P:	D	D	R	R	R	R	D	D	R	R	R	R	R	R	D	D	D	D	R	R	R	R	D	D	D	D	R	R
S:	D	D	D	D	D	D	D	D	R	R	R	D	D	D	D	R	R	R	R	S	R	R	D	D	D	D	R	R
H:	D	D	D	D	D	D	D	D	D	D	D	D	D	D	D	R	R	R	R	R	R	D	D	R	R	R	R	D

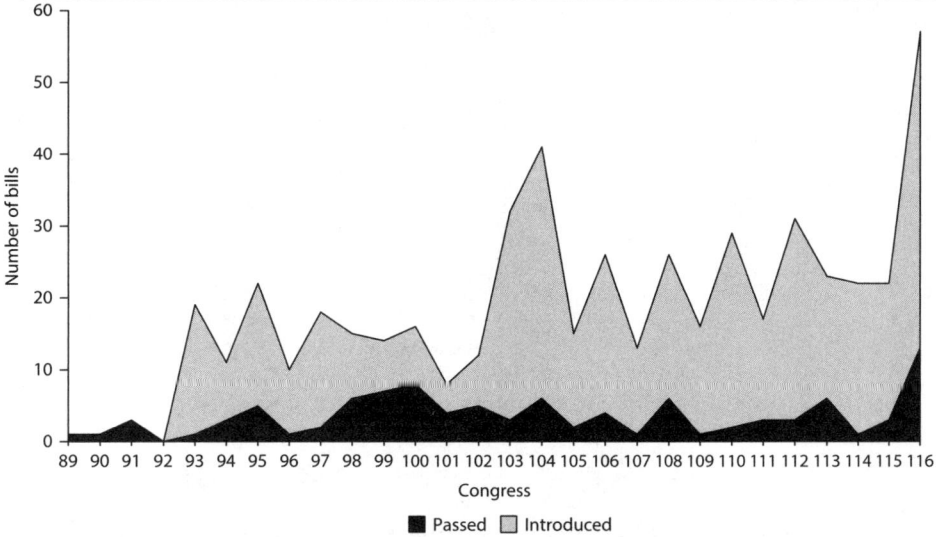

FIGURE 4.3. Civil legal representation bills considered and adopted, 1966–2020

partisan control of the presidency, Senate, and House during each Congress. In general, as figure 4.3 portrays, the number of civil legal representation bills considered and adopted by each Congress is greater now than immediately after the creation of the LSC in 1974, but the rate of adoption diminished as a percent of all proposed bills.

The greatest shift in these patterns centers on the 104th Congress—when Republicans retook a majority in the House of Representatives for the first time in four decades. Prior to the GOP takeover, the average Congress considered approximately twelve civil legal services measures and enacted 44 percent of those bills. Even if we remove the first three Congresses in the data, which considered no more than three bills per term on federal civil legal services and enacted them all, 29 percent of the proposed bills were adopted prior to the 1994 conservative revolution in the House. But the emergence of the Republican-led Congress in the mid-1990s ushered in a shift in legislative efforts. Beginning with the 104th Congress, the number of bills proposed jumped to an average of twenty-six per session, but the percent enacted declined by 30 percentage points to a rate of only 14 percent. The most notable spike in bill proposals came in the first Congress after Republicans regained

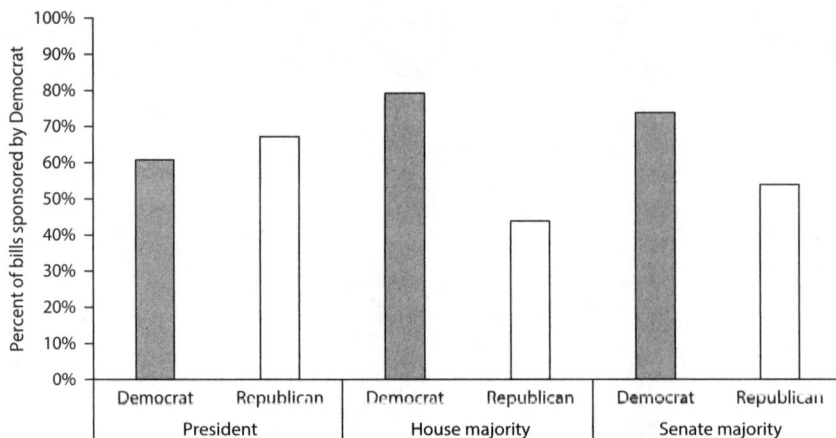

FIGURE 4.4. Composition of bill sponsorship by party control of federal government

their House majority. Forty-one bills were introduced during the 104th Congress—nine more than in any other Congress until the 116th, which proposed a slate of emergency funding bills to combat the COVID-19 pandemic—including fifty-seven that addressed civil legal services.

Perhaps unsurprisingly, the partisan composition of bill sponsorship has also shifted over time depending largely on which party is in control of Congress. Figure 4.4 illustrates the percent of all proposed bills whose primary sponsor was a Democrat based on the partisan control of the presidency, House, and Senate, respectively. Democrats were responsible for three-quarters or more of all bills proposed when their party had a majority in the House (79 percent) and Senate (74 percent). By contrast, Democratic sponsorship unsurprisingly dropped when Republicans held the reins in the House (44 percent) and Senate (54 percent). Notably, however, Democrats continued to sponsor a higher rate of bills addressing legal services when in the minority party relative to their Republican counterparts.

These patterns are consistent with what we might expect from an increasingly partisan environment for civil legal policymaking. Indeed, the fact that the biggest spike in legislative action for each party took place after regaining control of the House following a sustained period in the minority—the 104th and 112th Congresses for Republicans, and the 110th and 116th Congresses for Democrats—corresponds to this narrative. Given that structural transformation advocates are concentrated among Democrats and welfare retrenchment advocates are concentrated among Republicans (with procedural justice advocates representing a more bipartisan mix), it stands to reason that the spike in partisan legislating after regaining the congressional majority likely corresponds with efforts to undo what your respective antagonists have legislated in the previous regime. Thus exploring partisan patterns in legislation helps to understand how the balance of power shifts across the three approaches over time: predominantly Democratic structural transformation advocates, bipartisan procedural justice advocates, and predominantly Republican welfare retrenchment advocates. The volume of statutes alone gives us only so much leverage; it is necessary to consider what these statutes proposed too.

What Federal Legal Services Laws Propose

Is the policymaking activity to address civil legal representation consistent with the idea that Republicans in the 1990s ramped up their efforts to undermine—or outright eliminate—the LSC while Democrats fought to support it? What about when Democrats retook control of Congress in 2006? Examining the focus and target of the laws that were ultimately enacted clarifies how the different factions worked to achieve their political goals for federal LSPs. We conceptualize policy substance in two important ways. First, what does the law do? Figure 4.5 depicts the substantive goals of all legal services laws enacted from their origin in 1966 through 2020. The figure describes two important facets about policy substance. First, it shows the percent of laws enacted that address each category (the line). Second, it shows how many laws of each type (the bars) were sponsored by Democrats and Republicans, respectively. In combination, this information illuminates the relative significance of these different aspects of the laws, while showing differences in priorities by party.

Perhaps the most important aspect of legal services legislation concerns whether bills expand or restrict access to federal assistance through the expansion (restriction) of funding or service to different constituent groups. In general, laws were more likely to expand funding and service than to restrict them. About two-thirds of all laws expanded the provision of legal services either through appropriating more money than the previous year (67 percent) or by developing programs for new groups of litigants (29 percent). By contrast, only one in five laws restricted funding (20 percent), while fewer than 10 percent of laws restricted access to legal services to specific groups.

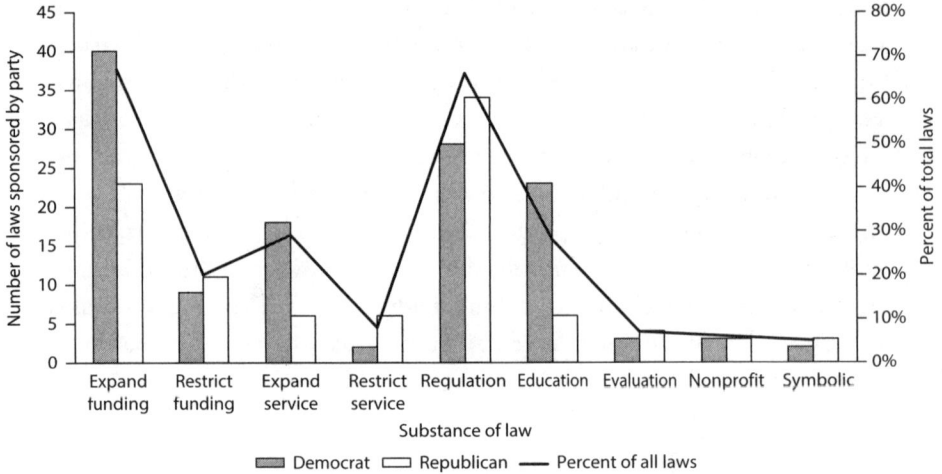

FIGURE 4.5. Substance of laws by rate and partisan sponsorship

There are interesting partisan similarities and differences in these patterns that correspond with distinct preferences for proponents of expansive legal services (either through a procedural justice or structural transformation approach) and opponents of the enterprise. It is crucial to note that both Democrats and Republicans were more likely to sponsor legal services laws that expand funding, consistent with the notion that procedural justice supporters of the program exist in both parties. On average, however, Democrats were more likely to sponsor laws that expanded both financing (68 percent of all Democratic-sponsored laws) and constituent services (31 percent) relative to their Republican counterparts (62 and 16 percent, respectively). The reverse is true for restrictions. Republican-sponsored laws were twice as likely to cut funding—30 percent compared to 15 percent among Democratic-sponsored laws—and more than five times as likely to eliminate services for specific groups—16 percent for Republicans compared to only 3 percent for Democrats. This confirms that opposition to federal LSPs was concentrated among Republican lawmakers.

After addressing the scope of service, regulations represent the next most popular element of legal services legislation, with 66 percent of laws incorporating regulations about how programs can operate. Because most of the regulations address debates over the type of cases that LSC-funded attorneys can bring along with the political and lobbying activities they can(not) engage in, exploring these patterns helps tease out differences in partisan support among proponents of a more transformational approach to policy versus a procedural justice approach. Notably, sponsors from both parties put forth legislation that regulated the activities of legal services grantees, but fewer than half of the Democratic-sponsored laws contain regulations on the use of LSC funds, while nearly all (92 percent) of the Republican-sponsored legislation regulates how funds can be utilized. This metric likely undersells the partisan differences because many of the regulations demanded by Republicans in the compromise to create the LSC have become path dependent—they appeared in Democratic-sponsored laws and persist in future legislation. The partisan mismatch in the use of regulations to control what LSC-funded programs can undertake both in and out of the courtroom provides strong evidence that relative to proponents of a structural transformation approach to civil justice, procedural justice supporters as well as opponents of the whole endeavor are more concentrated among Republican lawmakers.

Education initiatives were the next most common feature of legal services legislation, with about 28 percent of laws containing a provision to create or fund legal training or law clinics to expand the population of civil legal aid attorneys. Notably, such programs were much more popular among Democratic-sponsored legislation (39 percent compared with only 16 percent from Republican sponsors). This partisan difference maps onto the long-running opposition among both procedural justice advocates and outright opponents of legal services, who saw law schools, backup centers, and other legal services training programs as hotbeds of cultivation for law reform, and thus sought to minimize funding to them. Finally, only a small percent of laws explicitly implicates nonprofits, requires evaluation protocols, or incorporates symbolic gestures. While each is marginally more popular in Republican-led legislation, the numbers are quite small overall.

Who Federal Legal Services Laws Affect

Another way to measure what these policies are doing is to consider who they are designed to affect. Figure 4.6 illustrates the distribution of federal legal services laws by the populations they identify. As with the previous figure, it shows the overall percent of laws addressing each group as well as the number of laws for each target population by the party of the sponsor. Perhaps unsurprisingly, the most cited group are low-income people, with 45 percent of laws

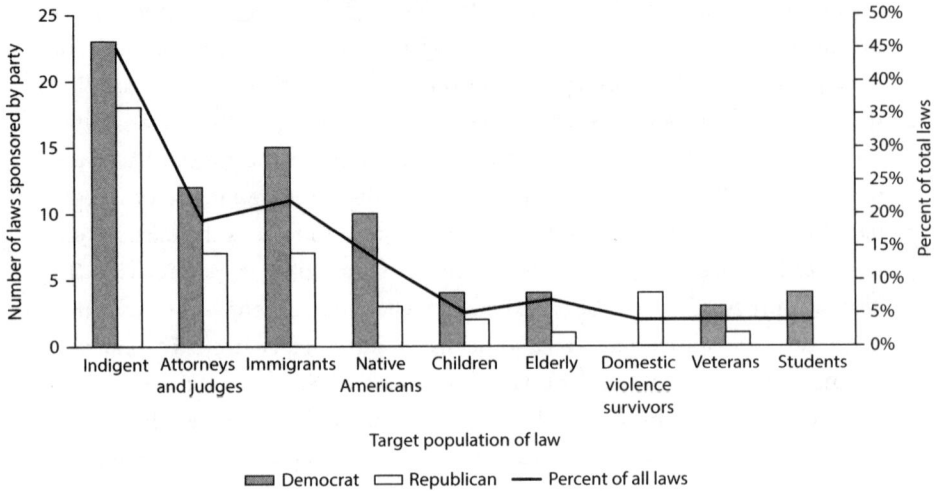

FIGURE 4.6. Target population of laws by rate and partisan sponsorship

specifically identifying this population. Three other groups comprise at least 10 percent of the laws enacted. About one in five laws (19 percent) prescribe behavior for attorneys and judges. While some of these mentions include funding to train attorneys, most are regulations to address the legal and political activities that LSC-funded attorneys can undertake.

Outside low-income people broadly, two groups of beneficiaries are most frequently targeted by legal service laws. Twenty-two percent of laws specifically address immigrants. For example, several appropriations bills carve out funding for migrant agricultural workers. Others impose restrictions on support for undocumented immigrants, while a subset lifts restrictions for grantees to use non-LSC funding to support undocumented immigrants who are survivors of domestic abuse. Native Americans are also singled out in about 13 percent of laws. Specific funds are often set aside to support legal service provision for tribal lands and official tribal members. Interestingly, veterans, the elderly, and survivors of domestic violence are rarely targeted by these interventions; despite representing some of the most adversely affected and severely underserviced low-income populations when it comes to civil legal problems (LSC 2022), each is targeted by less than 10 percent of federal legal service provisions. Once again, differences emerge in how the two parties incorporate target populations in the laws they sponsor. Democratic-sponsored legislation is more likely to target indigent clients, immigrants, Native

Americans, and students, while Republicans are the only sponsors of legislation to specifically address survivors of domestic violence.

But these partisan divisions cannot tell us whether legislation targeting each group is intended to expand, restrict, or regulate their access to or provision of civil legal representation. To consider this, figure 4.7 explores whether laws targeting the four most frequently cited groups—attorneys/judges, indigent clients, immigrants, and Native Americans—expand, restrict, or regulate the provision of civil legal services.[15] While expansions and restrictions of service obviously implicate attorneys and judges, regulations are the primary legislative tool to shape whether LSC grantees can engage in more or less law reform. Thus the partisan difference emerging in legislation targeting service providers, with Republicans more often enacting regulations compared to their Democratic counterparts, is notable. It suggests that Republican lawmakers are more likely to attempt limiting or restricting the activities of legal service providers to curtail structural transformation approaches. This partisan difference in regulatory language persists for each of the three client target populations, with Republican-sponsored bills enacting regulations in a larger percentage of laws relative to Democratic-sponsored bills.

Patterns in the expansion and restriction of service are particularly important for understanding how legislation provides for different target groups. As figure 4.7 shows, partisan differences once again emerge for this issue. For laws implicating both indigent and Native American litigants, Democrats are more likely to sponsor bills that expand service, while the two parties engage in expansion in roughly parallel trends in laws affecting immigrants. For restrictions, however, Republicans are considerably more likely to place limits on LSC programs in laws that specifically target all three client groups. While we ought to be careful about interpreting these patterns since most laws engage more than one substantive outcome and target group, it is still notable that partisan patterns continue to point to a preference among Democratic legislation for more structural transformation relative to Republican lawmakers.

Taken together, these patterns of bill substance and target population suggest a growing but complex partisan divide between Democratic and Republican lawmakers when it comes to providing access to civil legal representation for low-income people. Despite large bipartisan support in its infancy, the distinct approaches to legal services provision become apparent when looking

---

15. For this analysis, funding and group service are combined into two distinct binary variables for expansion and restriction.

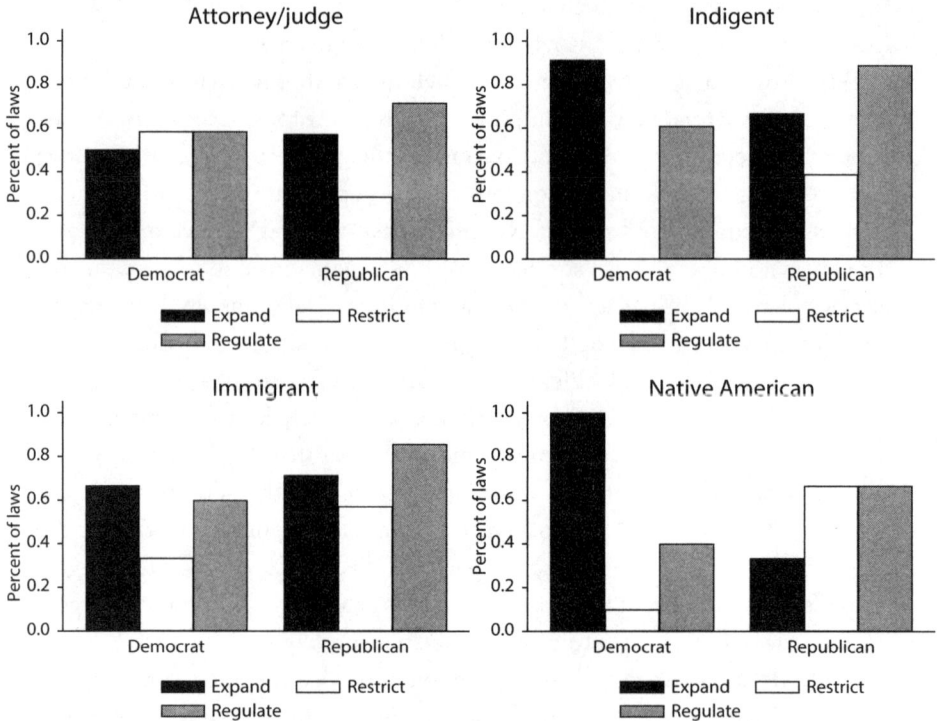

FIGURE 4.7. Target population of laws by substance and partisan sponsorship

at patterns of legislation. While both parties demonstrate at least some support for the procedural justice elements of the program through funding, Democrats are more likely to embrace a greater degree of funding and service provision. Democratic-sponsored legislation also points to a greater preference for facilitating law reform activities through more limited regulation and greater autonomy, while Republican policies are far more likely to restrict the activities of service providers to prevent LSC funding from being used to support structural change. And finally, welfare opponents attempting to curtail or eliminate federal support for either structural transformation or procedural justice appear to be concentrated among Republicans, as evidenced by increased efforts to restrict funding and service. The most significant efforts by Republicans to do so correspond with their emergence as the majority party in the House after half a century out of power. The mid-1990s spike in GOP-led proposals to weaken the LSC suggest it was part of the larger effort to retrench means-tested social welfare provision across the board.

The Policy Foundation for Inadequate
Civil Legal Representation

Why has "the most effective poverty program, dollar for dollar" failed to achieve its potential? What does this policy history mean for the larger political economy of civil justice? What does it mean for people like Quiana who cannot leverage legal services to forfend against basic incursions on their well-being? The history that we chart here reveals that the answer lies in the ongoing struggle among policymakers over three differing visions for what a program of legal representation for the poor can and should achieve. And these warring visions signal more than differences of opinion about the civil legal system; they reflect fundamentally distinct approaches to power relations in a political economy that historically privileges some at the expense of others. At one end of the spectrum exists support for using the civil legal system to fundamentally rebalance economic and political power in the American political economy. Proponents of such transformative goals see the expansion of subsidized legal representation to people living in poverty as an opportunity to use law reform to usher in policy and political change through the courts when legislative efforts to do so are largely stymied.

At the other end of the spectrum is a group of policymakers fundamentally opposed to expending federal resources to support groups at the socioeconomic and political margins. These opponents of civil legal service provision, and indeed the welfare state more broadly, seek to maintain existing power imbalances through the absence of federal social assistance. And situated in the middle of these two groups is a bipartisan contingent of policymakers who view legal services as a program designed to individualize social problems and channel them through the formal legal system rather than encourage political mobilization to tackle structural inequalities. While this group ultimately supports a limited, procedural justice model of federal programming, it does so to preserve the existing power structures in the American political economy. This difference is perhaps most evident in the way that its adherents draw stark distinctions between helping low-income people with their individual legal needs and helping to empower low-income people as a group that can exert political power for its own ends. Procedural justice advocates support the first, more paternalist form of help while fighting against the second, which would allow low-income people to help themselves on their own terms.

Interestingly, while these approaches reflect crucial partisan differences, the dynamics of policymaking described in this chapter do not suggest a completely polarized policy agenda. What emerges instead is a spectrum of policymaking consistent with the presence of these three distinct approaches: predominantly Republican opponents of federal support for civil justice, predominantly Democratic supporters of a structural transformation agenda, and a conservative leaning but bipartisan cohort of proponents who favor narrow proposals to fund procedural justice. As the political power of each of these groups has waxed and waned in Congress, so too has the federal effort to support civil legal representation, resulting in the preservation of an increasingly limited program of federally funded legal services that fails to fulfill its potential.

Importantly, these disagreements are not simply rooted in class-based preferences about who deserves access to the civil legal system. As this chapter has described, they are racialized as well. From debates over who sets the agenda for local programs of legal service provision and discussions about whether grantees can engage in lawsuits that fundamentally affect groups subject to a history of racialized policymaking—from school desegregation and voting rights cases to fights over what rights immigrants and welfare recipients ought to have in the civil legal system—the story of federal support for civil legal representation is integrally entwined with a racialized political economy. So what have the consequences of this policy tug-of-war been for the socioeconomic and political power of the millions of low-income people and communities of color who are frequently exposed to civil legal problems, but often lack the resources to successfully navigate the civil legal system in pursuit of justice?

Access to civil legal representation is a crucial resource for people who must traverse an increasingly dense network of civil statutes for a range of issues from protecting their housing rights and securing child support to negotiating financial difficulties, such as bankruptcy and debt collection. Hence such representation is imperative because it is a prerequisite for guarding a variety of economic, social, and civil rights nominally granted by the state. It is a key component of democratic citizenship in the United States that is neither fully realized nor fully rejected because of the tug-of-war among three policymaking approaches. Driven by conflicting visions of citizenship, deservingness, and marginality, proponents have sought either a procedural justice model of legal services or a more transformative model. In the face of a growing conservative opposition that ties legal services to the racialized welfare state it seeks to eliminate, it is likely that procedural-justice-oriented supporters will continue to prevail.

The consequences of this stagnant policy regime are severe, limiting the capacity of marginalized people to meaningfully access the protections and benefits that they are entitled to, and entrenching existing socioeconomic and racial hierarchies. In the previous chapter, we looked at the prevalence and substance of civil legal problems, concretizing their democratic implications. In many ways, the negative democratic consequences explained in chapter 3 reflect the dominant scenario should outright opponents of civil legal services prevail. Without adequate access to counsel, race-class-subjugated communities will either continue to lack access to the legal system to address their civil justice needs or navigate it alone, reducing both the perception and reality that they can meaningfully exercise their legal rights. As we demonstrated, this scenario is likely to further depress people's perceptions of their own legal and political efficacy, diminishing already marginalized people's political power.

In the ensuing chapters, we explore how the remaining two visions of the civil legal system manifest in the socioeconomic and political lives of low-income people who must continually confront the system of civil justice. Chapter 5 considers how low-income people's civil legal experiences are shaped by access to civil legal representation, highlighting the repercussions for their trust and efficacy. By examining the difference between having access to improved procedural justice or not, this chapter details the political tension between procedural justice policy advocates and the welfare retrenchment advocates who would eradicate even the bare minimum of federal support for civil legal representation. But it also highlights the limitations of individual-level legal counsel for addressing the underlying causes of precarity that disproportionately harm marginalized communities.

Finally, chapter 6 extends the ambit of civil legal institutions beyond courts and lawyers along with the policies that structure access to each. As a groundswell of grassroots organizing emerges to help people address underlying structural injustices that generate civil legal problems and channel people into the civil legal system to begin with, opportunities have emerged to shift the balance of power (Michener 2019b, 2022; Michener and SoRelle 2022). This community organizing, particularly from cross-class, multiracial tenant groups fighting for right-to-counsel and other critical legal rights expansions in states and cities around the country, is consistent with the aims of earlier law reform advocates, but it pushes beyond legal frameworks toward an even more transformative politics. Each of these chapters maps to a different vision of the US political economy, pointing toward disparate paths for the economic and political power of the most marginalized people.

5

"The State Is Supposed to Help"

THE POLITICAL BENEFITS
OF PROCEDURAL JUSTICE

WHEN SORA found herself navigating housing court, she was attempting to fight an eviction after her landlord refused to accept her Section 8 housing benefits. Her journey through the courts was first without counsel and then with the aid of a legal services attorney:

> When [the landlord] did the eviction, I was by myself. And that judge was very, very nasty, you know? . . . I mean it left me crying out of the courtroom, you know, and I just cannot believe this just happened. Like I have all the proof of everything, and the judge won't look at any. I printed off every text that I had in my phone. I had over fifty pages, and she wouldn't look at none of my things, but she looked at everything for [the landlord]. And so she was like . . . just picking the landlord. I'm, like, are you all serious? You know—I was just sitting there just distraught. . . . Like nobody was on my side. . . . [That] first time should have been when I really needed [legal aid] because everybody who read the judgment say this doesn't sound right. . . . [The second time with legal aid] it was fine because the attorney knew exactly . . . it worked out perfect for me . . . that part went so smoothly. . . . I was less stressed. It's like fine, great.

Sora's experience is neither isolated nor exceptional. Recall that the LSC (2022) estimates as many as 92 percent of people with civil justice issues receive inadequate or no legal attention, with significant consequences for peoples' legal outcomes as well as their attendant socioeconomic consequences (Seron et al. 2001; Tyler and McGraw 1986; Zimmerman and Tyler 2009).

While Sora's account highlights how low-income people's experiences with civil legal institutions—especially in the absence of counsel—can lead to negative legal outcomes, her struggles also exemplify how such experiences erode trust in governmental institutions. As Sora concluded of her experience,

> They're supposed to help you, but they belittle you, you know, like the judge. . . . [S]he got out there and she read what the problem was—where [the landlord] didn't fix anything—and then [the judge] is like, "This is a Section 8 case? Oh, oh, I need to get Section 8 on the phone. This is what always happens [with Section 8], and you're not going to allow her in when she tries to come and fix the house?"

Since Sora's situation aptly demonstrates the implications of negative civil legal experiences, it is worth going into detail to contextualize her circumstances further. Sora's landlord claimed that she refused her entry into the home to make repairs. But Sora explained during her interview that she had given her landlord many opportunities to schedule repairs. The reason repairs had not been made was because her landlord refused to give Sora sufficient notice. Instead, the landlord would call or text Sora out of the blue and say that someone was going to stop by to make repairs. At those times, the only person home was Sora's teenage daughter. Since Sora did not want her teenage daughter to be alone with unfamiliar men, she turned away her landlord's repairmen: "I gave her a date. I was there every other day. My daughter was there, [and] she was sending random men to my house." Sora tried to assert this in court, but the judge did not allow her to speak and did not take her concerns into account:

> I mean every time I talked, [the judge] would shut it down. You know, she just was on that landlord side like hard. And so she stopped court. We stayed in court to after 4:30, saying she needs to stop court to go call Section 8 and they need to pay [the landlord] her money because I wouldn't allow her to come in. But every text that we read shows [me saying], "Hey, what time are you coming?" She'd say this repairperson isn't going to work. I'm going to send this person. I said, OK. . . . The only thing I kept asking her, just give me a little notice. You work; I work. I can get someone there. I can't be there sometimes, but I can get someone there . . . but you can't keep sending random men to my house when I have a teenage daughter. And [the judge] was like, "Well, you're not complying. . . . She tried to do

it for the whole week." I said all I told her was we can get together December 28. I said but for the Christmas holiday, I spend with my family. And the judge was like, "You should have made time for her." . . . I highlighted where I gave her accommodations and you know [the housing authority] was like, well, you just need to move.

Sora's experiences with the judge and housing authority left her deflated, discouraged, and displaced from her home. Her perceptions of government institutions floundered as a result.

Like nobody was on my side. It's like they belittle you because you don't have a certain type of money. . . . It's like they give you such a hard time to even live. You know, the state is supposed to help you when you're on [assistance]. It's alright—for certain people—I'm not going to say all people but for me, it was already degrading; it was embarrassing to just know that we're living under Section 8. You know your kids look at you, like wow, you're super mom; you do everything but then you turn around and, like, I'm getting help from the government and I'm feeling even lower because they treat you so low. You know? You're in poverty, but then they treat you like you're in poverty. You know, so it's like—it's just—it's sad that the system works with the landlords instead of the people who work every day.

Sora's diminished trust in government brought on by her civil court experience was a marked change from the hope she felt when initially learning about federal housing programs she could benefit from. Having run away from an abusive home at twelve years old, and subsequently living in a string of foster placements and eventually on the streets until she was nineteen, Sora was elated when she first learned that she could get government assistance with housing:

I got the call that I was on the list. They allowed me to pick something out. They were like, "Hey, go pick a house out. This is your amount." And I'm young. So I'm like, oh, wow, I get a house. So I was staying in a little apartment. So I was ready to go. Got there and thought I was living a life because you know the rent wasn't that high, but you have a house.

Notwithstanding her initial excitement about having a home she could afford, by the time Jamila spoke to Sora, her numerous experiences navigating civil legal courts as a Section 8 beneficiary led her to a very different view of government: "Living in the streets for so long, you're like, OK, wow, they're going to help, but, you know, you didn't realize that was like signing your soul over." Throughout the interview, Sora talked about her goal of gaining independence from the state so that she would not continue to have demoralizing interactions with judges and housing officials: "Every year I'm like, OK, this year. I'm going to save some money to get out of the housing [benefits]."

It wasn't until Sora's second case—this time, with the aid of legal counsel— that she offered a different perspective on the state and her own personal trajectory. Later in this chapter, we elaborate on what happened after Sora's trip through the courts with an attorney, enabled through federal LSC funds. For now, we use Sora's narrative as an entry point for delving more deeply into the ways that legal counsel structures political efficacy and trust.

In the previous chapter, we charted the historical development of legal services, highlighting three distinct political visions that policymakers have imagined for civil legal representation over time: retrenchment, procedural justice, and structural transformation that fundamentally alters the balance of power in the larger American political economy. While a procedural justice approach to civil legal representation has prevailed—as reflected in sustained yet circumscribed federal investments in civil legal representation—federal funding remains insufficient and subject to ongoing attacks from proponents of welfare retrenchment. All the while, visions of a transformed economy and robust democracy have largely faltered. Chapter 3 confronts some of the material and political consequences of these historical realities by detailing the extent and nature of civil justice problems facing people in the United States, and the associations between those problems and various political outcomes.

In this chapter, we consider the upshots (and limits) of civil legal access for democratic life in race-class-subjugated communities. We investigate whether gaining access to counsel—a crucial element of procedural justice—bears on the relationship between civil justice problems and political engagement. While scholars have begun to address the myriad ways that having adequate access to civil legal counsel influences social and economic outcomes in the United States (Sandefur 2008), we know far less about the *political* dimensions of access to justice. In the pages to follow, we assess what obtaining legal representation means for how people experience and engage in political life. While civil legal problems can erode trust and efficacy, we expect that access to counsel can mitigate such erosion. Given the racialized dynamics of civil legal experiences, we also expect that these processes differ across racial groups, in part owing to very different starting points for people's trust in the government.

We once again take a mixed-methods approach to explore how the provision of procedural justice bears on people's trust and efficacy within the civil legal system. We return to the survey data described in chapter 3 to examine the breadth and type of civil legal resources utilized by economically stratified as well as differentially racialized groups in the United States. We then estimate the associations between access to counsel and civil legal trust and efficacy. Our findings suggest that while negative experiences with the civil legal process are correlated with diminished trust and efficacy in relation to civil legal institutions, certain forms of civil legal representation seem to serve as a modest corrective, generating small gains in trust and efficacy with respect to the courts. These efforts, however, operate at the level of individuals and do little to build broader political power.

To provide deeper insight into the processes underlying these statistical patterns, we turn again to qualitative data. Relying on interviews and participant observation, we describe the significance of counsel for people's experiences of the civil legal system. Our findings underscore both the importance and limits of procedural justice. While expanding access to civil legal representation for low-income people is important, it is ultimately insufficient for resolving the core issues that drive demand for such representation.

Political Consequences of Procedural (In)justice

We demonstrated in chapter 3 that experiencing civil legal problems generally has a deleterious effect on a person's civil legal efficacy as well as their broader sense of democratic belonging and political efficacy. But the presence of adequate legal representation can be a game changer. Access to counsel has the potential to serve as a political resource that may—though not always (as Deanna's story from chapter 3 suggests)—smooth the process of navigating the civil courts.

Following this logic, we expect that people who have legal counsel will generally have a more positive interaction with civil legal institutions. Not only will they have someone whose expertise can help them navigate complex court procedures and laws, but a lawyer may mean that tenants like Sora stand a better chance of having their evidence considered. Such gains may make litigants feel more like their voice is heard and that they are able to influence case outcomes—experiences that can improve people's evaluations of the court

(Lind and Tyler 1988; MacCoun 2005; Thibaut and Walker 1975, 1978). In this way, having access to counsel should boost people's sense of efficacy within the civil legal system. Such an outcome was, after all, a primary goal of procedural justice advocates who saw the provision of individual counsel as key to improving marginalized people's trust in the system and willingness to comply with it. By improving people's perceptions of the courts, they sought to prevent race-class-marginalized communities from pursuing collective political action as an alternative method to secure redress.

Beyond the resource that counsel can offer, increasing litigants' legal efficacy by providing publicly subsidized access to counsel may further improve people's sense that government works for them—especially if they understand that access as a policy benefit. When people receive and understand the source of benefits from government policymaking, scholars find an increase in political participation and efficacy across a range of issues (e.g., see Campbell 2003; Mettler 2011; SoRelle 2020, 2022). While the LSC has been chronically underfunded by Congress, those who are able to secure counsel through legal services grantees, which can include a range of actors from designated legal aid offices and pro bono private attorneys to law clinics, may experience positive resource and interpretive effects from gaining access to publicly funded counsel. Of course, this will depend in part on whether people are able to connect their access to counsel with government policymaking (Mettler 2011; SoRelle 2020, 2023). We use both surveys and interviews of people with civil legal problems to explore the link between access to counsel, internal and external political efficacy, and trust in the civil legal system as well as the limitations of that relationship.

The Political Correlates of Procedural Justice

In the survey data introduced in chapter 3, respondents were also asked a series of questions about the resources they used to address civil legal problems. All of those who reported at least one civil legal problem were asked, "At any time while you were dealing with any of these problems, did you or a member of your household try to get help from any of the following?" Answer choices included getting assistance from a paid private attorney; volunteer attorney; civil legal aid organization or attorney; community, nonprofit, or social service organization; law school clinic; legal hotline; online resource; or family member or friend. Respondents could check any that applied. In the following analysis, we will use these individual measures along with a binary variable to capture having access to any counsel, including those who reported at least one of the following: a paid private attorney, volunteer attorney, legal aid attorney, or law clinic. We use the same items described in chapter 3 to measure internal and external political efficacy as well as evaluations of citizenship.

Legal Counsel and Attitudes toward the Civil Legal System

Recall from chapter 3 that about one-third of survey takers (34 percent) reported that they or someone in their household experienced at least one civil legal problem in the previous two years, with notable variations based on racial and income background. Those who experienced such problems reported generally diminished internal and external efficacy vis-à-vis civil legal institutions. Does access to counsel, as procedural justice advocates would hope, mediate this diminished trust in the legal system? We anticipate that access to counsel might improve people's experiences with civil legal institutions, boosting their sense of efficacy and trust in the courts. But what percent of people who experience civil legal issues have access to counsel? And how do those rates vary by income and race? Table 5.1 describes the resources people were able to use to navigate their civil legal problems. It considers patterns for the full sample and racialized subgroups alongside those who make less than $30,000 annually for each cohort.

The most common resources people turned to were forms of information rather than legal counsel. More than four in ten respondents reported using online resources (45 percent) or seeking advice from family and friends (43 percent) to address their civil legal needs. This pattern is consistent across racial groups, including for low-income respondents. It is possible that some people may turn to these sources of information because they do not perceive their civil justice issues as necessitating legal recourse (see Sandefur 2019), but given the lack of access to adequate civil legal counsel, particularly for low-income people, it is almost certainly the case that many participants report turning to these outlets because they cannot secure access to counsel. For others, information and friendly advice may supplement counsel.

A paid, private attorney is the most reported type of legal representation when participant income is not considered, yet people report using several forms of volunteer or subsidized legal support at relatively comparable rates. When we restrict our analysis to low-income participants, paid, private counsel is most common only among AAPI respondents. Low-income White, Black, and Latinx respondents, by contrast, report some form of subsidized or pro

TABLE 5.1 Percent of Respondents Receiving Civil Legal Help by Race and Income

	Full Sample	White	Black	Latinx	AAPI
Private counsel					
Paid private attorney	16%/15%	17%/14%	16%/15%	16%/15%	16%/17%
Volunteer counsel					
Volunteer attorney	12%/14%	8%/10%	12%/14%	14%/15%	12%/14%
Legal services attorney	13%/15%	11%/13%	16%/17%	12%/12%	12%/14%
Nonprofit organization	13%/15%	13%/19%	14%/15%	11%/13%	12%/13%
Law clinic	3%/3%	2%/3%	4%/4%	4%/3%	4%/3%
Information					
Online resource	45%/41%	46%/42%	45%/42%	42%/37%	46%/45%
Legal hotline	9%/9%	7%/7%	10%/10%	10%/10%	9%/9%
Friends or family	43%/45%	45%/49%	42%/43%	42%/44%	47%/45%

Note: Number in columns represents percent of all respondents / percent of respondents with annual income below $30,000.

bono counsel as the most common (or an equally common) source of legal support. And across all groups, support from law clinics is the least commonly used form of counsel.

So to what extent does having access to these resources correlate with attitudes toward the civil legal system for people who experience civil justice problems, and how do those patterns vary by income and racialized positioning? Figure 5.1 reports the predicted associations between legal resources and civil legal efficacy—a person's perception that they can use the courts to protect their rights and are treated fairly by the courts. Among those who reported at least one civil legal problem, having access to any form of legal counsel corresponds with an increase in both their reported ability to use the courts to protect their rights and the perception that they are treated fairly by the courts. These results occur both for the full sample and those whose incomes fall below the sample median—a group of consequence if we are interested in the political ramifications of the extension of LSC funding to close the justice gap for low-income people. Moreover, that relationship is not only driven by people who can afford paid private attorneys. Other forms of counsel—like those supported by LSC grants—appear to matter for the relationship between legal counsel and political efficacy.

For the full sample, private paid attorneys generate a positive boost in people's perceived ability to use the courts to their advantage and the

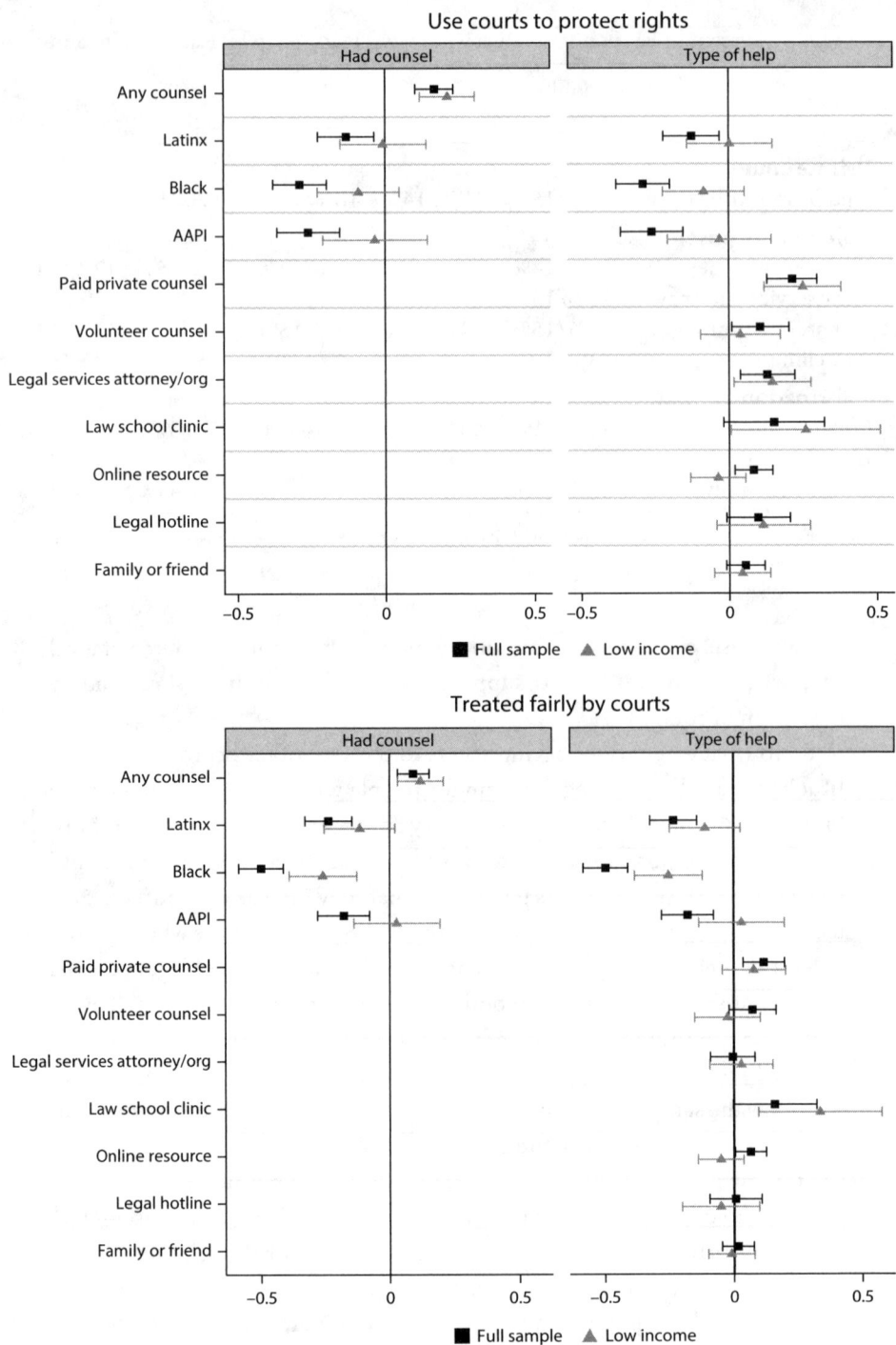

FIGURE 5.1. Legal assistance and civil legal efficacy by income
Note: Points represent coefficients from OLS regression; confidence intervals in bars.

likelihood that they will be treated fairly when doing so. The same is true for several forms of access to unpaid counsel and even online resources. The picture shifts somewhat when we narrow our focus to lower-income respondents. For those making below the median income, access to a paid private attorney provides the most significant boost to people's evaluation that they can use the courts to protect their rights, but low-income people with access to paid attorneys do not feel that they are treated any more fairly compared with their peers who do not have private counsel. Notably, among low-income respondents, the noncounsel resources do not correspond with improved measures of political efficacy. This is a particularly important finding as policymakers and some advocates have turned their attention toward solutions to close the justice gap that rely heavily on digital, self-help resources.

Being able to utilize a legal services attorney or law clinic   both of which are frequently supported through LSC grants—also produce positive effects on people's perceived ability to use the courts, but only access to law clinics correspond with feeling like litigants are treated more fairly in the process. Interpreting the distinctions across different types of unpaid counsel should, however, be done cautiously. It is likely that participants may be making somewhat arbitrary distinctions among civil legal services, nonprofit organizations, and so on, especially since the delineation on the ground is quite murky in many places. Because states fund civil legal services attorneys in such disparate ways—from private pro bono to law clinics and stand-alone legal aid offices—it is likely challenging for beneficiaries to identify the precise origin of their counsel. Thus for the remaining analyses, we focus on access to counsel as a binary rather than categorical measure.

Beyond income, the association between counsel and civil legal efficacy varies by respondent's reported racial grouping. Figure 5.2 explores the association between access to counsel and people's evaluations of their ability to use the courts to protect their rights by racialized group. A stark divide emerges when comparing White participants to their differently racialized peers. For White respondents, there is no statistically significant relationship between access to legal counsel and evaluations of efficacy vis-à-vis the civil courts. By comparison, Black, Latinx, and AAPI respondents report a positive correlation between access to counsel and increased efficacy in the courts. While the correlation between access to counsel and the perception of fair treatment is weaker, Black and AAPI respondents nonetheless evince a positive relationship between the two. The difference between how White and non-White respondents assess their efficacy with the benefit of counsel is especially

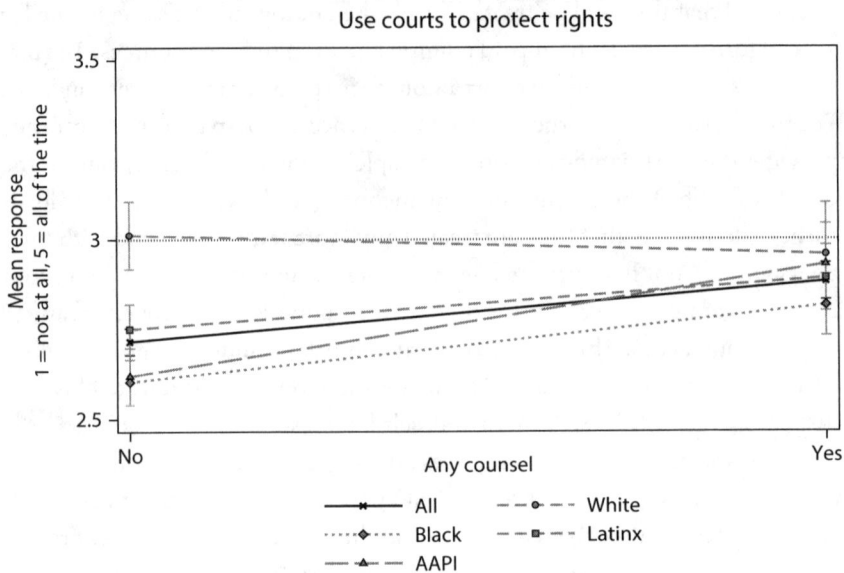

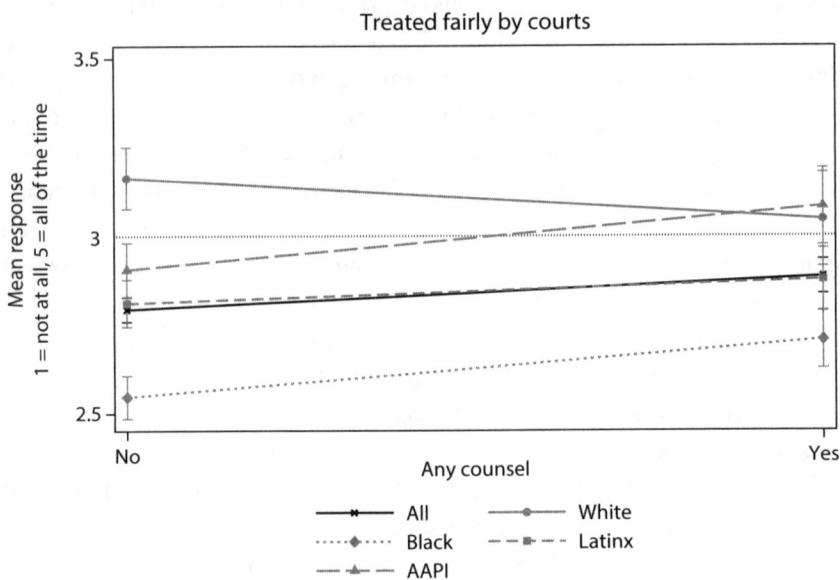

FIGURE 5.2. Legal assistance and civil legal efficacy by racial group
Note: Points represent marginal effects from OLS regression; confidence intervals in bars.

notable given the frequent observation from Black and Latinx interview participants in our study who navigate the courts alone that they feel disrespected as well as devalued by court personnel because of their racialized identity.

Taken together, these results suggest that access to counsel generally corresponds with a modest boost in civil legal efficacy. Critically for people of color, access to government-funded subsidized or free counsel contributes to that outcome. This offers some confirmation for procedural justice advocates' hopes that federal legal services may increase people's trust in the legal system. To what extent do these same patterns extend to broader feelings about political efficacy? Do people who navigate the civil courts with access to counsel similarly feel a greater degree of efficacy in their broader political engagement?

Figure 5.3 takes a broad approach to these questions, examining whether access to counsel corresponds with people feeling like they are full and equal citizens in the United States. Recall that participants in the survey were asked how much they agreed with the statement "I feel like a full and equal citizen in this country with all the rights and protections that other people have" on a seven-point scale, where one equals strong disagreement and seven equals strong agreement. Figure 5.3 shows the difference in people's perceptions that they are full and equal citizens between those with civil legal problems who had access to counsel and those who did not by racialized group.

Among White respondents, there appears once again to be no link between access to counsel and how much people agree that they feel like full and equal citizens. One possibility is that for the average White respondent, they already have a strong sense of efficacy—reporting a higher rate of agreement than any other racialized group. For AAPI respondents, who report feeling like full and equal citizens at slightly lower rates than White respondents, there is also no correlation between access to counsel and their feelings of efficacy. Black and Latinx respondents with access to civil legal counsel, on the other hand, report an increased perception of about a quarter point that they are full and equal citizens. This is especially notable for Black respondents with civil justice problems; they are the only racialized group that does not, on average, agree that they feel like full and equal citizens. That said, having access to counsel moves them substantively closer to feeling efficacious as citizens.

Another way that people might think about how efficacious they are as political actors is to consider whether they think politicians listen to their concerns. Those who feel more heard likely have a greater sense of external political efficacy—the belief that their actions can affect the political system.

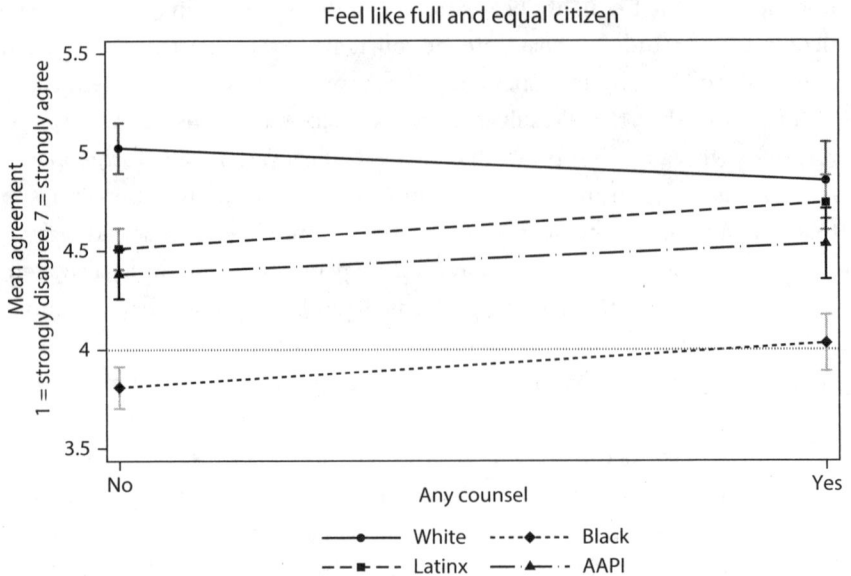

FIGURE 5.3. Legal counsel and perceptions of full and equal citizenship by racial group
Note: Points represent marginal effects from OLS regression; confidence intervals in bars.

Survey respondents were asked two key questions to help capture this sentiment. First, they were asked whether they agree with the statement "Politicians don't listen to people like me" on a four-point scale, where one equals strong agreement (and low efficacy) and four equals strong disagreement (and high efficacy). The top panel of figure 5.4 reports the relationship between having access to counsel and feeling like politicians listen to you by racial group for those with civil legal problems.

Notably, on average, none of the groups agree that they felt heard by politicians irrespective of whether they have counsel or not. Yet there are important distinctions among some groups that have access to counsel. White respondents, once again, demonstrate no difference in their evaluations of political efficacy based on whether they have counsel or not. Access to counsel similarly does not shape how Black respondents evaluate this question. For Latinx and AAPI respondents with civil legal problems, however, having access to counsel is consistent with a small uptick in the belief that politicians listen to them. But the size of that increase is quite small, and it does not substantively change whether either group, on average, feels listened to.

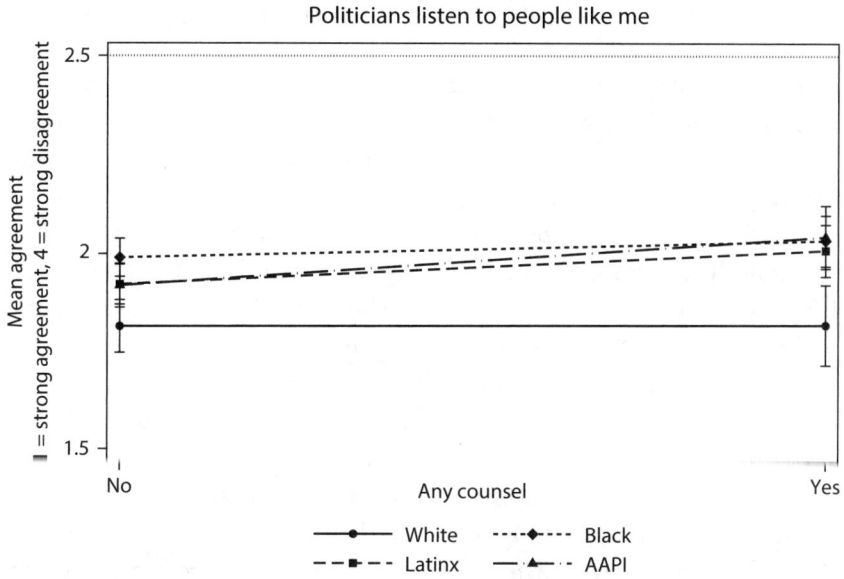

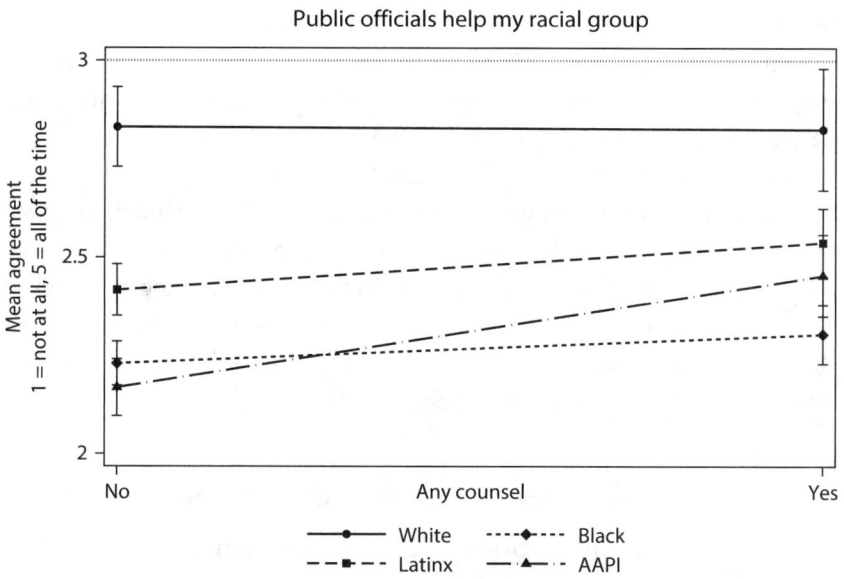

FIGURE 5.4. Legal counsel and political efficacy by racial group
Note: Points represent marginal effects from OLS regression; confidence intervals in bars.

Given the racialized disparities in who experiences civil legal problems and has access to counsel, we might also want to know how people's experiences of the civil legal system influence their feelings of group political efficacy. How do people from differently racialized groups evaluate whether politicians respond to appeals from their group as a whole? To answer this question, recall that respondents were asked to report how often they think politicians help people from their racial group on a five-point scale from "not at all" to "all of the time." The bottom panel of figure 5.4 reports these results. Once again, having access to counsel only increases feelings of racial group-based efficacy for Latinx and AAPI people with civil legal problems. And while these shifts are slightly larger than for the individual ratings of efficacy, they still do not change the fact that each group generally feels poorly represented by politicians.

These patterns suggest that while access to counsel can meaningfully, though modestly, spur feelings of political efficacy vis-à-vis the civil court system, most people with civil legal problems who gain representation do not reevaluate their ability to influence the broader political system in substantial ways. As such, access to counsel provides an institution-specific and limited increase in feelings of political efficacy. This is perhaps not surprising given the specific remedy that securing legal counsel supplies. But it is interesting because for at least some other policy domains, securing specific benefits can improve people's broader sense of political power.

Notwithstanding the value of these findings, there is still much to understand and unpack. What is happening in the lives of people with civil justice problems that explains the modest positive influence of receiving legal counsel on their perceptions of political efficacy? In the remainder of the chapter, we draw on in-depth qualitative data to delve deeper into the processes underlying the statistical correlations we observe.

A Qualitative Exploration of the Political Ramifications of Procedural Justice

Confused and Alienated: Navigating Civil Legal Processes without a Lawyer

The narratives of tenants who don't have legal assistance almost uniformly reflect profound confusion about how to traverse complex legal processes, suggesting diminished internal efficacy. They also convey striking mistrust in a wide range of state actors. Though we did not focus on trust in the quantitative analyses, it emerged as a central theme in the qualitative findings. Recall Sora's narrative of her first time going through the eviction process, in which she did not have access to counsel. Similar experiences were all too common among people without legal representation. Ray, who we heard from in chapter 3, faced eviction in the same Atlanta housing court that Sora traversed. He was given seven days to vacate the home he had lived in with his wife and children for the last seven years. Ray was initially supposed to have a legal aid attorney, but that attorney had a conflict of interest with the landlord's attorney and could not ultimately represent him. His local volunteer lawyers' program couldn't accommodate his case either, but they sent him an email with advice.

Given only this meager assistance, Ray's arguments did not prevail. Recall that Ray left the eviction proceedings believing the system was rigged against people like him. Not only did he express distrust of the judge, contending the trial was a foregone conclusion—"you're just a tenant and he's the landlord so I'm going to rule in his favor," but Ray further explained of the lack of counsel, "They sending me out to sea with just a small raft to fight the waves by myself. . . . They want you homeless, they want [Black people] on the street, they want us desolate." Ray expressed deep suspicion of the judge, suggesting that she represented bankers, and he made sense of this through the lens of being racialized as Black. He referenced "Black people" on several occasions, noted that "they do this stuff to us," and variably mentioned "our people" and "kinfolk"—which was particularly meaningful because he was being interviewed by a Black woman (Jamila).

Ray's experience was par for the course among interviewees without adequate legal support. Housing court is not designed for laypeople. As a basis for this research, one of us (Jamila) spent five years observing housing courts around the country, while the other (Mallory) has spent time observing civil debt collection court proceedings. Walking into a new court was *always* disorienting. Finding out where to go, what to do, and who to speak to—none of these were obvious or easy. Even for highly educated scholars dedicating years to understanding civil legal processes—and with no personal material loss at stake—being present in court was stressful and unsettling. Despite all the advantages of our positions as researchers, we often felt inefficacious in the context of civil courts and processes.

People facing the loss of their homes bear an incomparably heavier emotional and physical burden. Despite these gaping imbalances in power and positioning, tenants sometimes fought valiantly to be heard. But such efforts rarely bore fruit. Consider Candida, a Latina woman in New York City who attempted to stave off her first "notice of petition" for nonpayment of rent: "I get my first notice of petition that I am not paying my rent. And I'm like, 'What is this?'" If tenants ignore such notices, they do so to their landlord's advantage and their own detriment. Yet when tenants respond as directed by legal notices, they are brought into the morass of the housing court system. Some manage to secure legal representation (we'll talk about the implications for them in the next section). Others either delay contacting a lawyer, never do so, or are unable to secure one. The repercussions vary accordingly. Candida delayed representation. So for the first several years of her fight against her landlord, she navigated the courts alone:

> First court date is January 4 [during a] snowstorm. I go. The [landlord] don't show up. I get another date. I go by myself. I didn't have an attorney because I said, What is this? This is an error. *I'm going to state my truth, and I am going to be fine.* . . . I go back January 28, another snowstorm, and they don't show up. And then I start saying there's something wrong. I get dismissed without prejudice. . . . I didn't realize what the resources were in court. I didn't know who were court employees, who was representing landlords. I'm seeing the people calling out tenant's name; my name gets called out. I don't know what's going on. No one told me I had to check the board for my number and my index number. And I now start getting wrapped up into Bronx housing court nightmare. . . . My preconceived notion and my naiveness was that I was going to go January 4 and clear it and say, "This is an error. These are my rent statements. This is what I sent."

Candida had been paying rent and believed that there had simply been a mix-up. But it turned out that her landlord wanted to repurpose her rent-controlled apartment and needed to displace her to do so. He stopped cashing the rent checks, and after a while, tried to evict her. In her (self-confessed) naivete, she initially trusted the legal process, believing that presenting evidence of her on-time rent payments would resolve the matter quickly. She ended up in a protracted court battle. From the time she was initially served in late 2009 until late 2013, she struggled against her landlord alone. She went from court date to court date convinced that eventually her "truth" would win the day. It did not.

Marissa, an attorney and tenant advocate in New York City, explained why. Since Marissa had not been personally embroiled in an eviction battle, her vantage point was more institutional. She depicted the same NYC housing court that Candida experienced this way:

> What you see if you walk into the housing court, where it's sort of mayhem, and there isn't proper meeting spaces, and it's just . . . The space is challenging because there's just not adequate facilities. . . . Housing court's a place where they basically run the scam evictions. . . . That's just what it is—how it's functioned, it has not functioned as a proper court of law.

This description of housing court as "mayhem" and a place that often fails to function as a "proper court of law" was corroborated across interviews by people with legal problems, lawyers, and organizers. One consequence of dysfunctional housing courts was a lack of internal efficacy in relation to civil legal processes; people understandably do not feel equipped to function in the context of the kind of mayhem that Marissa describes. A second consequence is the erosion of trust as people developed cynicism toward the actors involved. This included judges, lawyers, and housing authorities. Candida, for example, derided the state housing division as "a bunch of incompetent people that make decisions about how tenants will be evicted based on not understanding information that's provided. Even if you write it sequentially like an educator, one, two, five hundred—they still can't get it." This speaks directly to the presumption that government actors cannot be trusted to do their job well and helps us to make sense of the inability of civil litigants like Candida to believe that they can be treated fairly within the system.

Aria, who we learned about in chapter 3, was similarly disillusioned by her experience in housing court. In January 2023, she came to court to fight her landlord's eviction attempt. She did not have a lawyer, but she did have reams of documentation. Recall that when her landlord's lawyer claimed that she did not pay rent for three months, Aria produced an official governmental record showing that the local Department of Social Services had directly paid it. Later, when the judge adjourned the eviction proceedings until the following week, Aria expressed to him that she was worried about having to take more time off from work. But the judge told her that regardless of those concerns, she had to come back next week. During an interview shortly after her court proceeding, Aria tearfully voiced the numerous ways that her living conditions undermined the physical and mental health of her family: "When you got a slumlord and you got to live in that and it's no help on the outside, what else do you expect for a person to do? You get depressed, like me. . . . I've never lived like this. . . . It's like a struggle, struggle, struggle. . . . I am so stressed out with where I live."

Aria had a lawyer briefly for a prior eviction case involving the previous owners of the same building, who also failed to ensure that the building was heated. When the owners switched, the case was dropped. Yet the new landlord soon continued the same practices. Aria tried to get a lawyer again, but she was unable to do so. By the time we spoke, she had a litany of complaints against her landlord: he had entered her home without permission, refused to make critical repairs, charged her for heating parts of the building she did not live in, and neglected hazardous conditions. Aria brought pictures and videos of the many problems in the home to court that day. She pulled out her cell phone during the interview and began to scroll through her photo evidence, narrating along the way:

> ARIA: Now you see [*plays video of her home on her cell phone; the video depicts the basement of the apartment*] . . . you're going to see my lights flicker on, let me rewind it. Now you see . . . these lights keep going on and off. This is the basement. . . . That should not be on my breaker. And see . . . this is my leak in the kitchen [*shows pictures of a clearly dilapidated kitchen ceiling covered in water stains*] . . . right next to my stove. It's large now. First it was just a little. . . . That's where you are cooking food. This is my tub. Just all lead [*shows picture of tub surrounded by some kind of substance*].
>
> JAMILA: Really?
>
> ARIA: Yeah.
>
> ARIA: This is the drainer [*shows picture of inside the bathtub, where a drainer should be, but there is no drainer*]. Don't have no drainer in it. They came and pulled it out, and never came and put it back. This is my life. I don't even have a light on in my room because I can't turn my switch off. In order for my light to come on, I got to go downstairs in the basement, turn my breaker on. When I want it to go off, I go back down in the basement and turn it off.
>
> JAMILA: Wow.
>
> ARIA: When we first moved there, we was moving the dresser in and my son slipped. This is how weak the walls is, he slipped and fell on the wall and went through the wall [*shows picture of a large hole in the wall*]. Now this has been like this since we moved here [two years ago].

Though Aria's video and picture evidence was copious, without an attorney, she never got an opportunity to present or even discuss it in court. Meanwhile, her landlord's lawyer "got all of this time" as the judge allowed him to recurringly speak at length.

Aria was hemmed in by unequal power dynamics. Her landlord initiated an eviction after two months of her withholding rent, but she suspected it was also retaliation for her attempt to get redress for her living conditions:

> ARIA: I called the [housing office] on them. . . . We have no gas in our apartment. So last winter, we went through two stoves because I kept my oven open. And that's illegal. That is unhealthy for the kids. Carbon monoxide or whatever. But at the time, we had no other choice. I didn't have no money to go to the hotel and stuff then . . . and then he turned the electric off on me [it was in his name]. And I lost a refrigerator full of food.
>
> JAMILA: He turned it off because you didn't pay rent?
>
> ARIA: Because I wouldn't pay the rent. And because I had called that office.
>
> JAMILA: And that office is where you make complaints?
>
> ARIA: Yes.

No one from the city office Aria called to lodge complaints about her housing helped her. Instead, she was being evicted and approaching the end of her capacity to cope. Though she was strong while standing up to her landlord's lawyer in court, she began crying less than an hour later, reiterating, "*I feel like I'm nothing.*" Toward the end of our conversation, Aria expressed a sense of hopelessness: "I just don't know which way to go now. I don't know how it's going to work. . . . I know in my heart that God is going to make a way for me. . . . He's going to make a way. That's what I just keep telling myself." Aria's faith in God kept her afloat, even while her faith in the state waned with each additional threat to her physical and mental health.

Effective legal counsel certainly would not have saved Aria from all of her troubles. Indeed, as we discuss throughout this book, procedural justice is a floor (and a low one at that) in the fight to secure justice for people facing precarity. Only fundamental transformations of our political and economic systems could fully address the range of harms perpetuated against Aria. Nonetheless, having a lawyer might have helped with some of her challenges. At the very least, Aria would not have been alone in the face of her desperate circumstances. When tenants like Candida, Aria, and Ray cannot access lawyers, conditions are ripe for their exploitation, which can deepen their cynicism toward the civil legal system and its associated actors. Marissa, the attorney quoted earlier, explains how this happens:

> For many tenants, the defining experience was [that] it's impossible to get an attorney—there's all of these signs about getting legal assistance, but when you call the numbers, you can't get through to anyone, or if you do speak to someone, they give you advice and then they say they can't help you . . . and many tenants will sort of start to say to themselves, "It doesn't seem like a court." Right? Many tenants will say, . . . "*I just need to make a deal* [with the landlord] *and be done.*" . . . Everything—I think everything about [the tenants'] experience so far is just that [getting a lawyer] would not be in their interest. That they would get the runaround, that it might just make things more hard—difficult, that it's going to take longer, that they'll be stuck at court longer and they won't get to pick up their kids, that they might get a lesser deal, or they'll get a crappy legal aid lawyer, or whatever.

This distrust toward the civil legal system can lead to harm. Even when lawyers can help, people sometimes forgo representation because of understandable frustration with legal processes. They thereby diminish their chances of having their cases arbitrated advantageously or at least *less* disadvantageously. For example, as Marissa suggests, tenants sometimes make informal "deals" with landlords that are harmful to their own interests. In states like Georgia, this outcome is even more likely because some counties have "mandatory arbitration" policies, requiring tenants to enter into negotiations with landlords before they can go before a judge. When they go into these negotiations without an attorney, which is called pro se, there are few benefits for the tenants and the terms are binding. Mary, a legal aid lawyer in Atlanta, laments that

> people will sign [a] consent agreement and there is really nothing we can do. . . . I don't see a lot of agreements that are great for the tenant, especially if they are pro se. I mean, 'cause sometimes we'll get in there and we're representing someone and it's worse than we knew, but then we can at least try to negotiate for more time. Whereas I will see a lot of agreements with pro se tenants where they basically agree to move out in a week or even less than a week, and you sit there and be like, "Seriously, you would have gotten the same amount of time or more time if you'd gone before a judge." . . . Sometimes it's a payment plan so in theory that's good for the tenant

because if they can make those payments, they can stay, but they've agreed to payments they can't possibly make.

In this way, to delay or forgo legal representation because of negative perceptions of legal actors can create damaging conditions for tenants. Of course, the inability to get a lawyer is often not a result of perceptions but rather that of inadequate resources stemming from the consistent underfunding of legal service provision. Either way, legal representation is a fork in the road. People with it have strikingly different experiences than those without.

The Difference Help Makes: Navigating Civil Legal Systems with a Lawyer

Just one day after returning home from a two-month hospital stay, Ronald was served eviction papers in front of his five children. His first instinct was to look for help. As a low-income single father in New York City, he relied on Section 8 housing vouchers for his subsistence. Still healing from a collapsed lung, he lacked the energy to fight his eviction on his own. Here is how he described what he did in the face of looming houselessness:

> I [got] up the very next day. I said, I've got to get outside. I've got to find out what am I going to do even though I was supposed to stay in. So I went to the corner store and I seen a friend of mine [Vance]. And I told him what was happening. So he said," "If you go down to [West Avenue], they've got an organization down at the bottom of the hill . . . [and] they got attorneys." So I went down there the very same day. I wasn't supposed to get seen that day, but I had told the receptionist of my circumstances and that I was sick and that I needed to talk to an attorney. So I don't know when I'm going to be able to get back out here. I don't know if my lungs are going to collapse again. I'm supposed to stay in. I had no business being outside. But I knew I've got five kids, and I had to at least take care of them. So through the grace of God and his mercy, I was able to see a lawyer that day.

Ronald talked about that day with an air of exultation because it was the beginning of a new stage of his life. The lawyer that represented him won his case. Ronald's landlord had long refused to do repairs in the apartment and had failed a recent inspection by housing authorities. As a result, the portion of the rent usually paid via Section 8 was withheld. Ronald kept paying his portion ($1,400 a month) and so his landlord did not have legal cause to evict.

Nevertheless, he tried to remove Ronald from the home rather than make the necessary repairs. Though the landlord was in the wrong, it is unlikely that Ronald would have prevailed without legal representation. During the time of his case, 99 percent of housing cases in New York City resulted in judgments favoring landlords. Ronald's victory in court reversed some of the harm that his children had suffered under the threat of eviction:

> I wound up winning the case. I'm in a brand-new apartment today. My daughter in the beginning [of us] going through this, she was an A and B student. Her grades dropped to Ds and Fs [during the eviction case]. . . . She's now a year and a half in college studying to be a nurse.

What's more is that Ronald's experience with effective legal counsel made him want other people to have similar support. He was so passionate about this that he got involved with a local tenant organization and became active in a citywide political campaign focused on providing low-income tenants with a right to counsel.

> I stood in that hallway of my apartment and tried to figure out where I'm going to put my stuff, where I'm going—what am I going to throw away? You understand that? Where am I going to go live? When I looked into my kids, their eyes, seen how frightened they were, you understand then how scared they were, the stress. And I don't know if I faked it good enough, being strong, but I was just as scared and fearful as they were. So I said to myself, [I want] to make sure tenants have lawyers, that this is the fight, something that I wanted to participate in.

In contrast to the mistrust portrayed by people facing the civil legal system alone, having legal representation spurred Ronald's belief in that system and motivated him to invest his energy into improving it. Indeed, the right-to-counsel campaign he became involved with was successful and spurred him to further political action. He remained involved with the local tenant organization, and eventually engaged more and more in statewide efforts—speaking at the state capitol to push for expansions of tenant rights beyond his city and across the entire state. Though Ronald was one of the first people Jamila interviewed, over the course of the six years following her initial conversation with him, he emerged again and again during ethnographic work because of his ongoing organizing activities.

This was a common theme that arose with interviewees who received legal counsel: they were emboldened to do more by their relatively positive experiences with the civil legal system. Tisha was a wheelchair-bound Black woman from Atlanta. She had limited income and required a round-the-clock health aid. She sat at so many intersections of structural disadvantage that one might erroneously assume her disempowerment. Yet with the support of an attorney from her local legal aid office, she was embroiled in an ongoing legal battle with her landlord over disability access. The speed bumps in front of Tisha's building were so steep they had caused her to fall out of her wheelchair, endangering her life and making it difficult for her to get around her neighborhood. Tisha sought help from a local disability rights nonprofit, which then connected her to legal aid. Once she found the support she needed, she was eager to fight her landlord. "I'm fighting. . . . I'm trying to fight for curb cuts, sidewalks, speed bumps, and crosswalks. I'm trying to fight hard to get them to do something like that."

Sora, whose multiple evictions we heard about at the outset of this chapter, responded to her eventual positive experience with legal aid by making a life-changing decision. Instructively, she shared this when we asked about how she participates in politics:

JAMILA: Do you ever participate in politics? Like do you ever vote or anything like that?

SORA: I vote. You know, I used to be class president, student government at school. I did go to college. I got my associates even after all of that. I got my associates and that was in my mid-thirties.

JAMILA: That's great.

SORA: And I'm a senior at [a state university] now getting my degree in paralegal studies.

JAMILA: Did [your experiences with legal aid] inspire you to do that?

SORA: It did. It really did. I really wanted to be a lawyer. I wanted to be a social worker and a lawyer in one because I wanted to help the people who was in my situation. . . . And it pushed me to want to be an attorney to help, and you know, that's what I've been working toward, and I want to open my own law firm, have a pro bono side for where people can't afford it.

Sora's career turn toward law was especially striking considering her personal background. After being abused and running away from home at only twelve years old, she consistently experienced government as callous and indifferent:

I've been through it; been through the foster system since I was twelve, [and] I was a ward of the state until I turned eighteen. So I was shipped over maybe three shelters, juvenile, ten foster homes, and I just left one day, and I never went back. So I've been through pretty much a lot of the different levels of government, and they don't care. You know, like my dad was abusive, and because he was a veteran, when the police came to assist or the judge would help, I mean you know the case, they're like he's a veteran; he would never do that. So I'm sitting here with marks, but because he's a veteran, we supposed to respect him. So everything in the system for me has never worked out.

Sora had every reason to remain mistrustful of government. Yet her positive experience with civil legal aid drew her into the civil legal system and oriented her toward engaging that system on behalf of others rather than avoiding it due to mistrust. Although Sora voted, elections were not the dimension of political life she focused on when asked about participation. Like many other interviewees, she painted a broad, rich picture of her political life that went beyond voting to the multifaceted ways that civil legal experiences came to bear on understandings of as well as engagement with the institutions of democracy.

The Merits and Limits of Procedural Justice

For tenants like Sora and Ronald, having access to counsel not only helped them to fight their evictions but also provided the spark for each of them to begin distinct paths toward building and exercising power to help others in their circumstances. Their stories represent a best-case scenario when it comes to how providing access to counsel can improve someone's political efficacy and engagement. But as our quantitative data and many of the other narratives we share in this book reveal, not everyone has such politically empowering experiences with procedural justice. Instead, it is more common for civil legal counsel to play an important but limited role in helping low-income people of color to feel as though they can use the civil legal system to their advantage. This chapter drew on extensive in-depth interview data to concretize the ways that people with civil legal problems come to have their efficacy eroded and how civil legal assistance in court can mitigate such outcomes.

The perspectives we present also point to the limits of a procedural justice approach to civil legal representation. While counsel can certainly improve marginalized litigants' feelings of efficacy within the court system, it is not a panacea. One potential concern about the effects of access to counsel on people's modestly improved feelings of political efficacy might be that it removes incentives to engage in other power-building activities—a "civilizing" outcome that many procedural justice advocates mentioned in the previous chapter might applaud. Moreover, in a political environment that perpetually underfunds such programs, procedural justice is not accessible to all who could benefit from it.

But the examples of people like Ronald and Sora suggest that at least for some people, access to counsel can help catalyze political empowerment beyond the walls of the courtroom. So what are the alternative pathways through which people facing civil legal problems can pursue justice and power? The next chapter explores this question, focusing on community organizing as a promising possibility.

6

"Where Liberation Is Actually Going to Happen"

LEGAL JUSTICE, TENANT ORGANIZING, AND TRANSFORMATIVE POLITICS

TAMARA HAD lived in the same neighborhood in South Louisville, Kentucky, for nearly her entire life. Over that time, she watched the conditions of her community go "all the way down." She lamented "the crime, the violence," but had few other options as a low-income single mother of two. Jamila met Tamara in the office of a civil legal attorney, Bryson. When Bryson heard about this research, he connected Jamila with Tamara and volunteered the use of his office for the research interview. On a mild summer day, Jamila and Tamara sat in Bryson's unassuming office in a careworn Louisville neighborhood, and Tamara shared a housing journey that was painfully bound up in the economic realities of segregated low-income communities.

Despite the physical and social decline of Tamara's neighborhood, the cost of housing was on the rise. Finding a stable, affordable place to live became tougher with each passing year. And Tamara wasn't the only one feeling the housing crunch. Many people in her community were desperate for stable, habitable, low-cost housing. That desperation was like blood in the water, and the sharks were drawn to it. Tamara became the victim of one such shark. A predatory housing scheme brought her into the crosshairs of the civil legal system. Bryson battled on her behalf and helped her greatly. But Tamara's situation exposed the limits of the law in a political economy that cultivates conditions of exploitation (Desmond 2023; Desmond and Bell 2015).

Tamara's experiences unfolded in a series of layered predicaments. Though idiosyncratic, the details illuminate the processes we have examined throughout this book. As we relay Tamara's hardships, consider the themes we have emphasized in the preceding chapters: the political economy of scarcity that generates acute material needs, vital role of civil legal representation in addressing some of the justiciable problems born of such needs, and implications of civil legal institutions for political life. Each of these elements are reflected in Tamara's story. But her path, and that of the attorney who defended her, registers a pivotal role for nonlegal actors—particularly community organizations—that structure, supplement, and ultimately supersede the civil legal system. More than any other dynamic that emerged from our extensive multifaceted data, the operations and activities of tenant organizations revealed distinct possibilities for transforming democracy in ways that hold hope for altering the conditions circumscribing life within race-class-subjugated communities.

————

Before things got bad for Tamara, they were hard but OK. Then they weren't. Tamara explained the change of course that thrust her into the civil legal system and brought her in contact with Bryson:

> The first time I met Bryson, I had been living in my house for like four years. And then COVID hit, and I was a security branch manager, so we never closed. So I ended up catching COVID. I was out of work [for a while], and I couldn't pay [my rent]. That's why my landlord filed for eviction.

Fortunately, Tamara evaded this first eviction. To do so, she navigated labyrinthine processes, and civil legal representation was key.

> The first time, like I said, I had COVID, and didn't work and didn't pay my rent for like two months. And my landlord filed an eviction because at the time, he wasn't working. Like normally me and him would work something out. . . . He was a great landlord, never had any other problems out of him or anything, but his money was tight. So he filed [an eviction], and I ended up getting hooked up with legal aid.

Tamara secured a lawyer through a legal aid society and had a hearing scheduled. The plan was for her and her lawyer to show evidence that she had applied for assistance through the Emergency Rental Assistance Program (ERAP) made available during the pandemic. This would be sufficient cause for the judge to halt eviction proceedings, which is what both Tamara and her landlord hoped for. Her landlord had only evicted her out of necessity, knowing that doing so would move her ERAP application to the front of the line and get him his money faster. No one expected this process to result in Tamara actually being forced from her housing.

Since this was during the height of the pandemic, the hearing was supposed to take place via Zoom. But when Tamara called the number provided on her hearing notice, she could not get through. She was never able to make it to the hearing. And despite her well-laid plans, the judge issued a default judgment against her, enabling an eviction.

> TAMARA: They had changed the Zoom call number, and they didn't notify [me]. . . . So [the judge] granted the eviction even though everything had been [changed].
> JAMILA: Even though you called the right number.
> TAMARA: Yeah. But they had changed it. So everything, the [ERAP] application and everything, like everything was supposed to get worked out that day in court. [But] I didn't have the right Zoom call number, so they granted the eviction.
> JAMILA: And later when you figured out you had the—and I guess they figured out too—that you had the wrong number, was there any way to get that reversed?
> TAMARA: That's where Bryson came in.

Bryson was not a standard legal aid attorney; he was a civil attorney who specialized in impact litigation of the sort that LSC-funded agencies are prohibited from initiating (recall the limits placed on legal services as elaborated in chapter 4). Impact litigation refers to the legal practice of taking cases that have the potential to influence a broader population or change an underlying structural issue rather than solving one person's individual claim. Since Bryson's organization did not receive federal funding, he was free to pursue distinct cases with the potential for affecting large numbers of people. Tamara's lawyer at legal aid put her in touch with Bryson. She noted that "legal aid contacted me and was like, 'It was a mistake with the court. They didn't give a whole lot of people the right number.'"

In a separate conversation Jamila had with Bryson, he explained the situation in detail:

The way this all went down was in January of 2021, the court switched its Zoom accounts. And the way that they switched the Zoom accounts meant that the old number wasn't going to work. They had sent out hundreds of eviction notices telling people to show up at this old number, but didn't have anybody in that room, didn't have access to that room any longer. . . . Instead of sending out new notices, they just proceeded along. . . . I mean, you can imagine the analog equivalent is to show up at courtroom 308, and then without providing any notice, they move it to courtroom 502. Obviously, a due process violation. You have to have notice and opportunity to be heard in your judicial proceeding.

And so, the way it went down was that [several community organizations] facilitated a . . . check-in every Wednesday. And I would get on those calls and just listen in. . . . That's sort of what we're doing a lot of times when we're on these community coalition calls. It's just like, listen, listen, listen, listen. . . . But then sometimes somebody says something where it's like, stop right here. Like we need to talk about this. And the city . . . was actually the one that said, "What happened in court today was really messed up. I can't believe that they are evicting people after getting the wrong number." And I said, "Stop. Let's talk about what's going on. Like what happened?" And I got with the legal aid society and found out more about what had happened to its clients. . . .

For a lot of people, they were going to show up via Zoom from Lowe's break room on their break. You know, we have a lot of people whom I've seen show up in their break room on the job for their eviction hearing. And so those folks didn't know to file a motion to alter, amend, or vacate the judgment or anything like that. So with Tamara as the class plaintiff alongside another woman who had the same experience, we filed a lawsuit in federal court, seeking an injunction that would require the court to issue new notices.

Though Bryson's aims seemed reasonable, the legal system said otherwise. As he recalls,

We ended up not getting an injunction. . . . We made the case to the federal court that we needed immediate protections for people. That hundreds of people each week were being evicted or facing eviction because of this wrongful notice. And unfortunately, the briefing schedule that the federal court laid out had us briefing this issue for five weeks instead of enjoining the behavior immediately. And as a result, we weren't able to protect those people. And we ultimately dismissed the lawsuit because at that point, the people who had gotten the wrong notice had already gone through the system. And the people who were getting new eviction complaints filed against them were getting the proper information. So we didn't get the relief that we needed.

When I asked Tamara how she felt about this failure of the legal system to provide redress, she expressed political cynicism: "It just fits with Louisville. It fits with the city. A lot of stuff goes on that no one is held accountable [for]." Like Aria, Sheila, and Deanna—Black woman whose civil legal problems were highlighted in chapter 3—Tamara was alienated from political institutions and mistrustful of them. And despite her ability to get a lawyer, the failings of the legal system still left her vulnerable to houselessness. Ultimately, it was not the law that saved Tamara but rather her landlord's willingness to "work it out." Once she was able to get the ERAP funds and pay her landlord the rent she owed, he declined to enforce the eviction. While this was a positive ending for Tamara, it rendered her dependent on the goodwill of the person profiting from her housing—something that most of the people whose stories we share in this book could not rely on. Several years later, when Tamara faced another perilous housing dilemma, her luck ran out:

> I ended up staying [in the first house] like another two years. [Then] we had a bad storm, and a tree fell on the house, and I didn't have any choice but to leave. Everyone was safe. It didn't hurt anyone. I just can't live in the house anymore if a tree falls on it. So then I found what I thought was my dream house, and it turned out to be a scam.

Tamara went on to explain the situation she was in when she began searching for new housing and the punishing road it led her down. While she does not use the language of "political economy," her story reflects the pernicious nexus of predatory market conditions and negligent (at best) political institutions. "I've been [working for the government] for going on three years, so I make good money. And I don't even qualify for a lot of apartments. . . . I make over $20 an hour. Like it's crazy. One single person in Louisville, you're not finding anywhere to live."

As Tamara was grappling with this plight, she stumbled across a Facebook Marketplace posting of a house for rent through a company called "Main Street Renewal." To Tamara's knowledge, "Main Street Renewal has a lot of properties listed online. Basically, if you want to live somewhere in Louisville, you have to go through them."[1] So she went through the company. Or so she thought. The ad online said Main Street Renewal, but what Tamara did not know was that the number listed connected her to someone entirely unaffiliated with it.

> TAMARA: And it was like contact this number. But it wasn't really the number for Main Street. It was the guy who scammed me.
>
> JAMILA: So you found the house on Facebook Marketplace. You call the number; you thought you were calling Main Street. Who did you end up getting when you called that number?
>
> TAMARA: The guy told me his name was Tristan. And that it was his property. . . . After being there for three months—then [the real] Main Street contacted me, and [it] was like, you're not supposed to be in this property; this is our property.

Tamara's realization that she had been unknowingly squatting in a Main Street property was devastating. She had paid "Tristan" a $1,000 deposit in April, moved in that month, and then proceeded to pay him $1,000 a month in May, June, and July. By the time she got a notice to vacate from the "real" Main Street at the end of July, she had lost $4,000 to a scam. Tamara tried to contact "Tristan," but could not reach him. When she realized that she had been defrauded, Bryson was the first person she called. Per Bryson's recounting, the problem was widespread:

> Main Street Renewal bought thousands of properties last year. And fraudsters like Tristan break in, change the locks, and then rent to people like Tamara for three or four months until Main Street catches up and says, "Hey, we're ready to rent this property, but it looks like there's somebody else living there."

Tamara confirmed this, recalling memories of when she moved in that did not seem suspicious at the time but became so in hindsight: "We met a locksmith there. It was [Tristan] and the locksmith, and I got a key. So I'm assuming it's

---

1. Even a cursory check confirms Tamara's understanding. A Google search of "Main Street Renewal Louisville" brings up a deluge of entries on Yelp and Reddit where people describe the company's pervasiveness ("It sucks, they have almost every home we've looked at"; "I live in Louisville, Kentucky, and unfortunately they own most of the rental properties"), and how predatory it is ("I can't imagine a worse rental company"; "Main Street Renewal is a nightmare of a company"; "They are so awful. I could write a book on the horrible experience I am having with them").

his house. Locksmith changed the locks like he proved this his house, right? No." The months following the revelation of fraud were chaotic.

> TAMARA: It was just a bunch of back and forth. . . . They filed for eviction like two or three times before, like a judge dismissed it. And I'm like, OK. And then we was working with them and they was going to accept [rent from me]. And then they didn't. They said they sold it again and the new people didn't want [to rent to me]; it was just crazy for months . . . from July until April.
>
> JAMILA: And that whole time, were you still in the property?
>
> TAMARA: I was in the property.
>
> JAMILA: Were you paying anyone? Because you stopped paying Tristan.
>
> TAMARA: I stopped paying Tristan. And I was going to pay Main Street, and at first, they was ready to accept it. And then they was like, well, no, we're going to do this. We're going to do that. And then they was like, they sold it. Like it was sold like four times while I was there.

Bryson explains his failed attempts to negotiate on Tamara's behalf:

> The deal that we wanted to make with them was, you know, she entered into a contract with this person because you didn't maintain the property in a way that protected people from harm. And so we want to just pay you the $1,000 a month rent. But they wanted to rent it out for something like $1,600. . . . And so that wasn't affordable [for Tamara]. And so we negotiated back and forth, and finally agreed to leave in April. But yeah. From July until April, they wouldn't accept rent.

When Jamila asked Tamara how that nine-month period of uncertainty affected her, she was frank: "[I was] extremely stressed. I even started going to therapy. . . . I had anxiety. I was depressed. So I was just seeking help." During that trying time, Bryson was a key support for Tamara. When she described the various legal proceedings and court cases that she had to engage, Bryson figured largely in her experiences:

> I showed up [to court], but I think one time that lawyer didn't show up and they rescheduled it. And then another time Bryson was like—because I work at night. So I had just got there—and Bryson was like, "I already talked to the lawyer. You can go ahead and go home and get some sleep." [Without Bryson] I'm pretty sure I would have been out of there a lot sooner than the months it took.

Despite Bryson's invaluable support, however, he could not delay the eviction forever. And when Tamara left in April, she faced the same treacherous housing market that had led her to be scammed the previous year (and did so with considerably more trepidation). Coincidentally, Bryson was renting out the residential unit above his storefront legal office, and right around the time Tamara was looking for some place to live, Bryson's tenant decided to leave. The stars aligned, and Bryson decided to rent the unit to Tamara. He called her and said, "It's not a house, but it would be a place for you to land." She and her children have been there since.

Once again, notwithstanding Bryson's personal commitment and considerable legal talents, Tamara's fate had been determined by the goodwill of a landlord (albeit in Bryson's case, one who was more invested in Tamara's well-being than he was in turning a profit). Along the way, Tamara learned again and again that the state would not protect her and tenants like her. Main Street Renewal faced few repercussions for buying up houses throughout the city (thus reducing supply and driving up prices), leaving those properties vacant and unguarded for months on end (thereby creating the conditions that enabled scammers like "Tristan"), or evicting the people who suffered on account of such neglect (saddling them with eviction records and housing debt that contributed to continued cycles of poverty and exploitation). Even worse is that the local police were aware of what was happening and did not act.

> I had called the police on Tristan because he was calling and threatening me [when I stopped paying him rent]. And when the police showed up, they was like, "You're like the fourth family that's been scammed in this house." Like they know that [people] used that house as a scam. The police know it. And they was like, "Well, you made it longer than anybody else."

Per Louisville law, the police had no affirmative obligation to prevent the fraud. Of course, the problem could be fixed legislatively. As Bryson pointed out,

> Louisville City Council could pass an ordinance that says, you know, when residents complain of fraud, real estate fraud or something like that, the police are required to file a report with the county attorney, and the county attorney shall cause notice to be placed on that property. Notice adequate to [convey] to someone who is physically on the property that this house may be used in a crime, and to contact so and so to make sure you're not a victim of fraud. But there's [no ordinance] like that.

Although she was now stably housed (thanks to Bryson), Tamara remained distraught over her ordeal, especially since the consequences had spilled over into her social network:

> I didn't even know what to do. Like I didn't know that you could be scammed and living in the house. Like that was unheard of to me. I was like, Are you serious? . . . And it's crazy because I had recommended Tristan to other people at work. So then I felt bad because I got my coworker scammed. . . . [That coworker is] still living in the hotel right now trying to recover. Like they gave him everything.

The issues precipitating the fraud were bigger than Tamara. They were rooted in a detrimental array of political-economic configurations: a housing market that was untenable for low-to moderate-income families, a welfare state that provided limited assistance securing housing, and a local government that inadequately regulated property owners. Since most of the people Tamara knew were also ensnared in this thicket of structures, it only made sense to share the good news with them when she found a "dream home" for an affordable price—a feat that felt almost impossible. By the time she realized that the dream had turned into a nightmare, it was too late to warn her coworker. When I asked Tamara if she thought an ordinance of the kind Bryson had suggested would ever happen, she was pessimistic:

> No. I contacted the council representative for the district that I was in. And he knew—he knew that Main Street . . . was buying all the houses in this district. It had been reported that the house I was in had been used as a scam. *He knew; he did nothing. He did nothing.*

Tamara was not apathetic. She entreated the police and called her local elected official. But the state actors who were meant to protect and represent her flagrantly failed her. Bryson confirmed that what happened to her was criminal fraud. In the eyes of the law, she was a victim. Yet there was no redress; she was still evicted. And no one was surprised. Bryson characterized this situation as the legacy of historical oppression, portraying the problem as "the inertia of history. I mean, the judges in Louisville felt like they could treat people like Tamara that way . . . because of the inertia. Because like, that's just like the water they swim in." Bryson was not deterred by this despondent reality, but the experiences of Tamara and other people like her—and his inability to help them through standard legal practice—taught him invaluable lessons that were sharpened by his interaction with tenant organizers. He poignantly articulated what he learned:

> Our experience with the district courts is a really good example of the *limits of lawyerly power and the need for grassroots solidarity* because the system is going to grind on, . . . some sort of a well-crafted lawsuit and a noble cause is not enough to change it. . . . Getting even the most obvious injustices corrected with the most modest interventions—stop these few hundred evictions for a few weeks, send these people the correct Zoom notice, and redo it . . . —we're totally incapable of getting that done, you know. . . . They just wanted to grind on . . . in some ways that's liberating because it clarifies for me what our job is. . . . It's like, boy, if we're losing on things like that, we don't have any choice but to go back to the grassroots and build power with the people this is going to impact. And it's the same thing with the district court litigation. It's like, boy, if the district court, these are the people who are supposed to be neutral, these are supposed to be the gate-keepers for justice in our community. And they just wanted to grind on. And so—that's been . . . a paradigm shift for our organization. . . . Being policy experts, and being the people who could file a lawsuit here and there to fix a problem and train legal aid attorneys, that's one job. [But this re-quires something different]. . . . If we are going to be a law firm for [the] growing movement of grassroots organizations and organizers, their people are going to need more support. . . . We're just not constructed like that right now . . . to be a place that can receive a lot of interfacing with directly impacted people or grassroots organizations.

Bryson had become acutely aware of the constraints on his reach as a civil legal attorney pursuing impact litigation and engaging in "grasstops" advocacy (e.g., offering policy expertise and filing public interest lawsuits). While he believed in the work he was doing, he had come to view it more soberly in the context of a local political economy that was captured by an "inertia of history" that privileged the interests of property owners and other economically advantaged (disproportionately White) power holders. Judges, police, and legislators all knowingly and recurrently failed people like Tamara. Bryson's legal representation could barely chip away at such problems and stood little chance of achieving more fundamental change. So he began to envision alternative uses of his legal acumen. Because he had relationships with community organizers (recall the community coalition calls he sat in on to scout out legal problems he might help with), he had been exposed to a different theory of change (bottom-up power) than what most lawyers espoused (top-down power). The bottom-up approach he was turning toward was not predicated solely on elite power brokering (e.g., advocating before legislatures and adjudicating cases before judges) but instead recognized the (complementary) need to build and exercise power in the communities most harmed by the status quo (Michener 2025a).

Tamara and Bryson offer a narrative that sensitizes us to the limits of civil law, the role for community organizations in bridging its inadequacies, and the prospects for extending beyond it toward more transformative political ends. The remainder of this chapter highlights how tenant organizations do this work, how their efforts bring them into engagement with civil legal systems, and how they push from within and outside those systems to struggle against the prevailing terms of the American political economy.[2] We do not focus our analysis on community organizing processes because they are the easiest, most obvious, or most salient path to political change. Rather, we center tenant organizations as an important institutional resource because they are an overlooked but *possible*—and promising—site of power from the margins (Michener 2020; Michener, SoRelle, and Thurston 2022; Michener and SoRelle 2022).

Consistent with the wider framing of this book, such organizations address the structural drivers of civil legal problems, tackling the political economy of civil justice from the demand side. While lawyers *supply* legal resources to address individual civil justice problems, community organizers build power to affect the governing and economic institutions that create the *demand* for such legal resources. Some lawyers (like Bryson) embrace an organizing approach and work within it (contra to a traditional lawyering approach).

We illustrate these practices and elaborate their logic by carefully portraying the ways tenant organizations respond to civil legal problems. In doing so, we chart the terrain of the possible. This is an important function of descriptive research: to foster political imagination by showing what can happen in the world and assessing such possibilities through clarifying analytic lenses. Even in structural contexts where political transformation does not appear probabilistically feasible, empirically grounded descriptive assessments of possibilities offer instructive (and even inspirational) insight on pathways of change.

---

2. The insights elaborated in the remainder of this chapter draw on ideas and analyses first published in Michener 2022.

Community Organizing and Civil Legal Systems

Local organizations that lie outside the scope of legal aid often participate in legal processes (Caulfield 1971; Golio et al. 2023; Gordon 2007). Such groups draw on courts, lawyers, and legal problems as a basis for community organizing. Organizing is "an approach to collective action that seeks to change individuals and groups into effective actors in the public sphere" (Han, Baggetta, and Oser 2024, 246). The main objective of organizing is power building, which can be understood as "the strategic development of political formations (groups, networks, coalitions) that equip people and communities to exercise collective power over the processes that affect their lives" (Michener 2025a, 194).[3] The processes that organizing can be deployed to gain power over include (but are not limited to) legal ones. Tenant groups are community organizing institutions that work within racially and economically marginalized communities to (among many other things) provide support navigating legal processes, obtaining legal representation, contesting unfair legal practices, and breaking the control of legal systems (Golio et al. 2023; Michener 2022). In this way, grassroots organizations act as civil legal institutions. Unlike the other civil legal institutions we have emphasized in this book (e.g., legal aid organizations and courts), nonlegal local organizations can operate both inside (to a certain extent) and outside the formal civil legal system. This gives them distinctive leverage as a power resource.

Scholars studying power and the welfare state have long identified labor unions as vital power resources that channel the collective ability of workers to balance power as well as shape the outcomes of struggles with employers (Jung and VanHeuvelen 2024; Korpi [1978] 2022; Milkman 2024; Refslund and Arnholtz 2022). We similarly conceptualize tenant organizations as power resources—focusing on their role channeling the collective energies of tenants to assert a balance between tenants' interests and those of economic elites who use housing as a vehicle for amassing wealth. Organizations like tenant unions are important civil legal institutions precisely because of the constraints that

---

3. Organizing is a distinct mode of political activity, marked by at least three features that distinguish it from either mobilizing or advocacy: relationality—people being organized have substantive relationships with organizing groups and with one another that go beyond episodic interactions; power sharing—people being organized have core decision-making power with the organizing group; and strategy—people being organized act based on tactically motivated political ideas about how to achieve change (Michener 2025a).

Bryson bumped up against in his work with Tamara. Like Bryson, community organizers recognize the limits of law and act accordingly. Consider the insistence of Tom, a tenant organizer in California, that

> even if you know all of your rights and you are 100 percent on the right side of the law, it's not really going to matter if your landlord has four attorneys and you show up in court against them, right? Even if you get a legal aid lawyer, like bless them, they're doing the Lord's work, but you know, they're just outgunned. So in terms of the legal system, . . . [it's] woefully inadequate.

As Tom makes clear, even while civil legal attorneys are "doing the Lord's work," they contend with resource deficiencies that leave them "outgunned." No matter the intentions or aspirations of lawyers or judges, the civil legal systems that they are embedded within place sharp limits on how much they can help people like Tamara.

Dan, a civil legal attorney in Detroit, gave us detailed insights into the nature of those limits. In our hour-long conversation, Dan enumerated a panoply of challenges. He pointed out that even one of the most popular and sought-after expansions of legal support—providing counsel to tenants facing eviction in housing court—does not ultimately allow for "a right to counsel" of the sort that proponents hope for. Instead, in the wake of Detroit's recent right-to-counsel law, things are just as hectic as ever. Dan explains why:

> I am [still] in [housing] court pretty regularly and it seems . . . just as chaotic as it was when I was there [before right to counsel]. . . . There's tons of turnover in those courts. They're asked to staff a whole docket on three days a week. So you can imagine if you're taking all of those cases, theoretically, how many attorneys you need when there are thirty thousand cases filed in Detroit alone? It's just—it's a lot of cases. . . . And then you start to think, OK, well, you are underfunded already. What they said they needed [for right to counsel] is already underfunded in Detroit. But even that amount, people were saying, that's not enough. . . . That's enough to pay attorneys like forty-eight grand a year. But if anybody gets any other job opportunity, they're going to take it, you know. So to get attorneys who are really invested, it's just not enough. . . . I was making seventy as a supervising attorney . . . but, you know, with my family, I was looking for other opportunities constantly because you just can't afford that . . . with inflation and all the stuff going on. So anyway, it's really hard to get people who are invested.

And then ultimately, even worse, they go and work for landlord attorneys who can pay them like a hundred grand. And then they know all the secrets, so to speak, and then they're able to screw us. . . . The reason [I moved to impact litigation] is because we were looking at the root of issues and not just trying to constantly hack at all the new branches that are coming out.

In the conversation that followed, Dan talked again and again about how his impact litigation firm worked with community organizations to identify the most pressing problems facing tenants, and coproduce solutions that went beyond the individual-level approach of legal services and pushed toward collective interventions. Despite being trained as a lawyer, Dan recognized that grassroots organizations were vital power resources. This theme emerged with nearly all the lawyers we interviewed. Whether prompted or not, civil legal attorneys clearly discerned the limits of legal tools, and some of them noted that when lawyers found themselves at an impasse, tenant organizations could step in. Such organizations fight to expand civil legal rights, support people with civil legal problems, and build power within racially and economically marginalized communities (Michener 2020; Michener and SoRelle 2022).

Though tenant groups do not chiefly focus on legal aid, the people they organize face housing problems that bring them into the web of the civil legal system. As a result, tenant organizations cannot ignore civil legal processes. They instead engage and (sometimes) challenge the civil legal system. The rest of this chapter elaborates four ways that this happens: through direct collaboration with lawyers and legal organizations; through the provision of court support to tenants; via direct action to disrupt court practices and outcomes; and through intentional and critical redirection *away* from the legal domains toward more structurally transformative pathways to change. Using these means, local organizations protect and cultivate the material well-being of tenants while planting seeds of reconfigured power dynamics in the US political economy. In doing so, they illuminate a conduit that goes beyond a supply-oriented (more lawyers) approach to addressing civil legal problems and toward a demand-oriented (more power) strategy for changing political-economic systems

Mechanisms of Engaging the Civil Legal System

The four mechanisms by which tenant groups engage civil legal processes to build power were distilled from a thematic analysis of qualitative interviews with members and leaders of tenant organizations (n = 78).[4] The rest of this chapter provides concrete examples of each mechanism. Descriptively elaborating on these processes allows us to better understand how local organizations operate in relation to civil legal systems to forge a more just political economy.

Direct Collaboration

When we asked tenant organizers about their relationship(s) to the civil legal system, they most often noted their collaboration with legal aid organizations. Legal scholars have long called for "collaborative lawyering," "community lawyering," "rebellious lawyering," "progressive lawyering," and other modes of legal advocacy that position lawyers as "partners in collective ventures to save the world" rather than as "saviors or champions" (Lopez 1992; Nickles, White, and Cole 2001; Piomelli 2006, 544; Villazor 2004; White 1998). These approaches vary in subtle ways, but they all orient around the imperative of communities "speaking and acting on their own behalf" in partnership with lawyers (Piomelli 2006, 544).[5]

While lawyers have written extensively about such lawyering practices, this chapter highlights the perspectives of people within tenant organizations, many of whom are living in race-class-subjugated communities. Both leaders and members within tenant organizations found consistent, wide-ranging ways of collaborating with lawyers to meet community needs as well as build their power. Collaboration included working with lawyers to ensure that tenant organizations' legal guidance did not run afoul of the law, coordinating community eviction defense trainings with legal experts, getting legal support in advance of taking risky organizing actions, and enlisting lawyers to file legal motions in conjunction with broader strategic organizing efforts.

Ali, a tenant leader in Georgia, recalled that when her group was developing guidelines to help tenants who were facing eviction, "we had like [the city's]

---

4. We used Dedoose to analyze the data. For the analyses in this chapter, we examined interview excerpts that were tagged with the code "civil legal system" or any related subcodes, which included "housing court," "lawyer/legal services," and "perceptions."

5. They also have roots in the ideas of 1960s' sand 1970s' poverty lawyers like Edward Sparer, who envisioned law reform and legal services as a vehicle to collaborate with and empower social workers, welfare recipients, and other community members to independently exert political pressure on their own behalf (Davis 1993; Lawrence 2014).

legal aid to help us with the legal jargon of it and all of that. So they would tell us you can't put that in there. You can say this, but you can't say that. That's illegal. We can't say this, you know, all of that." To comply with legal restrictions on the unauthorized practice of law, tenant organizations had to carefully balance between offering help to people with civil legal problems and providing legal advice, the latter of which is prohibited (Sandefur 2020). Collaboration with legal aid helps them to figure this out. Ariana, a tenant organizer from Texas, similarly explains the involvement of legal aid in tenant meetings and eviction defense training events:

> We started working with a legal aid community liaison, and so he would come to a few of our meetings and explain, "This is how we're able to work with you. Like we can do educational events, but it has to be several other organizations, it can't look like we're favoring you with your socialist leaning." And so next weekend they're going to do an eviction event training for us and teach organizers how to represent tenants in eviction court.[6]

Beyond trainings and guidance, legal aid attorneys and tenant organizations also collaborate in ways that enable the latter to pursue new and potentially risky strategies. For example, a group of tenants on the West Coast were dealing with a landlord who would often refuse to make repairs or replacements, creating barely habitable housing conditions. Juan, a tenant leader in the building, described it this way:

> This question of habitability, particularly in [this city] where disinvestment is a necessary part of speculation. . . . It takes so fucking long for the city and the courts to rectify a habitability situation. . . . Meanwhile, [tenants] have to live in those situations. . . . At what point will we get to the point where to be a tenants' association means to collectively pool your money, stop paying your landlord, and invest in the habitability. . . . The city is not going to do it for us; the local [tenant union] is going to do it for us.

Tenants can fight habitability deficiencies by withholding rent (like Josephine in chapter 1 who joked about sending her rent on vacation at hotel escrow).

---

6. Recall from chapter 2 that tenants in Texas can appoint almost anyone to represent them in housing-related legal proceedings, including nonlawyers without formal legal training. In this context, tenant organizations can train their members to represent one another in legal proceedings.

Withholding rent, however, poses a substantial legal risk (Super 2011). If a tenant withholds rent to pay for repairs, an eviction means losing both their home and the money they put into fixing the home. A (somewhat) less risky strategy is that of collectively withholding rent and pooling it to make major repairs. Tanya, a tenant from the same group as Juan, contextualized the dilemma:

> Landlords hate it when you do your own repairs; they get really angry. . . . Each of us have tried individually to do that in the past, and our landlord gets really angry and [aggressive], but this is the first time we're trying to do it collectively. How do we overcome that fear together by working together? We have the legal right to make certain repairs and deduct them from our rent. The reason we haven't done that isn't because we don't know our rights, it's because we haven't been organized before and we've been scared to do it.

Crucially, collaboration with legal aid informed the strategy underlying this type of collective action. Tanya made this observation as she talked about how her landlord removed all but one washing machine from her large apartment building. She explained why she and other tenants in the building were planning to use withheld rent payments to buy additional washing machines.

> [Having so few washing machines for the building] is *illegal*, and it's really tough during COVID. Everyone has been sick, and they don't want to go out to wash their laundry. . . . We have a lawyer who is willing to argue the case for that in court. . . . We are no longer waiting for permission. . . . We are building the confidence and trust to take risks.

Juan echoed similar sentiments, saying,

> This is the first time we're talking about doing this collectively. We know we have the legal right to make certain repairs and deduct rent. And one reason we haven't done it is because of fear. And we don't really know how this is going to play out in court. We have an attorney who said he would argue it—and it's up to us whether we're going to take this risk. One of the things we're talking about is laundry machines; there's one in the building and it's always broken, and there used to be more, but they took them away—which is illegal. For most of the pandemic, everyone has been sick. The idea [that] we have to go out and do laundry while we're sick because the landlord is cheap is insane.

As tenant leaders, Juan and Tanya decided on a strategy of collective risk in collaboration with a lawyer who mitigated that risk by offering to fight for them in court. In this case, Juan and Tanya approached a legal aid attorney for help and received enough support to reassure them to take a daring strategy. Absent the support of legal aid, the avenue of collective action that they pursued might have been untenably risky or seemed entirely out of reach. In this way, tenant organizations facilitated new and different forms of collective action by collaborating with legal services.

Relatedly, some tenant organizers emphasized how lawyers and tenant unions worked together through community lawyering arrangements that positioned lawyers to follow instead of lead (Ancheta 1993; Elsesser 2012). Rather than going to a tenant union and telling it what the group should do, community lawyering brings lawyers into community with tenants and deploys them in the service of needs identified by tenants. A tenant organizer from a large organization in Massachusetts described it in these terms:

> We work with standard legal services entities and also legal services that are connected with universities. . . . But those lawyers have developed a practice they refer to as "community lawyering." So not only are they kind of on the right side of the issue—they're representing the tenant not the real estate corporation—but they're representing the tenant in a way that's making the tenant a protagonist in their own drama. So they're saying, "Look . . . I'm the lawyer, and I'm here to advise you about your legal rights and maybe even represent you in some cases. But mainly I am deferring to the tenant association. I'm deferring to the members. . . . I'm deferring to the organizers to let us know what you want us to do."

Dan, the lawyer from Detroit quoted earlier, talks about what this kind of collaboration with tenants looked like from his perspective. His legal organization decided to oppose predatory landlords in Detroit on a collective level, upending the common dynamic of a single person (or family) facing off against a landlord who is committing wrongs against many disconnected tenants across the city. The organization was able to do this because it was being responsive to local organizers, who flagged the slumlords whom tenants were struggling against:

> We're working with community organizers who have been identifying slumlords who have properties all across the city. And we're trying to file proactive cases against those landlords on a mass scale. So not just one-offs,

but saying we've identified a hundred properties. Because Detroit is . . . not like New York, where it's mostly high-rises. We're mostly single-family homes, so it's hard for one individual to go against one landlord who has all the resources, and this person doesn't. So we're saying, OK, we're going to find these things that these landlords are doing that are wrong, and we're going to proactively file a case against all of these properties simultaneously with similar fact patterns and go from there, and then kind of knock the landlord back on their heels because these repair issues only come up in the eviction defense context once it's too late. . . . The reason I wanted to talk to you today is because I hope that in some part of this conversation, it can go to . . . what are we doing to actually try to really solve the problem in a substantive way . . . so that people don't ever get into court? Because truthfully, in Detroit, our issue is, why do we have thirty thousand people in these courts every year? And obviously the answer is people don't have money. But the other answer is like there are ways to keep people out of this court if we actually are able to be proactive instead of reactive.

Being proactive was only possible in partnership with organized tenants, who could systematically identify problems and facilitate strategies for addressing them. Sometimes, the most viable strategies were legal, as the lawsuit that Dan planned to file suggests. But more often, legal strategy was supplementary and subordinate to core organizing approaches. When Bruce, a tenant leader in Kentucky, explained the core work that a coalition of tenant organizations did to protect a group of tenants who were being displaced, he noted that the legal strategy was parallel and subsidiary:

> There's this trailer park . . . where a developer . . . had gotten tax increment financing from the city and county together to buy the trailer park with plans to evict everyone and build a shopping mall on it. . . . They get millions of dollars in public money in a city and county that doesn't have any public money, or that's what they tell everyone, you know? And it really is a really small budget and they're giving all of their tax money away. . . . And we ran this, like, rapid response campaign. . . . Oh, and [Bryson] was also involved. . . . He filed the lawsuit.

In implementing the insights relayed earlier in this chapter, Bryson had been working collaboratively with tenant organizers. And though he did not talk about this specific displacement case during our interview, the local tenant organizers I interviewed did. Their "rapid response campaign" involved canvasing the trailer park to get residents organized, planning rallies, attracting media, directly engaging both the landlord and developer, putting pressure on the city and county governments, building a mutual aid fund to support tenants, and more. Bryson's lawsuit was one small part of this larger work, and Bruce mentioned it only briefly and in passing. An organizer we interviewed from a different tenant organization in the larger coalition didn't even mention the lawsuit at all when she spoke of the campaign efforts:

> We are going every weekend and canvasing in that trailer park to get all the folks organized. And they have come up with a list of demands, and they're going to city council tomorrow. And they're going to the fiscal quarter[ly] meeting, which is like the county government meeting [later in the month].

Jamila conducted a dozen interviews and spent almost a week doing ethnographic fieldwork in Kentucky. She crisscrossed the state (Louisville, Richmond, Lexington, and Berea), hung out with tenants in cafés as they explained their challenges, attended a tenant union Bingo night, broke bread with tenant members at a local Mexican restaurant, and sat in the offices of several local attorneys. Many of the people she spoke with mentioned the fight against the developers seeking to displace the trailer park residents, but only one (Bruce) brought up the lawsuit. This wasn't because the lawsuit was insignificant. Instead, it was because the organizing efforts (e.g., canvasing, rallying, and tenants directly engaging elected officials) were the chief focus of everyone involved (even the attorneys).

Tenant organizations collaborate with lawyers to leverage their complementary but distinct roles in larger political processes. Such arrangements facilitate the engagement of tenant groups with civil legal institutions while addressing tenants' legal problems in ways that orient toward collective solutions that make strategic use of the law without treating it as a substitute for broader and deeper action to achieve change.

Court Support

Another way that tenant organizations engage civil legal processes is through courts. Courtrooms are confusing, alienating, and demoralizing places for many tenants. Recall Marissa's description (in chapter 5) of housing court as "mayhem." Tenant organizations support their members and would-be members in traversing such courtroom chaos. They do this by providing emotional, material, and informational resources. Audra, a tenant organizer in Wisconsin, observed how this worked in her group:

> We don't have a lawyer in our organization, but we do have a legal advocate, and we do provide advocacy, which sometimes is just showing up to court, which is on Zoom now. But sometimes just like having an advocate there from [the tenant union] can be beneficial. So we've been doing that. And then we sometimes refer out to [a] legal aid society, which can provide income-based legal help.

Audra describes how the tenant union offered to support members in court both via the emotional support that comes with having someone present and through the tangible support of a referral to legal services.

In Kentucky, Bruce coupled different forms of court support, not just for members of the tenant organization, but for whomever tenant members encountered in court:

> What we would do was sit in on the court processing and wait outside the courtroom for tenants to come outside, where we would, you know, talk to them, and the first thing we would do was offer to help them apply for rental assistance. The two: first, the statewide fund and then the [local] fund that were available. And then we would also get their contact information, so we could follow up with them and see how they were navigating that whole process. And then also just giving them our contact information so that in case they were having a housing emergency, they could contact us, or in case they needed more resources or more help down the line. And also just kind of working with tenants, where people would tell us their stories if they were going through a really stressful time. And we would kind of see where we could potentially have an "in" to go and assist further.

This example captures the role of court support in connecting tenants to options for financial assistance, emotional encouragement, and base building.

In some contexts, court support is especially crucial given state legal or policy structures. Ariana, the organizer from Texas, told us why Texas law made court support a central part of the work of her tenant organization:

> The way it works in Texas is you . . . don't have to be a lawyer to represent a tenant in an eviction hearing. . . . And then they don't make it easy at all. . . . I went to an eviction hearing yesterday with the tenant and the

judge. . . . It's just another world. . . . It's so hard to understand what's going on. So we are sort of trying to help break down that process for people because I mean, I'm nine months in, and I still have a hard time explaining [it]. . . . Up until [Monday] like I hadn't known the difference between a notice to vacate and the lease termination notice, but they're like two separate documents and you know there's like such a specific order for evicting someone. So trying to explain that, even in English, and then there's tenants [for whom] English is not their first language.

Riley, a leader from a tenant union in Massachusetts who also had experience with direct legal involvement in the courtroom, relayed how her organization stepped in to fill a gap when state funding for a legal program ran out:

I was an advocate with the volunteers for justice program underneath community legal aid, so I was there, assisting every[one] who was fighting . . . doing the tenant work . . . [when our] grant ran out. . . . There were no attorneys to help people, so we had to teach people how to navigate a system that is set up for attorneys. So we got really good at being paralegals. Thank God, in the state you don't have to be certified to be a paralegal, and we're lucky enough to have twelve movement attorneys who work with us that volunteer their time in the organization, and they take the direction from us.

Even in Massachusetts, a state that Riley described as having "progressive courts," funding for lawyers ran dry, compelling members of the tenant organization to take up the task of supporting fellow tenants (and in another example of collaboration with lawyers, "movement attorneys" supported Riley's group to help equip them for this courtroom work).

In some states, the law is so complex and so heavily weighted against tenants that tenant organizations engage in preemptive court support, reaching out in advance to inform tenants of the various ways they can be evicted and informing them of strategies to protect themselves from displacement. Owen, a tenant organizer in Virginia, shared about the way his organization

made efforts to call and canvas neighborhoods we knew [because of court records] were facing eviction rates. . . . We were distributing eviction information, making [tenants] aware of current laws and their rights as tenants, as well as information about food, utility, and rent relief for Virginians.

Rod, a tenant leader from Arkansas, explains this approach:

> Arkansas has terrible eviction laws. There are basically three ways to evict someone. The most common is through circuit court. It's a civil procedure, but there's a very small window for a tenant to respond. . . . In 2022 in Arkansas, there were eighty-three-hundred-plus civil evictions that we could find. . . . And just in the Little Rock area, there were over thirty-four hundred. . . . When the moratorium went off in '21 and then when the governor refused rental assistance . . . it just spiked. And for the civil procedure tenants are served . . . legalese that [is] almost completely deceptive. . . . It sort of sounds like you have thirty days to respond, but you really only have five days. . . . There is the second [way to evict] and . . . it is called failure to vacate, and it is a criminal eviction procedure that dates from the Jim Crow era. And it is used in some counties and tenants can be jailed. They're fined for every day they stay in the place. . . . There have been people jailed. . . . And then there's a third [way of evicting people]. . . . It's a small claims eviction and it's pretty quick. So yeah, during the pandemic, we reached out to four or five thousand tenants and had some saves and kept a few people in [their homes], but it was tough.

By reaching out to people before they got to court to inform them about these complex legal processes, Rod's group offered a form of precourt support in a context where many tenants would face eviction otherwise.

Altogether, court support was a common activity that tenant organizations reported undertaking. This begs a critical question: If tenant organizations aim to fight for change that transcends legal systems (which they do), why do they spend so much energy on the time-consuming work of court support? Tenant organizations offered three main explanations for investing energy in court support. First, the courtroom presence of fellow tenants was symbolically and emotionally meaningful. An organizer in Michigan underscored this by noting that

> the way the law is right now, it definitely weighs in favor of landlords . . . but even if you don't have the law behind you, you still have the community and the sense of right and wrong behind you. . . . What's really powerful is to pack the courtroom, [because] not only does that send a message to the judge but it sends a tremendous message of support to the folks who are facing eviction.

In the context of a political economy that often favors property owners and disadvantages tenants (as the three routes to eviction in Arkansas exemplify), the support of tenant organizations was especially meaningful.

Second, court support was viewed as a form of solidaristic mutual aid. Organizers at a tenant meeting we observed in Michigan exhorted their members to "be available and present for folks faced with this awful possibility [of eviction]." They encouraged those who were part of the tenant union to show "radical hospitality." This aligned with activists' assertion that mutual aid is a "form of political participation in which people take responsibility for caring for one another and changing political conditions not just through symbolic acts or putting pressure on their representatives in government but by actually building new social relations that are more survivable" (Spade 2020, 136). In this way, court support reflected vital sociopolitical functions of tenant unions.

Finally, court support was an organizing tool used to bring new people into tenant groups. Organizers made this clear by continually noting that courthouses were fertile ground for identifying people with legal problems and inviting them into the ranks of tenant members. For example, organizers in one Kentucky tenant union describe how they made decisions about where to canvas for new group members: "[We] look on the court dockets to find people's addresses. . . . That's one of the ways that we find people's addresses. We'll look where all the evictions have been and we'll be, like, OK, we're going to hit those neighborhoods."

Tenant organizations' court support was motivated by ends ranging from symbolism to solidaristic aid to base building. For these and other reasons, tenant organizations invested time in legal processes despite being nonlegal entities aimed primarily at building power outside legal systems.

Direct Action

Nonviolent direct action is another way that tenant organizations engage civil legal systems. Direct action involves participatory tactics that push beyond traditional modes of advocacy and political participation (e.g., voting, lobbying, and talking to a politician) by deploying the strategic, disruptive power of people in nonviolent efforts to challenge injustice and demand change. Examples of direct action include protests, boycotts, rent strikes, eviction blockades, and more. Direct action leverages "people power" to "exert pressure on governments or other powerful institutions" (Carter 2005). Organizing-based direct action stands out from more episodic mobilization (e.g., mass protests) insofar as it entails strategic intentionality and is targeted toward specific campaign goals.

Nearly all tenant organizations we spoke with use direct action as a tactic. The fundamental emphasis of tenant organizations was not on reforming or improving legal processes per se but rather advancing policies and political transformations that enable access to affordable, quality housing. Still, because eviction is a legal process mediated through courts, and other housing problems similarly have legal dimensions, tenant organizations orient themselves toward the law to be responsive to political-economic realities. For instance, an organizer in Michigan talked about being "out in front of the courthouse protesting evictions." Similarly, an organizer in Massachusetts described how they

> constantly hark back to this demonstration we had on March 12 last year [2020] in front of the housing court where we demanded that the housing court be closed. . . . The housing court is cheek by jowl people squeezed into rooms. And most of the people squeezed into those rooms are people of color and are putting themselves at huge danger of COVID. So two days later, they did close down the housing court. And so then we looked for a moratorium law, which we worked with various officials to get passed, and we passed what we think is the strongest moratorium law in the country.

In these and other ways, tenant organizations targeted courts when they perceived them as a salient and central source of harm to tenants. Generally, the goal of such direct action was to slow down or entirely halt court processes so that evictions could not occur. Tom, a tenant organizer in California, relayed one direct action that successfully pressured a local elected official:

> We did a direct action at an assembly member's house at Christmas. . . . The eviction moratorium was set to expire, and we hadn't heard anything direct from him. We had tried to make an appointment through his office, and so a bunch of us just went to his house and started singing Christmas carols outside his house. And he came out, and I mean, he's a son of the community. Like he was a council member for years. . . . He's an African American man, a member of the community, so we were like, sorry to interrupt your breakfast, but we have an urgent problem here. He talked to us for twenty minutes, and then we had a meeting with him shortly after that and he agreed to sign onto a piece of legislation. . . . He [later] signed on.

Targeted direct action focused on specific people, groups, or businesses with a strategic end goal in view is a hallmark of grassroots organizing. Sometimes, the best tack is to gently but firmly get the attention of a "son of the community," like Tom's group did. In less amenable contexts, direct action could involve more confrontational tactics. Tanvee, an organizer in Missouri, explains her group's action:

> We chained our fucking bodies to the doors of the courts, pissing everyone in town off. . . . There's no one in this town who we haven't pissed off in some way . . . and you know we've gotten our people arrested, we've like done all the shit. . . . We've taken people on rent strike, we've come up against corporations, and so on.

Later in the conversation, Tanvee describes her tenant organizations' pivot from more conventional strategies to confrontational tacks involving direct action:

> We were trying to move [political officials] by writing letters, lobbying people, doing vigils, blah blah blah, it didn't work. And we had to sit with ourselves. . . . We can either keep doing this shit and it's not going to work, or we can figure out how to shut the system down because our goal, right, we had to really meditate on this, our goal was not to win an eviction moratorium, our goal was to end evictions, and a moratorium would have been a great way to get there, but they weren't going to let us have it, right, so we had to figure out another way to do that. . . . These existing power structures are oppressive, were designed to be, it's not a broken system, it's working, it's a system working as it was designed to, and it's our job to either change them or if we can't change them, shut them down.

As Tanvee so lucidly clarifies, tenant members and leaders seek systems change that goes far beyond fixing courts. When they chain themselves to the court-house doors, it is not because they believe that legal paths are the most important ones; it is because they view courts as one of the "existing power structures" operating in "oppressive" ways in their communities.

Importantly, direct action is not always oriented toward courts. Tenant groups confront a range of actors complicit in civil legal processes. This includes political officials (as Tom explained) and even police (who enforce court-ordered evictions). When Jamila observed an "eviction blockade train-ing" hosted by Housing NOW, a tenant organization in New York City, the group talked about the experiences of a Black woman named Laura. Housing NOW had found Laura's number on the housing court roster, reached out to her, and offered to help her fight her impending eviction. Once Laura was on board, Housing NOW coordinated a "phone tree"—a group of tenants ready and trained to show up at a moment's notice should Laura be informed that the local sheriff was scheduled to remove her from her home. The members who showed up to support Laura each had designated roles (e.g., blockader, arrestable, police liaison, media contact, and chant leader). Tenants participating in the blockade were given guidelines on how to interact with journalists, communicate on social media, and most crucial, respond to the police:

> When the police come, we will stand our ground, continue chanting and singing. Arrestables will move to the front if police try to arrest us. . . . Non-arrestables will move to the back of the group recording and documenting the scene. Those who get arrested will have access to legal support and money to pay bail. National Lawyers Guild observing.[7]

Prepared and ready (including with the support of lawyers willing to observe), Housing NOW made sure the phone tree was activated every time Laura received notice from the sheriff. Trained group members then encircled her home in nonviolent resistance to her removal from the property. This tactic—known as an eviction blockade—stopped the local police from executing an eviction. It worked because sheriffs are legally obliged to notify tenants about when they will show up. Housing NOW was aware of these legal parameters and leveraged them as a means to defend tenants from displacement. Over the course of several years, Housing NOW had organized numerous eviction blockades on Laura's behalf. After the most recent one, Laura's bank gave up on trying to evict her. Instead, it decided to negotiate more favorable terms that allowed her to remain in her home.

Housing NOW's eviction blockade exemplified multiple key functions of direct action. Direct action was an organizing tool; it activated Laura politically. She spoke at the eviction blockade training, sharing her experience to motivate her fellow tenants. Even after her own housing situation had been positively resolved, she remained committed to the work Housing NOW was doing in the community. Direct action was also a lever of change; it catalyzed shifts in local political dynamics that were favorable to tenants throughout the city. Several local landlords preemptively halted eviction proceedings, worried that they may be next on Housing NOW's agenda. Local elected officials reached out to Housing NOW, looking to engage it in conversations about

---

7. Arrestables were people willing to be arrested if necessary. Housing NOW emphasized that these should be people without prior records (and therefore less likely to receive severe punishment) and noted that police would likely be easier on White women who appeared "safe."

housing policy. At least one of those officials eventually participated in an eviction blockade.

While eviction blockades are an especially striking example, it is one of many tools in a broader direct action tool kit. While each tool operates distinctly, they are all aimed at confronting countervailing legal and political structures that generate legal and material need—whether that means gently convincing a policymaker to sign an eviction moratorium, forcibly blocking entry to courts, or refusing entry for a sheriff to evict a neighbor.

Redirection toward Structurally Transformative Approaches

The mechanisms of civil legal engagement stressed thus far show how tenant organizations work within and against civil legal systems (e.g., by providing court support, collaborating with legal aid attorneys, and taking direct action). But tenant organizations also intentionally work outside the immediate purview of the civil legal system to tackle issues on different terms than are possible from within. Indeed, most of the tenant members and leaders interviewed expressed having little faith in civil legal systems, and did not view them as optimal venues for change.

Cynical views of civil law were common. Even as tenant organizations committed energy to working within the legal system to help tenants in the short term, they understood that more liberatory goals would require transforming, imploding, or transcending civil legal systems altogether. Tom is worth quoting again at greater length on this subject:

> Our tenant [legal] counseling is really like, it's designed to be like a backdoor into actual organizing. So it's not that we tell people don't get a lawyer or don't go to court. But really, the role of that interaction is to highlight the deficiencies in the system. . . . We have done a couple direct actions at the courthouse. . . . We want to offer people court support . . . but . . . there literally are no tenant attorneys and we have one legal aid organization. . . . So if you're looking for an attorney and you don't have any money, really, we tell people organizing is your best option, and we don't even mean that in terms of like our own ideology, we mean that literally like if you call legal services, nine times out of ten you're not getting a call back because they got twelve hundred calls that day. So . . . that's our relationship [to the civil legal system]. . . . Woefully inadequate, and uh, we've tried battling it. . . . We've just been humiliated and disappointed every single time.

A broad orientation toward systems change, combined with an acute aware-ness of the deficits of civil legal processes, pushed Tom's group to focus on organizing as the "best option." He was convinced that a legal approach simply would not suffice. Given the larger political economy of civil justice in which lawyers are scarce due to government disinvestment and legal needs are acute due to rampant economic precarity, only building power would be effective for achieving substantial change in the conditions tenants faced.

Some organizers perceived a tension between these approaches. They pre-ferred to focus on community power building, even while recognizing the need to engage civil legal processes. And they struggled to find a balance that prioritized the former despite the immediacy of the latter. Alice, the organizer from Texas, conveyed it this way:

> Evictions are happening, at like a crazy speed. [The court] was scheduling thirty to seventy eviction hearings a day, like just steamrolling through them, you know, so there's this huge need . . . this really emergency crisis happening, and then you know also this side of it, of trying to build people power. So it's kind of like this play between the two. . . . I've kind of strug-gled to bring the eviction defense side of it along with the organizing, but you really can't have one without the other because tenants have so few rights in Texas that even with a lawyer, you can get thrown out. . . . You really do have to have outside pressure on a complex to stop evicting people.

This was one of the most common dynamics that emerged in tenant organizers' framings of the relationship between power building and legal work. As a ten-ant organizer in Ohio put it,

> We're not spending all of our time at the courts because we don't really think that's *where liberation is actually going to happen*. But also, I mean, we got to realize that the courts do exist, and people are going to be there and people need help there, so you know, if a tenant wants our help . . . our sup-port is, I would say unconditional, you know? We're not going to say, we're not going to go to the court with you because we don't think it's worth it or that's not what's going to be effective. . . . At the end of the day, we want to keep people in their homes, and we're not going to do that without engag-ing with the courts in some way because that's just how things are right now.

An organizer from a large West Coast tenant union echoed this:

> We are at our strongest when we can do things ourselves, when we are not focused on some other mediator like the courts to do things for us. . . .

Nobody wants to be in a pathetic, supplicant position. . . . We've been talking for years and years about working with politicians and the courts versus doing everything else, but tenants facing evictions have to deal with the courts. . . . So we have to figure out a way to synthesize these things. . . . How do we make it so that once you're in a position where you have to deal with the court and the lawyers, we're doing it on our terms. . . . How do we get to the point where it's not just the schematic either-or.

Balancing such imperatives, tenant groups resisted allowing legal prerogatives to dominate their organizational platforms. For example, a group in Philadelphia that works directly with lawyers nonetheless remained sensitive to the risk of placing organizing on the back burner:

We have been really careful around like legal work to make sure it doesn't lead in our organizing. Once a month we do these renters' rights clinics, which are like a chance for people to like meet one-on-one with a lawyer, like in a private Zoom breakout room, and you know, we really see the law as like another tactic to us and the organizing. And we haven't been jumping it; we've been pretty timid around, like, bringing out lawsuits. . . . We try to think about how do we collectivize the legal process as much as possible so it's not so expert driven by the lawyer. And [the lawyer] is in most of our meetings, but like we try not to let her speak too much; we try not to let her facilitate too much—especially when we have new members and new meetings with lots of people. We really make sure not to emphasize the legal aspects, the legal tactics, too much. Because, you know, often we will ask people, "What do you think it's going to take [this corporate landlord] to change?" [and] maybe about a third of the time, people say, "I don't know, maybe a lawsuit?" which could be true, but that's not our theory of how political power is built. So we don't go down that road. . . . We have a whole power analysis, like a whole strategy chart that we use or we map— who has the power to get us what we want—and you know the politicians are on there because they have influence over our targets. . . . And we've met with a couple city council people to get them to put pressure on landlords, and it's worked to get some concessions and keep the pressure on.

Likewise, a tenant organizer in Michigan observed that

although paralegal work is useful and it kind of helps with the immediate problems up front, I think the choice to move to tenant organizing was to do a longer structural build of tenant power in the area. . . . That's why we're trying to do that transition away from [legal work]. I still think that we will still try to do things like that like . . . a little bit of paralegal work. We still have that committee going on. But also, we'll still do things like, if some bad things happen at a courthouse, we'll still do protests and stuff like that. But, uh, I see us moving more in that direction of building power through organizing.

At the heart of many tenant organizers' desire to move beyond the legal system was an abiding belief that the collective power of people is more vital for securing a just political economy than the procedural power of laws. Alice offered resonant thoughts, contemplating a strategy of disruptive protest in the vein proposed by Frances Fox Piven and Richard Cloward (2011), two scholars who seminally strategized about forcing change by overwhelming welfare state institutions with need-based claims:

> One thing that evictions during a pandemic make you realize is that policy and the legal system is the only protection that tenants have by themselves. . . . And because that's hard to navigate and hard to understand—it's actually very hard to win court—there's definitely an aspiration of, like, having the people power to block lawyers from getting into a courthouse; that would be amazing. Like to really throw a wrench in the system and really make it difficult to evict people. Like we've talked about, you know, like if all the people who had an eviction hearing on that [day], they actually showed up, they wouldn't be able to have court. . . . So like even just one day of everybody showing up, that could change how that court [works and] how that judge does his docket. . . . I believe in power, and . . . in pressuring someone with so much more power just by sheer coming together like there's all of these policies in play that just is a thumb just pressing down on them. . . . This is the power dynamic that people don't realize is going on.

Tenant organizers see that civil legal systems have embedded power imbalances that disadvantage tenants. As a result, they are not content to engage civil legal processes on their own terms—terms unfavorable to tenants. Instead, tenant organizers look beyond courts, even as they carefully managed how to operate within and alongside them, to meet the needs of tenants while building power to upend existing power imbalances.

The Democratic Upshots of Tenant Organizing

Local organizations working within race-class-subjugated communities are an important aspect of US democracy (Han, McKenna, and Oyakawa 2021).

Such organizations are an essential component of civil society. Tenant organizations, in particular, act as a vital power resource, fostering a more inclusive polity that incorporates the voices of marginalized groups. This chapter underlines the ways tenant organizations take part in civil legal processes. Attending to the interplay between tenant organizations and civil legal processes surfaces an important way that local organizations buttress democratic citizenship, and provide some level of relief to tenants struggling to navigate a profoundly unequal and exclusionary civil legal system (Sigafoos and Organ 2021; Sommerlad 2004).

The democratic benefits brought by tenant organizations map onto the structural transformation approach described in chapter 4. Tenant organizations are not primarily interested in procedural justice—and its individualizing of collective problems, though they will leverage its promise as needed to advance the interests of tenants. The ambit of tenant organizations' aspirations is inclusive of, yet broader than, procedural justice. The scope of tenant organizations' ambitions varies across groups, but the most powerful and effective groups are much more focused on structural transformations of the American political economy than the formal actors within the existing civil legal infrastructure. They are seeking pathways not just for redress (the promise of civil justice) but for liberation too. For this reason, tenant groups are an essential organizational modality within the civil legal landscape and a fundamental power resource within contemporary US politics, especially when viewed from the margins (Michener 2020; Michener, SoRelle, and Thurston 2022). In chapter 7, we conclude the book by considering the prospects for tenant organizations' power-building efforts to fundamentally transform the political economy of access to justice.

7

"I'm Going to Change It for Someone Else"

THE FUTURE OF POWER AND ACCESS TO JUSTICE

JANE IS a White, working-class, transgender woman from rural Kentucky. The bigotry she endured because of her gender identity has permeated her experiences with housing. Living on her own since the tender age of seventeen, she has recurrently confronted problems of serial displacement, eviction, and discrimination. All of this has unfolded within an oppressive local political economy, where key power brokers are insulated from accountability. In some ways, the specifics of Jane's circumstances are discernibly different from many of the other people featured in this book; Josephine, Aria, Sora, Sheila, Tamara, and Quiana are cisgender Black women living in cities, fighting to survive in the shadow of racial capitalism. But Jane's experiences widen and deepen the lens through which we understand the range and interconnectedness of marginalized people affected by a political economy of civil injustice.

Though different in important ways, Jane's case is like many of the others in this book insofar as it reveals layers of disadvantage enabled by legal and policy structures, exacerbated by oppression, and impossible to address solely via legal means. Jane benefited from legal counsel and expressed immense gratitude for it, yet when we met, she was houseless and despairing over her personal situation. Nevertheless, just days before that, she had attended her first tenant union meeting, intent on doing what she could to ensure that no one else had to go through what she did. In this way, the arc of Jane's experience—lack of happy ending and all—parallels the arc of our arguments in this book.

———

Jane and Jamila met on a warm summer afternoon in rural Kentucky at the office of Molly, Jane's legal services attorney. Jane's body language, facial expressions, intonation, and general comportment allowed for an organic, wide-ranging, informative conversation. Jane was funny, honest, heartbreakingly despondent, and doggedly determined. One of the first things Jane revealed was that she was currently houseless. At only twenty-five years old, she confessed that she was "bouncing around. . . . I just don't know if I want to live in a house anymore." Digging deeper, Jamila discovered a disturbing set of circumstances underlying Jane's displacement and ambivalence about ever finding a home again. When Jamila asked about Jane's experiences with housing, she went straight to the point:

> My experiences have been shitty. . . . I mean, people aren't nice. [Especially] not to me. So it's been pretty shitty. You know, people are judgmental. People are rude, and they use that shit against you, you know? People tear you down to fucking build themselves up.

Jane's voice and body vibrated with emotion when Jamila asked her to explain. She narrated a series of destabilizing experiences that had led her to move from place to place over the last eight years. As a rural, low-income Kentuckian from a resource poor family, Jane had to take what she could get. And that wasn't much. But she muddled through until she hit a wall with her most recent landlord and everything crumbled.

> JANE: I moved in with my friend, and then I ended up taking over her lease, and that was my last lease. That was my psychotic, crazy [landlord]. I swear to God, she tried to kill me. She tried to kill me. There's no way you can tell me that she didn't try to kill me. Threatened to kill me. And then four days later, a car drove over top of my bed. So four days after you threatened to kill me, then the car drives over top of the bed. I'm just like, "That's a big coincidence, babe." It's a really big coincidence. No. It's been shit. That was a shitty situation. It was bad. That's why I know Molly, because Molly's been fucking defending me for the past [three years] since 2020.

JAMILA: It started during the pandemic.

JANE: Yeah. And we have been going; me and this landlord are still going. I'm not in the house anymore. . . . And there's an open case of the . . . Commission of Human Rights. She's under investigation for discrimination against me. It's a big, huge thing. Right is right and wrong is wrong. And you were wrong.

JAMILA: What happened?

JANE: Less than a month into the lease, she was already saying stuff . . . just little things at first. And then she just put the eviction notice on the door. That's what it was.

JAMILA: What was the eviction notice for?

JANE: What did it say? Being a public nuisance or something like that. . . . Being a public nuisance was the means of eviction. . . . I don't even really understand this. . . . I just laughed at it because there's no way this is real. . . . And I could not understand it. . . . I was like, "Maybe I was too loud?" Couldn't really have been too loud living next to train tracks. The train tracks—literally the train ran right behind the house. So it was always loud because there's a train going by every hour on the hour. Yeah. I'm like, "I can't really beat that." So I don't really know what her thing was. And then I contacted Molly. And then Molly contacted her, and then she called me back and she was so mad at me. She was like, "People like you should have to learn the hard way." She said, "I work for everything I had in life." And she said, "And you think that just because you get a free lawyer." . . . She got so mad at me that I got the legal aid or whatever. . . . And then we went to court. I won that court case.

Though Jane avoided that eviction attempt, her relationship with her landlord deteriorated even further: "She told me I had gender issues. And who says that to someone. . . . Told me I had gender issues, and she didn't want any part of that." In response to those discriminatory comments, Jane called Molly again and also told her landlord, "My lawyer will be in contact with you." She then called Molly again for the second time.

I called Molly and we went to court. And then we requested another jury trial, as we do, because I love those [because] no one fucking White man's going to decide my fate. And all the court, all the judges, here are White. They're all White judges. I will never put the fate of my life in the hands of one singular White man. That is stupid. That would be ignorant of me to do that. I might as well just walk away if that was the case. . . . There's no chance in hell that that man is going to look at me and be like, "I'm siding with you."

Though Jane was White, her identity as a trans woman had sensitized her to patterns and processes of oppression. She ended up being glad that she did not leave her fate in the hands of a single judge because when she got to court, she found out that the judge was friends with her landlord:

They're friends with her. The judge was like, "Hey, Donna, I haven't seen you in a while. How are you?" And I'm like, how is this legal? How was this legal that they're sitting here talking to each other, know each other? . . . And I'm sitting here like, "Hey, judge. Hey. I'm here too." . . . [Anyway,] then we got our second court date. We requested a jury. And then they gave us the court date for the jury trial. And the day before we were supposed to go to court, a car runs through my bedroom, over top of my bed, directly over top of my bed.

JAMILA: Do they know whose car it was?
JANE: Oh, yeah. They do. She was twenty-three years old. This young girl was on some new medicine.
JAMILA: What happened?
JANE: Nothing was done. There was nothing done. It was just, she was just . . . she got off clear, and my landlord got one hell of an insurance check. And I was completely displaced from the house. [But] after that, the police were like, "Yeah. You can go back in there." So I went back in the house and then the landlord was like, "You're not allowed in there. My friend at the codes department [said so]." . . . So I was like, I just won't go in the back bedroom. I was like, this is still my house. All of my stuff's still here. You guys already pulled the car out. We've already put a piece of wood over. I get it. And they were like, "It's not structurally safe." . . . There's literally one part of the house that's damaged, but still I was like, you want me to leave anyway? . . .

This is just very convenient. I'm not just giving up because a car came through the house. . . . Just because the car came through the house doesn't mean I'm leaving all of a sudden. We're still going to the court. Like we're still doing the whole eviction process that you wanted to do so dearly. We can do that. You wanted to do it. So we're doing it. And just think that a car came in the house does not mean I had to leave.

So they called the codes department, which was her friend. . . . And as this lady's putting the note on the door, the landlord's right behind her, telling her, "I messaged you on Facebook last night. Did you get it?" And then they turned around and she was happy. And gave each other hugs. . . . So she was like, "You're not allowed back in the house." And I was like, "All of my stuff's in the house." And she was like, "You'll have to schedule a time with the codes department to get your stuff out. Well, someone will have to go in there with you because you're not allowed in the house anymore."

At that point, Jane had nowhere to go and few resources for relocating. She called Molly and racked her brain about what to do. Then she got an idea.

JANE: I was like, "Is the driveway still mine?" And [the code enforcement lady] was like, "Yeah, why?" And I was like, "Well, I have a van outside, a minivan, so I'm going to go put my seats down in my minivan and put a mattress in the back. And if I can't stay in the house, I will stay in the driveway."

JAMILA: Oh my gosh. You are so tenacious. I love that.

JANE: So that's what I did. I said, "Yeah." I said, "Give me a minute." I said, "I have to grab something." So I went inside, and I grabbed my mattress. And I put the back seat of my van down. And I said, "My lawyer said that you're [right and I'm] not allowed in the house, but I do still have a lease here. So this driveway is still mine. So I will be staying in the driveway. If you guys need me, I'll be right there." . . . And that landlord got so pissed. So do you know what the city went and done? It put a restraining order against me. . . . The whole city went and put a restraining order against me. I don't know how that one happened.

JAMILA: Against you? Restraining you from going around who?

JANE: The whole house. They restrained me from the whole entire area.

JAMILA: What happened after that?

JANE: They fixed it, and now she rented it back out and jumped the rent up to $800 a month for the new tenants. And I paid $400 a month when I lived there. And the new tenants paid $800 a month.

JAMILA: So even if you win the case, there are people living there.

JANE: Yeah, looks like. I just don't know. I mean, I really don't get it. And then when we went in court, her lawyer was calling me he and him. . . . It was just the most blatant . . . and he's also the lawyer for the city. . . .

Who knows what the next situation could be? Really good. Really fucking bad. So I just haven't even tried to rent a new place. I just been, whatever. I've just been floating, staying here, there, everywhere. Friends. I've been seeing my sister some too, but that's a whole different relationship. It's terrible. I shouldn't even have to stay with her. I put my emotional stability on the back burner just to be able to have somewhere to sleep at times. Because she's not very, they don't really accept me fully. They're kind of closed-minded themselves. But sometimes when I have to have somewhere to stay, I have to put up with it and deal with it, and it is scary, . . . and I loved that house. I did like it. I loved it a lot. It was such a good little space. It was. I had it decorated. It was pretty. It was like my space. All of my stuff up there, I was like, I did that. And then I was like y'all took that.

When I asked Jane where she could go from here, she confessed that she had recently gotten involved with a local tenant union recommended to her by a former tenant of her landlord who had also been evicted by her:

Yeah. Just recently I went to my first [tenant union] meeting. It was the Thursday before last. It was that day that I had court. It was right after my court. They had a meeting over at the park after that. And I went to that as well. And I'm going to go with them door-to-door on Sunday and start knocking on some doors. Then they asked me if I wanted to go to—what else is it? They're doing something in September. He asked me if I wanted to go to a seminar somewhere or something. I have no clue, but I'm about to be a part of it. I might as well. . . . *I'm going to change it for someone else.* Make sure no one else has to go through what I went through. No one deserves it. It sucks. It's fucking shitty. But I mean, I got through it. But just because I got through it doesn't mean the next person will get through it. Not everyone has that. Because I mean, I'm from Kentucky. I'm a fucking trans woman in the mountains of Kentucky. . . . I've got a backbone.

Jane had found a place to channel her will to fight. While the courts were initially her way of pursuing justice ("I want justice," she insisted), her experiences in that realm left her seeking other alternatives. That was the case despite Molly being an outstanding lawyer and Jane holding legal aid in high regard:

The thing is, [legal aid] people are justice warriors. Really, at the end of the day, we call them legal aid. But they are justice warriors. They're just people who are defending people who aren't able to defend themselves and don't have the financial stability to defend themselves. That doesn't make them any less than or make them some kind of like—it's not government assistance. They're good people . . . doing . . . good work. If saints were a real thing, these are saints. That's what these are. These are justice warriors, they're doing good. Molly's fucking standing on her own two feet, but also standing for like fifteen other people. That's a lot of fucking people to stand up and hold on your shoulders.

Notwithstanding that full-throated, compelling depiction of legal aid, Jane had not experienced the civil legal system as a haven of justice. The judge had misgendered her. The city had opposed her. The police had used the law against her. And the letter of the law had fallen appallingly short:

> You're not even allowed to use discrimination [as a defense] in eviction court, which is something that we're trying to change right now. That was one of the things that we brought up at our last court hearing because it shouldn't [be]. You're not allowed to use discrimination? . . . I just don't understand why it would be illegal to discriminate against someone, but also, you're unable to use that in court. What's the point of it being illegal? You might as well make it legal if there's no consequences for their actions, you might as well let them fucking do it. Just let them do it then.

Even outside the courtroom directly, the institutions responsible for enforcing nondiscrimination had proven frustrating for Jane as well as an affront:

> The Fair Housing Council, they gave me a piece of paperwork, which I haven't even really looked at it, but they were like, "It's just to estimate your damages." For I guess, money or something like that. . . . But how do I even put a price tag on my dogs or on my livelihood? My sense of stability. . . . She literally took me in front of a group of people and tore me down in a courtroom and called me he, him. How do you put a price margin on that, on being publicly humiliated and your character being defamed in a courtroom? How do you put a price on any of that? I haven't even looked at that piece of paperwork because I don't even know. How do you price your dogs that you had? Your dogs that you had a bond with since they were puppies? How do you put price margins on that because you had to get rid of them because it was not healthy for them? The least you could do was give them a good home because you didn't have one. So everyone wants a dog. Not everyone wants a tranny. I mean, it's the sad truth. . . . I just don't know how you put a price on that. What am I supposed to do, start tallying

it up? Who do I call? An estimator? What the fuck? Where do I get that appraised at? Who appraises that? Who appraises my emotional pain? Do I go to the doctor? Or do I have a therapist and like, "Hey, can you put a price margin on this?" How much is like my fucking sanity worth? I mean, looking over my shoulder for months to follow because I thought she had a hit out for me [and] was going to kill me because a car just drove through my house. . . . No. I don't know how you put a price tag on it. I don't even really know where to even start with any of that. I haven't even looked at that piece of paperwork because there's just so much that was lost in the moment. I mean, yeah, it's OK now. Well, I guess not. It'll never be OK. But I mean, it is what it is.

Like Tamara, Jane narrated an agonizing trail of disappointing, disempowering experiences with nearly every state institution she encountered. But she still planned to wake up on Sunday, head out into the rural community that had harmed her severely, and canvas with her fellow tenants. Collective organizing was all she had left. And while Jane's fate remained uncertain, her willingness to join a tenant union underscored a horizon of possibilities open to even intensely marginalized people, in devastatingly difficult places, facing seemingly impossible odds.

The Political Economy of Access to Justice

Uncivil Democracy tells the story of the political economy of access to justice with an eye toward the people who hold power over it (like the elites whose political maneuvering we traced in chapter 4), and most importantly, from the vantage point of those whose livelihoods and citizenship are indelibly shaped by it. In doing so, we explore how civil legal systems structure and can be structured by political power in the United States. While scholars and practitioners have paid increasing attention to the legal, economic, and social causes and consequences of access to civil justice, they have not suitably attended to the myriad ways that politics influence who can attain, wield, and bend the power of civil legal systems to address their needs. Scholars have also neglected examinations of how access to justice itself has profound consequences for political power. We have attempted to fill this void, offering an account of the civil legal system that is grounded in a substantive political economy framework and centered around the experiences of the people—like Josephine, Leo, Quiana, Aria, Sora, Tamara, and Jane—who must navigate

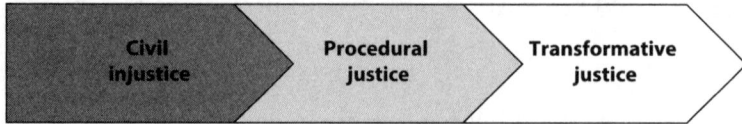

FIGURE 7.1. Political economy arrangements for access to justice

civil legal pathways to survive precarity. Our findings extend beyond the ambit of the civil legal system itself; they have implications for the American political economy and the contours of US democracy.

Access to justice is a prominent concept in scholarship on the civil legal system. It entails a much broader goal than addressing unmet legal need—the specific problem of access to counsel for civil cases. Access to justice refers to the idea that people can attain lawful resolution to civil legal problems—whether through formal legal processes or not—in expansive and equitable ways (Sandefur 2019; Wallat 2019). The core premise is that irrespective of structural positioning, people ought to be able to pursue and secure fair outcomes for their civil legal problems. This is a markedly more capacious goal than simply ensuring access to lawyers in the courts.

The narrative that unfolds in *Uncivil Democracy* suggests three possible paths for the wider political economy of access to justice, each with distinctive consequences for meeting the goals of equitable civil justice. As figure 7.1 illustrates and the previous chapters have detailed, we can think of these possibilities as a political economy of civil injustice, procedural justice, or transformative justice. While these alternatives exist along a spectrum rather than as discrete choices, they are worth considering independently.

The Political Economy of Civil Injustice

A political economy of civil injustice occurs, as chapter 1 describes, when existing public policy regimes generate structural inequalities that manifest in the widespread, unequal experience of socioeconomic precarity. This precarity gives rise to civil justice problems (Michener 2023a). Recall that more than a hundred million people in the United States are estimated to be living with civil justice problems that affect their ability to survive and thrive (Sandefur 2016). These problems become matters of civil law given the United States' unique reliance on the courts to adjudicate issues of social policy, civil rights, and the basic functions of the welfare state (Farhang 2010; Hadfield 2010; Kagan 2019; Zackin and Thurston 2024). In a system of civil injustice, however, the resources available for people to pursue justice for these claims are severely limited.

In chapter 4, we described the efforts of a growing contingent of conservative policymakers who view public funding for civil counsel for low-income people as part of a profligate welfare state. Year after year, these policymakers have worked to strip away any federal support for access to counsel to weaken the power of people experiencing civil legal problems and shrink the footprint of the welfare state. As our historical evidence reveals, the result is a dramatically reduced budget in real terms since 1981 for the LSC—which remains the largest funder of low-income civil counsel—even as the number of eligible clients has grown (Sandman 2015). In the wake of these developments, millions of people have been deprived of access to counsel, never mind access to justice. Indeed, scholars have noted a sharp uptick in self-represented (pro se) litigants in state civil courts over the last several decades. For example, estimates suggest that between 70 and 98 percent of landlord-tenant disputes involve at least one pro se client (Steinberg 2014).

And as chapter 3 showed, the consequences of abundant civil injustice are not only damaging to people's well-being but detrimental to democratic citizenship too. The experience of civil justice problems corresponds with diminished internal and external efficacy for the civil legal system as well as the broader political system. People with civil justice problems feel less like their citizenship is valued, and many also feel as though policymakers are not prepared to help people like them. The result—as people like Aria and Ray confront the courts without counsel—is that participation in politics feels futile, and they are left feeling disempowered both economically and politically.

And these experiences aren't interpreted as artifacts of individual circumstance. Instead, it is apparent that the legal institutions are systematically rigged against people at the racial and economic margins—and in favor of their predominantly White, affluent, and in cases such as Jane's, socially embedded landlords and property owners. Thus a political economy of civil injustice is politically disempowering and demobilizing in ways that are racially as well as geographically disproportionate—a far cry from securing access to justice.

These experiences don't simply translate to diminished feelings of efficacy. They correspond with diminished political life as well. Returning to the survey data, figure 7.2 explores the association between experiencing at

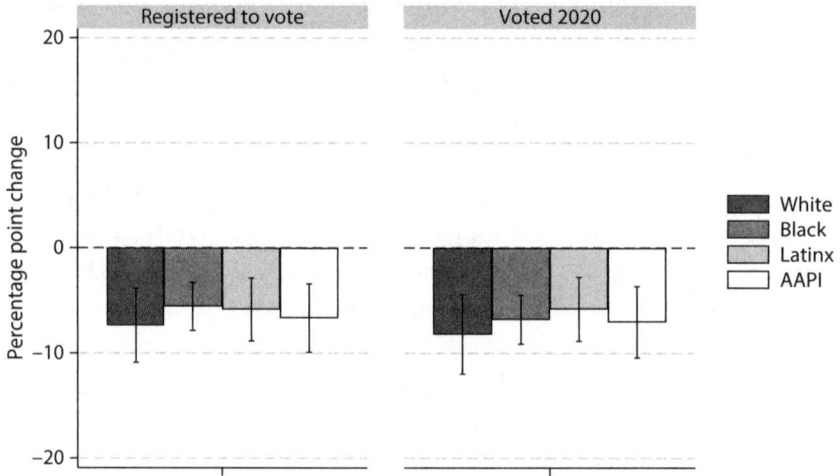

FIGURE 7.2. Experiencing civil justice problems and voting by racial group
Note: Bars represent coefficients from OLS regression and include 95 percent confidence intervals.

least one civil justice problem and people's likelihood of registering and turning out to vote.[1]

As shown, experiencing at least one civil justice problem corresponds with a reduction in the rate of voting by between roughly 5 and 8 percentage points for participants from each racial group. In practical terms, that means that holding constant other demographic characteristics that shape voting such as education, age, and income, people who experience civil legal problems are less likely to make their voices heard through the electoral system. In this way, a political economy of civil injustice leaves the very people who most need redress without a fundamental forms of political voice to demand policy change.

The Political Economy of Procedural Justice

The second political-economic arrangement we describe in the book is one of procedural justice. This occurs when support is in place to provide low-income litigants with access to civil legal counsel to address individual legal needs

---

1. This analysis once again employs coarsened exact matching to hold constant other demographic characteristics—like age, education, and income—that can influence political behavior.

without addressing the underlying demand that causes civil court dockets to overflow. Pursuing expansive procedural justice has been a hallmark not only of the legal profession but among policymakers across jurisdictions too. At the federal level, the Obama administration established the Office of Access to Justice within the Department of Justice with the aim of ensuring "access to the promises and protections of our civil and criminal legal systems for all communities." The first of its three guiding principles is to "expand access to legal systems by increasing the availability of legal assistance, supporting public defense, and eliminating barriers that exclude people based on economic, demographic or geographic factors" (Office for Access to Justice 2023). Almost all states have followed suit, with more than forty creating access to justice bodies (Wallat 2019).

Extending procedural justice also features prominently among popular policy solutions, chief among them the so-called civil Gideon or right-to-counsel laws. Named after the US Supreme Court case that affirmed the right to counsel in criminal cases, civil Gideon laws typically propose a right to counsel for certain types of cases deemed to significantly affect the well-being of civil litigants. As of 2024, for example, seventeen cities, five states, and one county have adopted right-to-counsel laws for low-income people facing eviction proceedings (Benfer et al., 2025). These locations vary with respect to region, size, and socioeconomic as well as demographic characteristics. On the positive side, right-to-counsel provisions have generated significant gains in tenant victories in eviction proceedings (National Coalition for a Civil Right to Counsel 2025). And as chapter 5 demonstrated, when people have access to counsel, they typically evince stronger feelings of trust, political efficacy, and democratic citizenship compared to their peers who must navigate the courts without counsel.

This came through clearly via interviews we had with tenants living in right-to-counsel cities who had experience with the program. Lily, a low-income Black woman from Detroit, explained why Detroit's RTC program was meaningful to her:

> [The legal aid lawyer] was just pretty amazing. He took on my case . . . and then he ended up getting me through the legal aid process. . . . He took away the worry and the stress. Honestly, that's a very stressful situation. . . . He told me all of my options. . . . He asked me exactly what I needed. He let me know how the court date worked. He was in person. He obviously was there and represented me. Like, I didn't have to say really anything. He

handled it. . . . I knew someone had my back. . . . The legal system, they're never kind of clean-cut. It's always like, well, who you know or what words to bring up or what programs to bring up. Like, it's very specific. Like very specific language that only lawyers know how to speak. And so because he was there, I was able to even get that thirty-day extension. . . . I didn't know anything about that, so I definitely wouldn't have been able to get that thirty-day extension that was well needed to figure out what to do. . . . My experience [working with legal aid] was just really great. . . . I didn't have to pay out of pocket. I didn't have to give a retainer. Like, obviously, I can't afford that in the first place. So the lawyer was very nice . . . very genuine person. I could tell he just wanted to help.

What's striking is that legal representation did not save Lily from eviction. She ultimately could not afford to continue renting her home and had to give it up. Lily was able to afford rent during the pandemic because she received more robust support through state and local programs. But once those resources waned and scarcity again pervaded political-economic relations, she could not afford rent. Though having counsel could not solve the fundamental problem of economic precarity that created her housing insecurity, it nonetheless gave her a sense of support ("I knew someone had my back"), relieved the burden of managing complex legal processes ("He handled it"), and offered her a tangible gain ("I was able to even get that thirty-day extension"). What's more is that this also gave Lily a distinct view of government relative to what she learned from other experiences. When we asked her whether her experience with eviction and the legal system changed her view of government, she answered affirmatively,

> [Yes], a little bit. I will say I've always been kind of, like, I don't want anything to do with the government. Like, I don't really trust the legal system. But my experience was so good. . . . They weren't as harsh as I thought they were going to be. . . . The judge was willing to even give me that extension. . . . In my experience, like they did honestly just want to help someone who fell on hard times.

When we then asked Lily if she perceived any of these experiences as political, she expounded, offering her understanding of the connections between legal counsel and a racialized political economy:

> I definitely still do [view the legal system as political], even though that was a great kind of experience for me. I guess just because of my ethnicity

[Black] . . . I would 100 percent associate politics with the legal system. I think with at least socioeconomic status when you can afford a lawyer—it's great that I had legal aid—but when you, when you can afford a lawyer, your outcomes are better. But everyone can't afford the lawyer. So I'm very grateful that because I'm low income, I was able to get legal aid. . . . So I think socioeconomic status does matter because when you have representation, your outcomes are better. And then I think with ethnicity, unfortunately, when you look at certain ethnicities and you see an eviction, your first thought is, oh, they're lazy or they deserve this, or the eviction is because of them, because of that person. I feel like due to certain ethnicities . . . the legal system is not going to incorporate, OK, well, maybe this person is an honest person who works and just fell on a hard time. . . . I feel like those things kind of get overlooked because of the color of your skin, unfortunately. And when you see an eviction . . . I don't think that it's as much leniency. Like, they don't think that's an honest period in someone's life. They might just write them off as, oh, they're lazy or they're a scam, or they don't want to work. Like, just evict them or they're not going to come up with the money. Like, just evict them. It's just not as much leniency, I feel like.

Lily's view of the legal system as political was based on a nuanced understanding of racism and class disadvantage. She viewed both as important (but distinct) barriers to fair outcomes—one a result of the inability to obtain representation, and the other because of racial stereotypes and perceptions of deservingness. So "even though" she had a "great" experience, she still recognized the structural limitations of the legal system. Indeed, she had several friends who fared differently than her, making her cognizant of larger dynamics:

I do know other people who have gotten evicted. And they, like, they weren't even given a chance. . . . I don't think they had lawyers. . . . I think legal aid had taken too long or something like that. They just weren't able to get a lawyer in time. And so they didn't have any representation—they got evicted right away.

The fuller context of Lily's experiences points toward the crucial limitations of procedural justice (as chapters 4 and 5 describe). First, the implementation of right to counsel does not address the basic fact that there are not enough attorneys to provide civil legal representation, even in the face of legal requirements to do so. For example, Lily was able to get representation, but her friends were not. According to estimates from Gillian Hadfield (2010), less than 1 percent of all US attorneys offer civil legal assistance to low-income clients— roughly 1 attorney for every 9,000 people living below 125 percent of the poverty line. By comparison, there is 1 attorney for every 429 people living above the poverty line (LSC 2022). Unless the supply of civil legal services attorneys is dramatically increased, right-to-counsel laws will continue to struggle with implementation (Benfer et al., 2025; Holder, Capps, and Hawkins 2023). That means access to basic procedural justice will continue to be uneven at best— especially if policymakers who are opposed to civil legal services continue to cut funding for education and training. Recall Sora's account in chapter 5 high-lighting the very different outcomes for her case when legal services could mus-ter the resources to provide her with a lawyer versus when it could not.

Logistical issues are not the only limitation to this procedural justice ap-proach to access to justice. A second concern emerges when we consider the fact that right to counsel can only supply access for those whose problems channel through the courts. As studies show, however, most civil justice needs do not end up in court (Sandefur 2016, 2019). Sometimes, this is the result of a person's inability to find a lawyer, at other times people don't think of their problems as legal in nature, and at still other moments, people do not have the time or capacity to engage the legal system in the context of fast-moving pro-cesses of displacement where there are incentives as well as threats pushing them to comply with the prerogatives of landlords without getting the courts involved (Sandefur 2009, 2016). Cari, a tenant we interviewed in Detroit, was swiftly displaced from her apartment in the middle of the winter:

> I was living in a building, and the building was sold. . . . I couldn't get enough other neighbors to rally. That's how I got familiar with the [legal aid organization]. I was trying to get them to give us more time . . . [but] they collected December's rent, and then they gave us a notice. . . . It was a really brutal January and February. So me and another tenant . . . we were the last two holdouts, and we just wanted our time. . . . We felt like we should have had more time because they—the building was sold, and they were going to renovate the building. But, you know, they didn't even work on the build-ing for six months. . . . It was almost two years before that building was renovated and opened up and people moved in. . . . And then of course, when it reopened . . . the rent was, what, three times what we were paying at that time.

Though Cari had attempted to engage legal aid, she was thwarted by both how quickly everything happened and her inability to "rally" her neighbors. The latter was because the company that purchased the building "told the people, . . . oh, yeah, we'll offer a stipend to get people resettled." Instead of pushing for more time, most of Cari's neighbors took the small stipend and moved out. Only Cari and one other neighbor held out for as long as they could. This is not an exceptional scenario.

There are a wide range of factors discouraging tenants from pursuing legal recourse, even when they have good reason to do so. Cari's professional experiences reinforced this point. As a community health worker, she helps low-income Detroiters to secure housing and health. Among the many resources Cari shared with her clients, she made sure to inform them about Detroit's right-to-counsel program whenever the opportunity arose· "I will say . . . 'Detroit has the right to counsel. You can ask for legal representation instead of going to court and not having any representation.'" Notwithstanding such efforts, Cari remained skeptical about the impact of right to counsel, noting that

> most of the people who I see are . . . already beyond going to court . . . they've left, they've left where they live, and they're now staying with someone. . . . They've lost their place to live. And are, you know, looking for another place. . . . That's kind of pretty much how it goes.

Even as a supporter of right to counsel, Cari recognized that access to counsel cannot provide justice for those who are "beyond" the courts.

A third key limitation of procedural justice solutions is in their intentionally limited focus on the supply side of the civil justice equation. As chapter 4 described, proponents of access to counsel often viewed this solution as a way to intentionally individualize what are systemic, structural inequalities. Procedural justice is thus consistent with a neoliberal policymaking tradition in which means-tested government benefits are provided in a manner that individualizes responsibility for what are realistically collective problems requiring collective solutions (e.g., see Hacker 2006; Soss, Fording, and Schram 2011; SoRelle 2022).[2] Underscored by the stories of people like Quiana, who could retain counsel to fight her eviction, but not to address the underlying problem of unsafe housing conditions that threatened her family's health and precipitated her nonpayment of rent, procedural justice often focuses on narrow,

---

2. It is further constrained by a process of judicial retrenchment in which particular types of rights-based claims have been winnowed away (Staszak 2015).

individual remedies for those considered deserving of help, especially remedies that are unlikely to reshape structural inequality.

In some crucial ways, a political economy of procedural justice is an improvement over the alternative of insufficient resources for representation that ultimately exacerbate civil injustice. Yet this approach preserves the existing power structure that privileges some while leaving others to contend with persistent precarity. Indeed, resources for procedural justice still funnel race-class-subjugated people into legal institutions that reify the harmful, extractive practices endemic to racial capitalism. Consider the experiences of Rachael, a Black woman from Detroit who benefited from ERAP, meant to prevent evictions, and then when she was evicted anyway, got an attorney through the city's right-to-counsel program. Though Rachael had received resources meant to ensure procedural justice, she was harmed more than helped through these mechanisms.

> I applied [for COVID eviction relief] and I got the funding, and [my landlord was] paid off. . . . I got the funding twice. . . . The first time I applied for funding, they paid the rent and it was current, but COVID—we were still experiencing stuff with COIVD, so I wasn't working, I had health issues . . . so I got behind again. [The eviction relief program] reached back out to me because they had additional funding, and they paid the majority of [my back rent]. . . . And the landlord accepted the funds. And then [the landlord] said, "We don't want to work with you on the balance." And they threw me out. . . . I had an attorney through right to counsel during that time, when I was getting the [COVID relief] funds and going through the eviction. However, the city of Detroit, what they did was they employed landlord or property owner counsel. . . . That's who was representing the tenants. . . . So what you had was landlord or property owner attorneys who were assigned to the right-to-counsel program to help people like me, but yet they did the opposite.
>
> What they did was they advocated for me to move. They didn't try to work on my behalf at all. It was like they were still working for the landlord or the property owner, even though legally they were representing me. . . . I was assigned to this attorney through the [right-to-counsel] program. I tried to reach out to him for months before the court date. I didn't talk to him. . . . I showed up at the court date, and he wasn't there. . . . It was virtual, but I sat in court for hours, and I think I had to be there at 9 or 10 in the morning. It was like 1 p.m. [and] he still hadn't showed up. So the judge or

the magistrate, whoever was in charge, they adjourned my case to go call and find him because I told them I had been trying to reach him for months. I couldn't reach him; I didn't know how to get ahold of him. And eventually he showed up to court. . . . He wasn't prepared. I mean, he was late to court, and then when he showed up, it was just like, "Move." That's what he was telling me, you know? And I'm like, "Wait a minute, aren't you supposed to advocate for me? Aren't you supposed to find out what's going on?" "Move, just move."

That's what he kept telling me . . . so I went to the city. This is how I found out he was a former landlord or property owner attorney because I went to the city, and I complained. I said, "Hey, y'all got this right-to-counsel program. Y'all saying y'all going to represent people, but this guy isn't representing me at all. You know, listen, look at how he's talking to me. Look at what he's saying." And that's when someone I spoke with told me that they didn't have enough attorneys and basically, they just brought on anybody, you know, to fill those roles. And that's how he got that spot.

To secure procedural justice for tenants like Rachael, the City of Detroit increased the supply of lawyers through all means possible. This included bringing aboard inattentive attorneys with clear conflicts of interest. The city elided the fundamental and enduring power dynamics at play between tenants and landlords, and offered "representation" in only the thinnest, most cynical sense. Under the guise of offering access to justice, the city exposed Rachael to further harm and frustration. What's more is that Rachael explicitly perceived this as a stripping away of power for herself and other tenants like her:

That's how the right to counsel kind of [works] in a nefarious way, or unscrupulous way: *it strips people of their power.* Because you have people who're relying on these—on these counselors to help them, to guide them, to tell them what their rights are, to tell them what their options are, and they're essentially doing the opposite. . . . So that, in effect, you're stripping my power, my rights away. People are going down there to court and being inadequately represented, like in my case. How do you ignore me, not talk to me for months, and then you show up to court hours late on the day of court? And how do you think that gives me fair and adequate representation? You don't even know as the attorney what the hell is going on. So how does that make me—put me in a better position? It doesn't. You know, that's why I say it's a facade, because it's actually hurting people. And I don't know the statistics. Perhaps there are some people who have had positive experiences. . . . But I do a lot of advocacy work here in this city. I testified . . . in our state capitol. I'm involved at the grass roots. I talk to people, and I know through the hundreds of people that I've . . . interacted with that more often than not, it doesn't work out for the tenant. . . . The whole system is a facade.

Whether right to counsel works out well—as it did for Cari—or devolves into disaster—as it did for Rachael—a pervasive theme that emerged from our conversations with people about their experiences with civil legal problems is that access to procedural justice is not enough.

The Political Economy of Transformative Justice

Transformative justice is a distinct vision that can only be achieved through foundational changes to the American political economy. This approach, espoused by early supporters of law reform and facilitated by community organizing efforts, has the most potential to build power among those in the crosshairs of the systems that generate civil and related injustices. As we've shown, the early reformers pursuing federal solutions to civil justice were interested in cases that had the potential to not only address individual client needs but also reshape social policies to be more equitable in the absence of the legislative will to do so. While such cases produced incredible successes in the early days of the LSP, the necessary tools to peruse law reform—like class actions, administrative participation, and specific types of cases (e.g., welfare and voting rights)—have been slowly carved away from federal programs.

If law reform efforts represent a top-down approach to pursuing structural transformation, the cross-race, cross-class tenant organizing discussed in chapter 6 represent a bottom-up force in the fight for transformative justice. Identifying tenant organizations as both civil legal institutions and power resources has significant implications for democracy. For people such as Josephine, Ronald, and Jane, who scholars are frequently quick to assume will be politically powerless because of the intersection of their racial, gender, and/or class positioning, organizing around civil legal problems has given them a platform from which to build political power.

For those who have access to local community organizations, civil justice problems can move from a disempowering to a power-building political experience—one that not only shapes individual circumstances but has the capacity to improve collective outcomes too. By tackling collective rather than individual civil justice problems, a transformative justice approach that allows community organizing to flourish holds the most liberatory promise. While chapter 6 conveyed the tremendous potential of this model, it is still relatively uncommon compared with the other two models of political economy. Moreover, collective organizing to support people experiencing other types of civil legal problems outside the realm of housing may introduce distinct challenges (e.g., the lack of geographically bounded communities that enable face-to-face organizing). Despite these obstacles, the last several years have seen efforts to do just that, such as with the rise of groups like the Debt Collective, which is organizing to build a nationwide debtors' union sharing similar principles as the tenant organizations we explore in this book. Indeed, one tenant organizer Mallory spoke with during the research process for this book was also a member of the Debt Collective. He viewed both his local tenant organization and participation in the nationwide Debt Collective as interlocking pieces of a larger project to build power among race-class-marginalized people experiencing economic precarity and exploitation.

The political economy of access to justice in the United States balances precariously on the knife's edge between a system of civil injustice and one of procedural justice. But momentum toward a political economy of transformative justice is growing in communities across the country as grassroots, community-based organizing among tenants builds collective power in pursuit of more systemic solutions to eradicate civil justice problems. The implications of that movement have considerable consequences for how power building can feed back into transforming the structural conditions that cause civil legal problems.

The Feedback Potential of Power Building

The analytic focus of this book has converged on how interactions with the civil justice system shape democratic citizenship, and what that means for who has and can wield political power. But the model of political economy depicted in the first chapter highlights another feedback pathway: political power can reshape future efforts to reform the social policy infrastructure that creates unequal civil justice burdens. While not the primary empirical emphasis of this book, it is worth considering the opportunities for and obstacles to power-building efforts to generate policy change moving forward.

When Political Power Reshapes Public Policy

The theory of policy feedback postulates that experiences with public policies and institutions reshape the politics of constituents with consequences for how people engage in future efforts for policy reform. Consider two cases in which positive and negative feedback processes unfold: Social Security and consumer financial protection. Social Security, which provides near universal income benefits to older people in the United States, exemplifies a positive policy feedback process. It instigates resource effects (from the cash benefits supplied and incentives for people to mobilize to maintain those benefits) that correspond with increased political participation among recipients (Campbell 2003). Moreover, the design and implementation of the policy constructs beneficiaries as deserving of help, improving their sense of efficacy (Campbell 2003). It also offers a direct, highly visible government benefit run by a relatively efficient government agency, making it clear to beneficiaries that government is helping them, which improves people's evaluations of government efficacy (Mettler 2011; SoRelle 2016; SoRelle and Mettler 2021). All of these features coalesce to build power among Social Security recipients. As a result, they have become one of the most ardent, steadfast voting blocs in the United States and are quick to engage in other forms of political activity to preserve their programmatic benefits (Campbell 2003). Thus policymaking efforts to reform or privatize Social Security have largely floundered in the face of steep political resistance. This feedback loop, bolstered by the political power of beneficiaries, has worked to maintain perhaps the most robust social welfare policy in the United States.

The case of consumer financial protection presents a contrasting feedback process. Consumer financial protections that regulate everything from bank accounts to credit cards to prepaid gift cards rely primarily on information disclosures rather than protective economic remedies (Hyman 2011; SoRelle 2020, 2023). Hence these protections rarely produce resource gains for consumers; in fact, by allowing companies to charge high fees and interest rates as long as they are disclosed up front, regulations frequently perpetuate economic losses for borrowers. Moreover, information disclosures largely obscure government's role in regulating the financial industry, leading most borrowers to the conclusion that disclosures are the product of company and not policymaker decisions (SoRelle 2020, 2023). They also teach people that problems with credit are the fault of poor decision-making or bad financial planning by individual borrowers themselves (SoRelle 2022). The result is that consumer financial issues are largely dealt with as individual, market issues, meaning borrowers rarely exercise political power to address predatory lending (SoRelle 2020, 2023). This demobilizing process induces a feedback loop wherein policymakers continue to adopt weak protections in the absence of voter mobilization to do otherwise (SoRelle 2020).

Both of these examples highlight the processes through which people experience public policies and institutions in ways that shape their political power as well as feedback into future policymaking. The same dynamic plays out in the case of access to justice. In a political economy of civil injustice, where people are largely disempowered, they may become more reluctant to engage in formal political activity such as voting and are unlikely to organize for change to the broader social policy landscape. In this way, structural inequalities that give rise to unequally distributed civil justice problems and inadequate access to justice to address them are both likely to be reinforced.

In a procedural justice system, those who gain access to counsel may see improved resources because of positive legal outcomes and more positive experiences of a state institution. As we demonstrate, this can lead to modest gains in political efficacy and feelings of democratic citizenship, which are typically prerequisites of political engagement. But procedural justice is also an individualizing approach; it does not bring people into the orbit of community-based, collective organizing. While some individuals may engage politically at slightly higher rates, legal access is unlikely to spark collective action on a scale necessary to achieve political transformation. This is especially likely if policymakers turn their focus toward providing digital information tools in lieu of legal counsel to encourage people to solve their own problems. As in the example of consumer financial regulation disclosures, information-based benefits like these can even further individualize how people perceive and navigate their problems, with deleterious consequences for political empowerment. A political economy of transformative justice, however, generates the potential for positive feedback that can fundamentally reshape underlying policy structures.

Positive Policy Feedback from Transformative Power Building

When community organizations intervene in the civil legal process and bring otherwise politically dormant litigants into collective movements that are explicitly working to build power, the prospects for positive policy feedback proliferate (Michener 2022; Michener and SoRelle 2022). Tenant organizations that build political power can channel that power in ways that countervail dominant political economic configurations and drive change (Andrias and Sachs 2021; Whitlow 2018, 2022, 2023). Take, for instance, the right-to-counsel laws that were enacted in both San Francisco and New York City. Local tenant groups played a critical role in both cases, leveraging their political power to persuade policymakers to adopt right-to-counsel provisions (Michener 2020). This pattern has been repeated in cities small and large across the country. Tenant groups have helped to secure a range of remedies from concessions from property managers to local—and in some cases, statewide—policy changes (Michener 2023c). In Minneapolis, United Renters for Justice, organizing a predominantly Black community, secured significant concessions from private-equity-backed Progress Residential, the largest single-family rental provider in the country (Morgenson 2023). In Kansas City, Missouri, KC Tenants worked to secure a citywide right-to-counsel law for evictions, adopted in 2021, and then backed four of six successful candidates for city council, including a member of the union (Calacal 2023; Webster 2023). In California, Housing Now CA, an organization coordinating tenant groups across the state, helped to win statewide tenant protections against unfair evictions and rent gouging (Blount et al. 2023).

These are only a small number of an ever-expanding list of victories won with support from robust tenant organizing. And unlike the individualized benefits of procedural justice, these wins—prohibitions against source of income discrimination, limits on price gouging, tenant bills of rights, good cause evictions, and more—work to address the underlying conditions that give rise to civil justice problems broadly, moving the needle toward liberation, where justice is more real and lawyers are less needed.

Obstacles to Positive Feedback

Despite these gains, tenant organizers face several hurdles in their journey to transform the American political economy. While other critical civil legal institutions, like courts and legal aid organizations, are directly (if inadequately) funded by federal, state, and local governments, tenant organizations plug the gaps of those institutions with no equivalent financial backing. Although government funding is not necessarily the best way to support tenant organizations, these groups' role as institutional players in the civil legal

system does warrant reflection on what forms of support (e.g., legal and financial) are useful for reinforcing their work (Balz 2024).[3]

The powerful actors against whom tenant organizers are contending are not
simply going to step aside in the wake of new policies to protect renters.
Instead, landlords, property developers, and other well-resourced interests
utilized many tools to thwart change in the existing balance of political and
economic power. For example, while laws nominally exist in most states to
prevent landlords from retaliating against tenants for pursuing legal remedies,
it hasn't stopped property owners from attempting to evict tenant organizers
and union members in an effort to halt their progress. One potential tool to
combat union-breaking evictions would be to enact a "Wagner Act" for tenant
unions, conferring collective bargaining rights to better position tenant
organizations to build power.[4] Derived from the landmark labor law that facilitates private sector unionization, a tenant-style Wagner Act would create
the conditions for tenants to unionize without retaliatory action. For instance,
such a law would ban evictions in the face of rent-striking tenants.

Beyond the obstacles presented by individual landlords, the potential for
positive feedback is further challenged by policymakers themselves. One of
the most notable tools that policymakers have at their disposal to fight against
a rising tide of localized tenant activism is the use of legislative preemption.
Preemption occurs when one level of government removes or restricts
policymaking authority for an issue from a lower level of government. It is a
hallmark of policymaking in federal systems where authority is split across
different levels of governance. And preemption in the US context has grown
rapidly over the past half century (Zimmerman 2008; SoRelle and Walker
2016; Riverstone-Newell 2017; Hicks et al. 2018). While the cities that have
adopted protenant ordinances vary with respect to their partisan makeup, they
are, on balance, more liberal leaning. In an all-too-common pattern (Flavin
and Shufeldt 2020; Barber and Dynes 2023; Goodman et al. 2021), conservative state governments have begun to use preemption to roll back those local
ordinances.

3. As Michener and SoRelle (2023, 222) find, tenant organizations prioritize financial
independence and go to "great care to protect their autonomy, prioritizing it even over resources
that might afford them greater capacity."

4. For an example of the conferral of collective bargaining power for tenants, see Klearman
2022; Kennedy et al. 2023.

Florida provides a compelling example. The Sunshine State was home to the second-highest rate of eviction filings in the nation in 2022 (Seecharan 2023). Despite that alarming trend, Florida governor Ron DeSantis signed the Residential Tenancies Bill (H.B. 1416) into law on June 29, 2023. The benignly named statute preempted a variety of local ordinances, with the potential to eliminate more than forty recently enacted tenant protections across thirty-five cities in Florida. These bills, which included protections like tenant bills of rights, fair notice provisions, and source of income antidiscrimination measures, to name a few (Schueler 2023), were originally adopted with significant organizing and mobilization from tenant groups. The use of state-level preemption to potentially erase the positive efforts of tenant organizing has considerable consequences for organizational capacity and strategic incentives to organize in future (Michener 2023d; SoRelle and Fullerton 2024). One possibility to overcome the effects of the state preemption of tenant protections would be to enact a federal tenant bill of rights that would provide uniform legal protections and facilitate the work of tenant organizing (e.g., see Johnson 2021).

There are many other legal, policy, and political strategies that could strengthen and protect tenant power (Balz 2024; Whitlow 2018, 2022, 2023). Given this book's emphases and approach, specific policy proscriptions are not appropriate without the leadership and input of tenant organizations. Nevertheless, the findings of *Uncivil Democracy* set the stage for a robust consideration of the role that the state, philanthropy, and other powerful entities could and should play in buttressing tenant organizations—and bottom-up organizing efforts in other domains—as purveyors of countervailing power that can beneficially (in terms of democratic equality) balance the concentrated power of elite economic actors (Andrias and Sachs 2021).

Pushback against efforts to fundamentally reshape power relations in the American political economy is, of course, to be expected. And how community organizations navigate those challenges will have significant consequences for the future of a transformative justice approach to addressing civil legal needs. Notwithstanding these complications, *Uncivil Democracy* demonstrates how this bottom-up approach to power building offers the most promising pathway to achieve broad, equitable access to justice. By addressing both the demand and—through fights for access to counsel—supply sides of the civil justice problem, a political economy of transformative justice holds great potential to build political power and reduce precarity for people like those who have shared their experiences in this book.

The Future of Power and Access to Justice

On an unusually warm, sunny September day in fall 2023, a motley group of people convened in an event space on the southern end of Roosevelt Island in New York City. Present were members and leaders from tenant organizations across the country, housing justice advocates, academics from several disciplines (including both Jamila and Mallory), and even a funder or two. The people sharing community that afternoon were diverse, not only with respect to their professions, but also their hometowns, backgrounds, and lived experiences. What brought this seemingly incongruous cohort together was a shared commitment to building power and pursuing policy reform through tenant organizing.

The location of the meeting was particularly apropos of the day's agenda: farther north on Roosevelt Island sat Rivercross and Westview—both large housing complexes that were initially built as part of the Mitchell-Lama program (before exiting the program to convert to private co-ops). Created by the Limited Profit Housing Act in 1955, Mitchell-Lama was designed to give low- and middle-income New Yorkers access to affordable rental and co-op units. Buildings were developed with publicly backed low-interest loans along with considerable tax breaks available to developers. The catch was a cap on rent, and for co-op units, the sale price. It was considered by many to be New York City's most effective affordable housing program, with some calling for a "Mitchell-Lama 2.0" to address the current housing shortage crisis (Barron 2024). Sitting in the shadow of these historically significant buildings, participants gathered with the purpose of exploring how this diverse assemblage—much like the cross-race, cross-class membership of tenant groups themselves—could supply mutual assistance to move their collective work forward.

The conversations that day were emblematic of several themes in *Uncivil Democracy*. While the term "American political economy" wasn't bandied about in conversation, the range of topics discussed—equity-backed real estate development, rental debt relief, local elections, and social housing, to name a few—played out in real time the idea articulated in this book that civil justice problems stem from a larger ecosystem of structurally unjust political-economic arrangements. During the afternoon, a breakout group gathered to brainstorm specific ways that tenant groups could build more power in their communities, focusing on everything from philanthropic support to financing mechanisms that could be leveraged to support tenant groups.

These twin conversations—of political economy and power building—are central to the ideas we present about the political economy of access to justice in the United States. By bringing politics and political power to the study of civil legal inequality, and civil legal processes into the realm of politics and political power, *Uncivil Democracy* makes novel contributions to our collective understanding of US political economy, racialized policy feedback, and the role of tenant organizations in disrupting politically disempowering processes in race-class-subjugated communities.

But the conversations shared that afternoon on Roosevelt Island also demonstrate that these concepts of political economy and power building are not isolated to academic spaces. Instead, they are prevalent in the concrete strategies and goals of groups working to ameliorate systemic issues of injustice in people's everyday lives. As people like Josephine, Aria, Quiana, Jane, Tamara, and Ronald along with the many tenant organizers we spoke with convey, ideas about who has and does not have power to address their precarity through the civil justice system are pressing matters on the ground.

To be sure, there is more to know. The political economy of civil justice is a vast and complex space, and we have only begun to peel back the layers of how politics operates within it. It is also a terrain that is changing rapidly in real time. The growing power of tenant organizations and reactionary efforts to thwart them suggest this. Nonetheless, *Uncivil Democracy* offers a novel exploration—centering the perspectives of the people whose thriving is inhibited by the inadequacies of US civil legal systems and pointing toward a horizon of liberation, where justice and power are possible for those who have too often been excluded from access to either.

Quantitative Appendix

2020 CMPS

The 2020 CMPS surveyed 14,988 US respondents between April 2 and August 25, 2021. To explore people's civil justice problems, respondents were randomly assigned to one of three batteries derived from the LSC Survey of Legal Need. The following is the survey protocol for each of the three civil justice problem batteries:

TABLE A

In the past two years, did you or any member of your household experience any of the following problems:

Split A [general]
- Problems with a landlord (for example, eviction or threat of eviction, maintenance and upkeep, dispute over security deposit, denied accessibility accommodation)
- Problems with a bank, lender, or debt collector (for example, deceptive lending practices, denied credit or loan, harassment from debt collection)
- Other financial problems (for example, bankruptcy, identity theft, repossession or wage garnishment, utilities disconnected over billing dispute or nonpayment)
- Problems with medical care or health insurance (for example, billing dispute, denied insurance, insurance coverage)
- Problems obtaining or keeping government benefits (for example, unemployment, SSI, SNAP, disability benefits, Medicaid)

(Continued on next page)

TABLE A *(continued)*

In the past two years, did you or any member of your household experience any of the following problems:

	• Problems with an employer (for example, wage theft, unsafe working conditions, denied workplace accommodation, unfair job termination)
Split B [rental housing]	• Landlord or someone associated with landlord destroyed or removed personal property without permission, or violated tenant privacy in some way
	• Landlord denied a reasonable accommodation for disability or medical condition
	• Landlord failed to provide basic services, repairs, safe accommodation, or meet other terms of lease
	• Evicted or threatened with eviction
	• Threatened by landlord for exercising tenants' rights
Split C [consumer financing]	• Problems with misleading, unfair, or deceptive lending practices
	• Problems getting access to credit or loan
	• Problems with identity theft
	• Problems with terms of repayment or interest rates charged by lenders
	• Problems with harassment by creditors or collection agencies, including threats of criminal prosecution
	• Had a home go into foreclosure
	• Filed or considered filing for bankruptcy

Matching Analysis

Description of Binning Process for Matched Covariates

Coarsened exact matching improves the balance between treatment and control groups by matching observations based on a specified set of criteria. In this analysis, observations are matched based on race, gender, income, education, and age of the respondent. To prune the sample to eliminate observations with unmatched covariates, specific "bins" or cut points must be specified for the matching criteria. The analysis in chapters 3 and 7 uses the following binning process for the matched covariates for the treatment:

TABLE B.1 Binning Cut Points for Coarsened Exact Matching

Variable	Binning cut points
Race	Coarsened as White (1), Latinx (2), Black (3), or AAPI (4)
Gender	Coarsened as man (1) or woman (2)
Income	Coarsened using the software's default binning algorithm, Sturge's rule
Education	Coarsened as some high school (2), high school degree/GED (3), some college / associate's degree (5), bachelor's (6), or graduate degree (7)
Age	Coarsened as 18–29 (2), 30–39 (3), 40–49 (4), 50–59 (5), 60–69 (6), 70+ (7)

Below are tables describing the tests of imbalance after matching as well as the size of the full and pruned samples for the analysis in chapters 3 and 7:

TABLE B.2 Univariate Imbalance (L1) of Treatment Group after Preprocessing

Covariate	L1	Mean	Min	25%	50%	75%	Max
Experienced civil legal problem treatment							
Race	0.02478	0.02478	0	0	0	0	0
Gender	0.0548	−0.0548	0	0	0	0	.
Income	0.0386	−0.21693	0	0	0	0	0
Education	0.01723	−0.01723	0	0	0	0	0
Age	0.04936	−0.04936	0	0	0	0	0

TABLE B.3 Sample Sizes for Full and Pruned Samples

	Treated	Untreated
Full sample	5,086	9,902
Coarsened exact matching sample	5,053	9,843
% matched	99%	99%

Statistical Results Tables

TABLE C.1 Tabular Results for Figure 3.2 "Correlates of Experiencing Civil
Justice Problems"

	Any problem	Number of problems
Latinx	0.059**	0.115**
	(0.011)	(0.037)
Black	0.136**	0.276**
	(0.011)	(0.037)
AAPI	−0.023*	−0.084**
	(0.055)	(0.039)
Income	−0.001**	−0.002**
	(0.000)	(0.000)
Education	−0.021**	−0.061**
	(0.002)	(0.009)
Age	−0.054**	−0.168**
	(0.002)	(0.008)
Gender	−0.039**	−0.169**
	(0.008)	(0.025)
Born in United States	−0.022**	−0.086**
	(0.009)	(0.031)
Constant	0.714**	2.027**
	(0.023)	(0.075)
N	14,872	9,902
R^2	0.08	0.09

Note: Numbers in columns represent coefficients of OLS regression with standard errors in parentheses; **$p < 0.05$, *$p < 0.1$.

TABLE C.2 Tabular Results for Figure 3.3 "Civil Justice Problems and
Civil Legal Efficacy"

	White	Black	Latinx	AAPI
Use courts to protect rights				
Any problem	−0.309**	−0.239**	−0.271**	−0.372**
	(0.047)	(0.031)	(0.035)	(0.042)
Income	−0.001	0.001**	0.000	0.002**
	(0.000)	(0.000)	(0.000)	(0.001)
Education	0.089**	0.025**	0.070**	−0.007
	(0.016)	(0.011)	(0.012)	(0.015)

TABLE C.2 (*continued*)

	White	Black	Latinx	AAPI
Age	0.064**	0.082**	0.141**	0.099**
	(0.014)	(0.010)	(0.013)	(0.014)
Gender	0.038	0.002	0.028	−0.058
	(0.045)	(0.030)	(0.035)	(0.041)
Constant	2.566**	2.483**	2.250**	2.844**
	(0.118)	(0.067)	(0.084)	(0.109)
N	2,557	5,161	4,152	2,874
R^2	0.04	0.03	0.06	0.05

Treated fairly by courts

Any problem	−0.276**	0.125**	0.211**	0.224**
	(0.043)	(0.029)	(0.033)	(0.038)
Income	−0.002*	−0.000	0.001**	0.001
	(0.001)	(0.000)	(0.001)	(0.001)
Education	0.089**	0.015	0.055**	0.014
	(0.014)	(0.010)	(0.012)	(0.013)
Age	0.066**	0.053**	0.121**	0.105**
	(0.012)	(0.009)	(0.012)	(0.013)
Gender	0.016	−0.097**	−0.017	−0.061
	(0.040)	(0.029)	(0.032)	(0.037)
Constant	2.697**	2.610**	2.411**	2.917**
	(0.107)	(0.063)	(0.079)	(0.099)
N	2,557	5,161	4,152	2,874
R^2	0.04	0.01	0.05	0.04

Note: Numbers in columns represent coefficients of OLS regression with standard errors in parentheses; **$p < 0.05$, *$p < 0.1$

TABLE C.3 Tabular Results for Figure 3.4 "Civil Justice Problems and Perception of Citizenship"

	White	Black	Latinx	AAPI
Any problem	−0.183**	−0.162**	−0.151**	−0.234**
	(0.061)	(0.051)	(0.050)	(0.056)
Income	−0.001	−0.003**	−0.001	−0.001
	(0.001)	(0.001)	(0.001)	(0.001)

(*Continued on next page*)

TABLE C.3 (*continued*)

	White	Black	Latinx	AAPI
Education	0.095**	−0.083**	0.019	−0.014
	(0.020)	(0.018)	(0.017)	(0.020)
Age	0.089**	−0.069**	0.118**	0.118**
	(0.018)	(0.016)	(0.018)	(0.019)
Gender	−0.027	−0.335	0.307**	−0.124**
	(0.057)	(0.049)	(0.049)	(0.054)
Constant	4.382**	5.217**	4.763**	4.533**
	(0.152)	(0.108)	(0.119)	(0.146)
N	2,557	5,161	4,152	2,874
R^2	0.03	0.03	0.02	0.05

Note: Numbers in columns represent coefficients of OLS regression with standard errors in parentheses; **p < 0.05, *p < 0.1

TABLE C.4 Tabular Results for Figure 3.5 "Civil Justice Problems and Political Efficacy"

	White	Black	Latinx	AAPI
Politicians listen				
Any problem	−0.069**	−0.067**	−0.106**	−0.130**
	(0.034)	(0.024)	(0.025)	(0.029)
Income	0.002**	0.000	0.000**	0.001
	(0.001)	(0.000)	(0.000)	(0.001)
Education	0.024**	−0.010	0.009	0.005
	(0.011)	(0.008)	(0.008)	(0.010)
Age	−0.000	0.012	−0.024**	−0.021**
	(0.009)	(0.008)	(0.009)	(0.010)
Gender	0.046	−0.016	−0.052**	0.016
	(0.032)	(0.023)	(0.025)	(0.028)
Constant	1.679**	2.091**	2.168**	2.102**
	(0.084)	(0.051)	(0.060)	(0.075)
N	2,557	5,161	4,152	2,874
R^2	0.01	0.01	0.01	0.01
Help my racial group				
Any problem	−0.005	−0.113**	−0.059*	−0.022
	(0.051)	(0.027)	(0.032)	(0.036)

TABLE C.4 (*continued*)

	White	Black	Latinx	AAPI
Income	−0.002*	−0.002**	−0.002**	−0.001
	(0.000)	(0.001)	(0.001)	(0.001)
Education	0.056**	−0.018*	0.029**	−0.028**
	(0.017)	(0.009)	(0.011)	(0.013)
Age	−0.124**	−0.013	−0.006	−0.025**
	(0.015)	(0.009)	(0.012)	(0.012)
Gender	0.060	−0.112**	−0.071**	−0.059*
	(0.047)	(0.027)	(0.031)	(0.035)
Constant	3.000**	2.684**	2.554**	2.631**
	(0.127)	(0.058)	(0.077)	(0.094)
N	2,557	5,161	4,152	2,874
R^2	0.03	0.01	0.01	0.01

Note: Numbers in columns represent coefficients of OLS regression with standard errors in parentheses; **$p < 0.05$, *$p < 0.1$

TABLE C.5 Tabular Results for Figure 5.1 "Legal Assistance and Civil Legal Efficacy by Income"

Use courts to protect rights

	Any counsel		Type of counsel	
	Full sample	*Low income*	*Full sample*	*Low income*
Any counsel	0.165**	0.209**	0.092**	0.119**
	(0.032)	(0.047)	(0.031)	(0.045)
Latinx	−0.132**	−0.007	−0.238**	−0.117*
	(0.049)	(0.074)	(0.046)	(0.070)
Black	−0.289**	−0.090	−0.499**	−0.259**
	(0.046)	(0.071)	(0.044)	(0.067)
AAPI	−0.260**	−0.035	−0.179**	−0.027
	(0.054)	(0.090)	(0.051)	(0.085)
N	5,014	2,360	5,014	2,360
R^2	0.03	0.02	0.05	0.02

(*Continued on next page*)

TABLE C.5 (*continued*)

Treated fairly by courts

	Any counsel		Type of counsel	
	Full sample	*Low income*	*Full sample*	*Low income*
Latinx	−0.126**	0.003	−0.234**	−0.111
	(0.049)	(0.066)	(0.046)	(0.070)
Black	−0.290**	−0.085	−0.497**	−0.253**
	(0.046)	(0.071)	(0.044)	(0.067)
AAPI	−0.261**	−0.032	−0.179**	0.031
	(0.054)	(0.090)	(0.051)	(0.085)
Paid private counsel	0.214**	0.250**	0.117**	0.079
	(0.043)	(0.066)	(0.041)	(0.063)
Volunteer counsel	0.106**	0.039	0.073	−0.025
	(0.049)	(0.069)	(0.047)	(0.065)
Legal services/org	0.130**	0.147**	−0.005	0.029
	(0.047)	(0.066)	(0.045)	(0.063)
Law school clinic	0.152*	0.259**	0.160*	0.336**
	(0.087)	(0.159)	(0.083)	(0.122)
Online resource	0.083**	−0.038	0.065**	−0.051
	(0.033)	(0.048)	(0.031)	(0.045)
Legal hotline	0.098*	0.115	0.006	−0.051
	(0.055)	(0.081)	(0.052)	(0.077)
Family or friend	0.055	0.044	0.016	−0.010
	(0.033)	(0.049)	(0.032)	(0.046)
N	5,014	2,360	5,014	2,360
R^2	0.03	0.03	0.05	0.02

Note: Numbers in columns represent coefficients of OLS regression with standard errors in parentheses; **p < 0.05, *p < 0.1

TABLE C.6 Tabular Results for Figure 5.2 "Legal Assistance and Civil Legal Efficacy by Race"

	White	Black	Latinx	AAPI
Use courts to protect rights				
Any counsel	−0.055	0.213**	0.140**	0.309**
	(0.088)	(0.054)	(0.059)	(0.071)
Income	−0.000	0.002**	0.001	0.003**
	(0.001)	(0.001)	(0.001)	(0.001)
Education	0.103**	0.007	0.066**	−0.018
	(0.028)	(0.019)	(0.019)	(0.024)
Age	0.049**	0.040**	0.125**	0.062**
	(0.025)	(0.017)	(0.021)	(0.023)
Gender	−0.026	0.051	0.029	−0.034
	(0.083)	(0.053)	(0.057)	(0.066)
Constant	2.35**	2.326**	1.990**	2.506**
	(0.226)	(0.114)	(0.138)	(0.175)
N	786	1,755	1,494	979
R²	0.03	0.01	0.04	0.03
Treated fairly by courts				
Any counsel	−0.117	0.161**	0.066	0.177**
	(0.081)	(0.052)	(0.057)	(0.068)
Income	0.001	0.001	0.002*	0.001
	(0.001)	(0.001)	(0.001)	(0.001)
Education	0.139**	0.029	0.062**	0.033
	(0.026)	(0.018)	(0.019)	(0.023)
Age	0.042*	0.019	0.074**	0.067**
	(0.023)	(0.016)	(0.020)	(0.022)
Gender	0.005	−0.080	−0.105	−0.054
	(0.076)	(0.050)	(0.055)	(0.063)
Constant	2.297**	2.458**	2.434**	2.551**
	(0.208)	(0.109)	(0.133)	(0.168)
N	786	1,755	1,494	979
R²	0.05	0.01	0.03	0.02

Note: Numbers in columns represent coefficients of OLS regression with standard errors in parentheses; **p < 0.05, *p < 0.1

TABLE C.7 Tabular Results for Figure 5.3 "Legal Counsel and Perceptions of Full and Equal Citizenship"

	White	Black	Latinx	AAPI
Any counsel	−0.165	0.225**	0.232**	0.152
	(0.119)	(0.091)	(0.090)	(0.112)
Income	−0.000	−0.003	−0.002	−0.002
	(0.002)	(0.002)	(0.002)	(0.002)
Education	0.127**	−0.099**	0.012	0.009
	(0.038)	(0.031)	(0.029)	(0.037)
Age	0.067*	−0.145**	0.042	0.067*
	(0.034)	(0.029)	(0.032)	(0.037)
Gender	−0.195*	−0.481**	−0.335**	−0.186*
	(0.112)	(0.089)	(0.086)	(0.104)
Born in United States	0.050	0.100	0.012	0.053
	(0.200)	(0.174)	(0.094)	(0.106)
Constant	4.385**	5.217**	4.853**	4.341**
	(0.364)	(0.108)	(0.241)	(0.301)
N	786	1,755	1,494	979
R^2	0.04	0.06	0.02	0.01

Note: Numbers in columns represent coefficients of OLS regression with standard errors in parentheses; **$p < 0.05$, *$p < 0.1$

TABLE C.8 Tabular Results for Figure 5.4 "Legal Counsel and Political Efficacy"

	White	Black	Latinx	AAPI
Politicians listen				
Any Problem	0.004	0.044	0.087**	0.124**
	(0.063)	(0.042)	(0.043)	(0.050)
Income	0.001	−0.000	0.000	0.000
	(0.001)	(0.001)	(0.001)	(0.001)
Education	0.009	−0.017	−0.001	0.020
	(0.020)	(0.014)	(0.014)	(0.012)
Age	−0.005	0.032**	−0.001	−0.023
	(0.018)	(0.013)	(0.015)	(0.017)
Gender	0.007	−0.021	−0.023	−0.005
	(0.057)	(0.041)	(0.041)	(0.047)
Constant	1.760**	1.980**	1.971**	1.889**
	(0.160)	(0.088)	(0.101)	(0.124)

TABLE C.8 (*continued*)

	White	Black	Latinx	AAPI
N	786	1,755	1,494	979
R²	0.01	0.01	0.01	0.01

Help my racial group

	White	Black	Latinx	AAPI
Any Problem	−0.006	0.074	0.121**	0.285**
	(0.095)	(0.048)	(0.056)	(0.065)
Income	−0.005**	−0.001	−0.002**	−0.000
	(0.002)	(0.001)	(0.001)	(0.001)
Education	0.096**	0.008	0.063**	−0.039*
	(0.030)	(0.016)	(0.0118)	(0.022)
Age	−0.168**	−0.016	−0.018	−0.026
	(0.027)	(0.015)	(0.020)	(0.021)
Gender	0.044	−0.151**	−0.088	−0.096*
	(0.089)	(0.047)	(0.054)	(0.061)
Constant	3.044**	2.488**	2.369**	2.631**
	(0.243)	(0.101)	(0.131)	(0.161)
N	786	1,755	1,494	979
R²	0.06	0.01	0.02	0.03

Note: Numbers in columns represent coefficients of OLS regression with standard errors in parentheses; **p < 0.05, *p < 0.1

Qualitative Appendix

Research Design

Ethnographic observation and qualitative interviews are essential sources of data for *Uncivil Democracy*. We collected qualitative data over the course of six years (2018–24) in a sequential, inductive process that enabled us to build and deepen our knowledge over time. Though we started with a broad interest in the politics of civil legal inequality, we did not begin this project with specific hypotheses that we aimed to prove or disprove. Instead, drawing on the logic of grounded theory, our arguments and emphases were emergent, developing as we observed civil legal processes and spoke to civil legal actors (Glaser and Strauss 1967). This inductive tack allowed the core findings of *Uncivil Democracy* to be generated from the "bottom up"—a methodological approach that parallels the book's substantive case for the importance of power in marginalized communities (Michener, SoRelle, and Thurston 2022).

Ethnographic Observation

Ethnographic observation pivotally shaped our interpretation of our interview, historical, and survey data. It also facilitated our recruitment of interviewees and contributed to the analyses that produced our core arguments. We began ethnographic observation in housing courts in New York City in 2018. Since civil courts are (for the most part) public spaces, observation consisted of selecting a city, identifying a courthouse, finding a courtroom (we focused on housing court), and sitting in that room for several hours—taking detailed notes on all that we saw and heard.[1] Our notes described a wide range of things, including who was present in the courtroom, what their body language and affect were like, what verbal exchanges occurred, what the outcomes of cases were, and more. Courtrooms were confusing, bustling, procedure-laden spaces that we did not understand well at first (just as tenants do not). In time, however, we came to know the practices, language, and processes of courtrooms quite well. This knowledge enriched our other qualitative work as well as our understanding of the processes we were studying.

We selected New York City (Queens and the Bronx) as a starting point for observation because its housing courts process over two hundred thousand cases each year, making it one of the largest and most active contexts for civil legal proceedings. Moreover, in 2017, New York was the first city in the country to enact a right-to-counsel law that attempted to ensure legal representation to all low-income New Yorkers facing eviction. As a city with a high demand for civil legal resources, a relatively high number of attorneys, robust grassroots organizing infrastructure, and substantial public resources devoted to providing counsel, New York was an instructive outlier (Michener 2020). Starting with a distinct case gave us a sense of how large, active, and relatively liberal (in terms of legal protections for tenants) courts operated. Eventually, we expanded to other parts of New York, observing civil legal proceedings in small and medium-size courts in very different cities, including Ithaca, Long Island, Rochester, and Syracuse. This helped us to achieve a theoretically relevant range, sensitizing us to similarities and differences across different kinds of (within-state) geographies.

Over time, we also extended this range to two additional states. First, we aimed to observe courts in a state that was distinct from New York in terms of politics and policy, so we selected Georgia. We observed courts in several Georgia counties of varying sizes and composition (Cobb, Fulton, and Gwinnett). We found important differences from New York, but we were struck by the similarities that seemed to pervade every court we observed (lack of clear direction or information, lots of waiting time, the disproportionate presence of Black and Latinx women, etc.). Finally, we observed court in New Jersey (Essex County). As a state that was close (geographically) to New York and had pursued

---

1. Sometimes tenants, landlords, judges, or other court actors noticed our presence and asked what we were doing. Our practice was to tell the truth: that we were researchers studying civil courts. This sometimes spurred further conversation, giving us another (unexpected) source of learning and perspective.

right-to-counsel policy too, but had less robust grassroots organizing infrastructure, fewer attorneys, and fewer resources committed to civil legal representation, New Jersey allowed us to have a near (but distinct) comparison.

Altogether, we spent more than one hundred hours directly observing in courts across the country.[2] We took detailed notes during court, using an "observation log" that included information on the date, time, and location of the court as well as a detailed description of the cases that were processed, outcomes of the cases, and nature of the courtroom interactions. Ultimately, observation helped us to better understand what we were studying. We learned about civil legal processes in ways that went beyond the technical details of courtroom procedure. Observation captured the look, feel, and experience of real-time reactions as well as interactions among lawyers and tenants. It also alerted us to aspects of civil legal processes that we had not otherwise recognized. For example, when we began this project, tenant organizations were not on our radar. In time, however, we became convinced of the importance of tenant organizing because we observed organizers in court offering tenants support and using courts as a springboard for building power. Tenant organizing and power building would not have been a central part of our larger argument were it not for our ethnographic observation.

The insights yielded from ethnographic observation compellingly demonstrate the substantive value of "mixed methods." Learnings from observation shed distinct light on the other kinds of data we collected. Our emphasis on tenant organizing and power building—inspired by ethnographic observation—gave us a lens through which to distinguish the structural transformation approach to civil justice that emerged in our historical analysis (see chapter 4). Relatedly, ethnographic observation gave us a clearer understanding of what people told us about their experiences when we interviewed them, making the interviews themselves more fruitful (because we could engage interviewees on terms that reflected our concrete, experiential knowledge of the institutions they navigated), and informing our coding and interpretation of the interview data. For instance, when Aria (whose courtroom experience was relayed in chapter 3), asked, "Why doesn't the judge recognize how many people this [landlord] has at court?" Jamila grasped her inquiry more fully having sat in the same courtroom and seen the same troubling patterns that Aria puzzled over.

2. Most of the observations were done by Jamila, but we also employed trained research assistants to help with observations in New York (Syracuse and the Bronx, respectively).

In addition to courtroom observation, we observed tenant meetings and gatherings, tenant rights trainings, and other tenant organizing events. Jamila embedded herself within communities of tenant members and leaders for extended periods of time between 2020 and 2024 (Burawoy 1991; Gillespie and Michelson 2011). Since this observation began during the pandemic, most of it was virtual (though Jamila did spend time in person with tenant organizers in Georgia, Kentucky, and New York). Being consistently present in spaces where tenant organizing actively unfolded helped us to understand organizing processes better, establish rapport and trust with the tenants and tenant organizers that we subsequently interviewed, and confirm some of the things we were told by research participants. So when people like Josephine (in chapter 1) talked about how poignant and emotional tenant meetings could be, it was even more compelling to sit in those meetings—seeing, hearing, and feeling what tenants meant when they spoke of the possibility along with the promise of tenant organizing.

Interviews

We conducted qualitative interviews with 124 people connected to civil legal processes. These interviews formed the fundamental basis for the arguments and structure of *Uncivil Democracy*. Interviewees were heterogeneous in many ways, but they fell into three broad categories: tenants who were not part of tenant organizations, tenants who were members or leaders of tenant organizations, and lawyers (see table D.1). The demographics, recruitment processes, and interview protocol for each group were distinct. The logic for including each was directly connected to the aims and focus of our research. We describe the details below.

Tenants who were not part of grassroots organizations faced civil legal problems with only the hope of procedural justice as their protection. Roughly half of the (nonmember) tenants we interviewed had legal counsel at some point (48 percent), while the others (52 percent) were never able to obtain a lawyer (of this latter group, some tried to get a lawyer and failed, while others never tried). Seventy-six percent of our nonmember tenant interviewees identified as women, 76 percent identified as Black, 8 percent identified as Latina, and 12 percent identified as White.[3] Interviewees hailed from five states (Colorado, Georgia, Kentucky, Michigan, and New York).

---

3. One of the twenty-five nonmember tenants we interviewed identified as nonbinary, and one identified as mixed race.

TABLE D.1 Interviewee Composition

Interviewee category	Number interviewed
Tenant (nonmember)	25
Tenant (member/leader)	79
Lawyer	20
Total	124

Interviews with nonmember tenants were meant to lend insight into the struggles of people with civil legal problems who did not have support from community organizations. The experiences of nonmember tenants represented a default baseline (most tenants who face civil legal problems are not members of tenant organizations), revealing the ways that tenants who navigated civil legal problems either alone or with only the support of an attorney made meaning of the processes they encountered. We asked these tenants about the nature of their civil justice problems (e.g., what was happening), what experiences (if any) they had with legal representation, and how they viewed their experiences as related to government and politics (e.g., whether they thought the government had anything to do with what they experienced). We recruited (nonmember) tenants for interviews at courthouses (by approaching them directly as they left housing court), through legal aid organizations (which sometimes shared information about the study with clients), via snowball techniques whereby people we already interviewed referred us to others who qualified for the study, and through targeted Facebook advertisements in cities where right to counsel had been implemented.[4] Despite this wide range of recruitment strategies, tenants who were not members of community organizations were a difficult group to recruit. As an acutely precarious, low-income group of people with good reason to be distrustful, these tenants were more disconnected from social networks and more hesitant to engage us. Despite such challenges, the twenty-five interviews we had with nonmember tenants were informative, helping us to get a clear sense of how and why tenants without support often felt adrift as well as alienated within civil legal institutions, and how they made sense of this in politically relevant ways (think of Aria, Sheila, Delilah, and Ray from chapter 3, or Quiana from chapter 4).

4. The latter recruitment strategy (targeted Facebook advertisements) was also part of a related but distinct research study on the implementation of right to counsel.

As the project advanced, our ethnographic observation highlighted the important role tenant organizations could play in civil legal processes. In response, we turned our attention to tenants who were embedded within tenant organizations. We interviewed seventy-nine members and leaders of tenant organizations.[5] The tenant members/leaders that we interviewed hailed from twenty-five states and forty localities. The states spanned every region of the country and ranged from large, populous states to smaller, less populated ones.[6] Similarly, tenant members/leaders were from a wide range of cities in terms of size, geography, demographic composition, and political context.

To recruit tenant members/leaders for interviews, we started by identifying tenant organizations throughout the country via searches across several platforms (Facebook, Twitter, Candid, and Google). We searched for the words "tenant" and "renter," often combining these terms with the names of specific states and cities to further refine our search parameters. After establishing a baseline set of organizations, we used a virtual snowball approach, reviewing organizations' websites and social media for relevant mentions of additional organizations. We initially identified approximately 134 tenant organizations across the country.[7]

We reached out to all the organizations for which we found contact information (via email, Facebook, or Twitter direct messages). In the first phase of interviewing, we received responses from forty-two organizations and completed interviews with members of thirty-eight organizations (about 28 percent of the original group of organizations identified). As we spoke to more organizations, however, we became known among the tenant organizing community, which created opportunities to speak to additional organizations.

5. Since many tenant organizations are explicitly nonhierarchical, the member/leader distinction was not always clear, and it generally did not seem relevant to what we learned. Tenant members who did not have official leadership positions in their organizations could sometimes tell us as much (or more) as organizational leaders about how and why their organizations engaged civil courts and legal processes.

6. Larger states included California, Florida, New York, and Ohio. Since some of the smaller states and some of the cities have few tenant organizations, we refrain from providing a comprehensive list of all states and cities where we conducted interviews.

7. This number changed throughout the project as new tenant organizations were started and old ones sometimes ended. We updated our listing of tenant organizations as we went, but surely missed new and budding organizations that emerged toward the latter part of our research.

By the end of the project, we had interviewed tenant members/leaders from forty-eight organizations.[8] While we did not aim to get a "representative sample" of tenant organizations, we did seek to learn from a wide range of organizations that varied in terms of geographic context and organizational contours.

Having wide-ranging cases in these regards allowed us to capture a heterogeneous array of perspectives. As we showed in chapter 2, civil legal systems in the United States are fragmented and diverse in substance as well as structure. The same is true of civic/organizational infrastructure (de Vries, Kim, and Han 2023). Together, these structural realities underscored the importance of geographic context for understanding the nature and experience of civil legal systems along with how grassroots organizations respond to them. Geographic range mapped onto variety in the racial contexts of tenant organizations too. We interviewed tenant members/leaders across a spectrum of racialized contexts from majority Black Southern cities, to cities with significant Latinx populations, to racially diverse northern and western locales, to largely White rural areas. Given the centrality of racialization in our rendering of the political economy of civil justice, this scope generated pertinent insights on the ways that racialization operates similarly and differentially across place.

The interviews occurred via Zoom or over the phone, depending on what was possible for us and preferred by the participants. Most interviews were with one participant, but sometimes multiple tenant members would join (we had up to four at one time). Moreover, some people would refer other members of their organization to speak to us, so on numerous occasions we separately interviewed different people from the same organization.

Tenant members/leaders frequently recounted similar legal problems as nonmember tenants. But when we turned to talking about what, if anything, could be done to address these problems, tenants who were members of organizations offered much richer and deeper thoughts on pathways to change. It's not that they were (comparatively) optimistic or Pollyannaish in their estimation of power dynamics and political possibilities. It is just that they had developed theories of change that positioned them and other tenants as active political actors with the capacity to affect the structures

8. The relational embeddedness of the qualitative work meant that we sometimes spoke to tenant members more than once, remaining in continual conversation with some of them as their organizations developed.

that most acutely affected them. We asked tenant members/leaders about themselves and their civil legal problems (taking a similar approach as we did with tenant nonmembers), but we also asked them about the work, activities, structure, and logic of the tenant organizations they were part of. The results were fruitful perspectives about how people experienced civil legal problems, and how they organized to confront as well as change civil legal and other system. (For a more detailed descriptive account of the activities and structure of tenant organizations, see Michener and SoRelle 2022.)

Our final group of interviewees were lawyers. We interviewed twenty lawyers from seven states and ten cities.[9] We interviewed lawyers in each of the cities where we did ethnographic observation in courts, plus in several additional locales. Lawyers offered complementary perspectives on civil legal systems and processes. Most (85 percent) of the lawyers we interviewed were involved in the direct provision of legal services through LSC-funded organizations. A few were focused on impact litigation meant to shape precedents and legal practices for large numbers of clients (like Bryson and Dan in chapter 6). Two attorneys were also members of tenant organizations—one cofounding a tenant group after becoming frustrated with the limits of the law.

We recruited attorneys through direct outreach to legal services organizations and snowball techniques (getting referrals from other lawyers). We sought their distinct viewpoints on the civil legal systems that they were such an integral part of. And while we learned a lot from attorneys, we were struck by how similarly they spoke across place (despite distinctive legal contexts). For example, attorneys in Georgia said many of the same things as attorneys in New York. We also noted that nearly all of what lawyers said reinforced the things that tenants told us. We ended the interviews with attorneys on reaching the point of saturation (when we no longer heard new things from them). That point came more quickly than we expected, in part because we found so little daylight between the basic substance of what lawyers told us and the experiences relayed by tenants.

---

9. The states were Florida, Georgia, Kentucky, Michigan, New Jersey, New York, and Virginia. Since some of the cities where we interviewed lawyers were small and/or had only a few legal aid attorneys, we withhold a full listing of the cities to protect the identities of the interviewees.

Historical Analysis

We conducted historical analysis to understand the political development of federal support for civil legal counsel. Political development refers to the study of durable shifts in governing authority over time (Orren and Skowrnek 2004). By paying careful attention to the timing and sequencing of institutional and policy evolution, a political development approach can help to identify key moments that represent new political and policymaking equilibria (Orren and Skowronek 2004; Pierson 2004). This method was critical for identifying and understanding the historical roots of the three orientations to the political economy of access to justice we describe in *Uncivil Democracy* (civil injustice, procedural justice, and transformative justice).

We rely on three main types of data to chart the historical process of political development for subsidized access to civil legal representation in the United States. The book has already described (in chapters 2 and 4) the detailed sampling and coding scheme we used to collect both state and federal legislation addressing civil legal representation. In addition to these original policy datasets, historical analysis of federal policymaking was supplemented by the careful identification and analysis of primary source documents, including congressional hearings and other primary source archival material.[10]

To identify major congressional debates about the provision of federal support for civil legal representation, we systematically explored congressional hearing transcripts for both the LSP and the formation and reauthorization of the LSC. We used ProQuest Congressional to identify any congressional hearings with the term "legal services program" held between 1965 and 1980, and "legal services corporation" held between 1969 and 1998. These search terms returned a population of 571 results for the LSP and 1,414 results for the LSC. Next, all entries were removed in which either the LSC or LSP was not the primary focus of the hearing (e.g., the 1973 hearing on the National No-Fault Motor Vehicle Insurance Act). This substantially narrowed the search to about 40 hearings (2 for the LSP and 38 for the LSC). Finally, the results for the LSC were narrowed to focus on hearings that reflected each of the major moments of policy change (e.g., hearings on the 1996 appropriations described in chapter 4) as well as two key moments of failed policy reauthorization. The latter is consistent with the notion that policy failures also play a critical role in

---

10. Most of the historical primary source data collection and analysis was conducted by Mallory with some participation from student research assistants.

political development because they set the stage for future political possibilities (Zackin and Thurston 2024). A final sample of eight congressional hearings, held between 1969 and 1996 across five different Senate and House committees with jurisdictional oversight, were carefully read in whole to identify recurring themes and debates.

While the legislative analysis provided insight into major congressional considerations (along with testimony from organized interest groups and executive branch policymakers), archival research offered deeper insight into the executive branch, including both the presidency and the relevant federal agencies involved in the administration of the LSP and LSC, respectively. Archival research was conducted at the Lyndon Baines Johnson and William Jefferson Clinton presidential libraries, with additional material drawn from previous archival research at the Consumer Movements Archives.[11] Prior to each visit, relevant material was first identified using the archival finding aids. Additional material was identified in conversation with the archivists, both prior to each site visit and with follow-up conversations on arrival. All boxes and folders identified as potentially relevant were pulled for examination, and Mallory inspected each file in person to determine whether it was relevant to the research at hand. In addition to extensive field notes from the in-person archival research, all documents deemed relevant to the study were subsequently scanned with a program that applied optical character recognition to translate the documents into machine-searchable text. The final sample of documents captured for systematic analysis included 58 from the LBJ library—primarily from the White House Central Files JL7 (Judicial-Legal Matters / Lawyers-Legal Aid) subject files and several collections of personal papers—and 75 documents from the Clinton library, the majority of which were from the Personal Papers of the First Lady, and spanned her time both as chair of the LSC and the First Lady. Each of the 133 documents (a majority of which were multipage communications, memos, or reports) was carefully read to identify themes and debates (both public and private) in the creation and administration of legal services programs. The archival material also offered concrete programmatic examples that informed our historical analysis.

11. We originally planned to include the Nixon and Reagan presidential archives as well, but COVID restrictions prevented us from doing so. Nonetheless, we were able to incorporate considerable material from the congressional hearings for these administrations along with secondary historical narratives.

Logic and Purpose of Qualitative Approach

Mixed methods can be invaluable in the larger tool kit of effective research approaches (Small 2011; Spillman 2014). The value of mixed methods, however, hinges on which methods are being combined, how they are informing one another, and for what purposes. Mixed-methods research should not be akin to throwing spaghetti at the wall to see what sticks. Instead, there should be both a logic and process to combining distinct methods, as there was in this study (Spillman 2014). We did not select the methods deployed in *Uncivil Democracy* because we assumed that mixed methods were necessarily or inherently appropriate. Nor did we presume that multiple triangulated methods necessarily improve on the quality of evidence. Rather, we integrated distinct methods based on what we sought to learn.

At the start of this project, we realized that there was relatively little political science research focused on access to justice, right to counsel, and the justice gap. Legal scholars (many of whom we cite and engaged throughout the development of this project) had studied these matters, and political scientists (whom we also cite extensively) studied topics related and adjacent to them. But there was little available in our discipline directly assessing the political economy of access to justice. Given the dearth of existing knowledge on this front, ethnographic observation with a grounded theory approach was the most appropriate place to begin. We had insufficient bases for proposing specific hypotheses and inadequate understanding to support strong causal propositions. Indeed, as noted above, we did not even fully understand crucial players in the civil legal landscape (e.g., tenant organizations), so we were not well positioned to formulate sound causal questions from the outset. We realized early on that identifying causal relationships was not the best aim for this research. Instead, we decided to hone in on description—a crucial, if undervalued, contribution in domains where there is still much to be learned about how processes unfold, how people make meaning of them, and what implications those meanings imply.

J Seawright (2016b, 49) critiques triangulation as insufficient insofar as it "provides multiple, somewhat incommensurable answers to causal questions." We agree that this is sometimes true. Yet we do not take up Seawright's (2016a, 47) push for social scientists to move toward "integrative multimethod research" in which "two or more methods are carefully combined to support a single, unified causal inference" where "additional methods are used to test or reframe the assumptions behind the central causal inference." Such an integrative approach is undoubtedly valuable in certain circumstances. Yet, Seawright's preoccupation with causal inference is misaligned with our core aims. Our central research goals are focused on deep description, elaboration of potential causal mechanisms, developing noncausal explanations to support constitutive arguments, and charting political possibilities. It is worth elaborating briefly on these goals given that some of them do not neatly fit within the standard confines of political science (although none of them are novel, and all of them have origins that well predate our research).

Deep description of experiences and processes was our starting point. What we learned by observing in courtrooms and talking to people gave us a clearer sense of the phenomena we sought to study along with their embeddedness within other institutions (e.g., federalism), connection to other political processes (e.g., community organizing), relevance to other research literatures (e.g., policy feedback), and political meaning. Deep description involved gathering detailed, specific, multifaceted information on what happens in civil courts, with legal aid lawyers, and among community organizations that are engaging civil legal processes. It also included engaging with historical legislative analysis and archival research methods, which provided a critical understanding of the process of political development that foregrounds the current institutional and political setting we sought to understand. Such description helped us to understand, explain, and contextualize civil legal processes, and shaped the development of our research. It was the essential foundation of *Uncivil Democracy*.

Though causation was not our primary goal, we nonetheless view this research as a basis for better comprehending the processes that structure the relationships between civil legal experiences and political power. Our qualitative description proved useful for elaborating potential causal mechanisms, even if it does not offer dispositive conclusions about causal relationships. Our correlational analyses suggested linkages between civil legal problems, civil legal representation, and various political outcomes (as detailed in chapters 3 and 5). While our research design doesn't enable us to make claims that these relationships are causal, our findings shed light on the relevance of mechanisms stressed in existing literatures (e.g., interpretive effects in the policy feedback literature) and lay a helpful foundation for researchers who can build on what we've learned to design studies that facilitate causal inference.

Beyond causation, our research highlights the importance of noncausal explanations (Navarrete 2024; Pacewicz 2022). Following, Josh Pacewicz (2022:933), we focus on constitutive arguments, which can be understood as "analytical descriptions about the makeup and useful categorization of social phenomenon, which commonly focus on existence (i.e., X exists), casing (i.e., X is a case of Y), or categorization (i.e., X consists of subcomponents A and B)." Importantly, constitutive arguments offer knowledge claims that are distinct from causal claims, though the two are often related and interdependent (indeed, as emphasized above, the formulation of sensible causal claims relies on constitutive knowledge). Crucially, however, the value of constitutive knowledge does not lie solely or even primarily in its ability to inform causal argumentation. Constitutive claims have independent significance, informing our "understanding of empirical reality absent any causal account" (Pacewicz 2022:934). Constitutive accounts do this by telling us about what happens in the world (X exists), where such happenings fit analytically (X is a case of Y), what such happenings consist of substantively (X consists of subcomponents A and B), and what meanings we might make of such happenings (X has implications for W, X, Y, and Z processes). All throughout *Uncivil Democracy*, we develop constitutive knowledge that makes these useful contributions.

The fourth and final research goal we focused on was charting political possibilities. As we noted in the main text, social scientists have come to emphasize causal probabilities, relying on quantitative statistical or experimental evidence to establish them. This is important, but it is not the only function of research. Researchers have the time and space to think beyond likely or probable outcomes. We can also consider what is *possible*, even if it does not appear to be frequent or probable. This is part and parcel of the role scholars play in broadening the scope of ideas, cultivating political and social imagination, making others aware of prospects that they might have otherwise remained indifferent to, and even inspiring new perspectives.

Uncivil Democracy admittedly marches to the beat of its own drummer when it comes to the layered and sequenced methods deployed in the research. We have no fidelity to methods (of any sort) as such. Instead, we committed only to knowing the corner of the world we sought to understand (civil legal institutions and processes) better than it had been known before, assessing that corner through distinct and theoretically productive analytic lenses (e.g., a focus on political economy and power), and creating knowledge that could both inform and inspire. With these goals in view, we drew pragmatically and ecumenically on a variety of methods. We did so as rigorously as possible, and in ways that were systematic and rooted in clear logics. This approach yielded rich insights, and a book we are proud of.

REFERENCES

American Bar Association (ABA). 1965. "Resolution Adopted by House of Delegates." White House Central Files, box 41, Lyndon Baines Johnson Presidential Library.

———. 1966. "Joint Statement before the U.S. Senate Subcommittee on Employment, Manpower, and Poverty." White House Central Files, box 41, Lyndon Baines Johnson Presidential Library.

Ancheta, Angelo N. 1993. "Community Lawyering." *California Law Review* 81:1363.

Andrias, Kate, and Benjamin I. Sachs. 2021. "Constructing Countervailing Power: Law and Organizing in an Era of Political Inequality." *Yale Law Journal* 130: 546–635.

Balz, Greg. 2024. "Tenant Union Law." *Yale Law and Policy Review* 43 (1): 1–94.

Baranski, John. 2007. "Something to Help Themselves: Tenant Organizing in San Francisco's Public Housing, 1965–1975." *Journal of Urban History* 33 (3): 418–42.

Barber, Michael, and Adam M. Dynes. 2023. "City-State Ideological Incongruence and Municipal Preemption." *American Journal of Political Science* 67 (1): 119–36.

Barnes, Carolyn. 2020. *State of Empowerment: Low-Income Families and the New Welfare State.* Ann Arbor: University of Michigan Press.

Barnes, Jeb E., and Thomas F. Burke. 2015. *How Policy Shapes Politics: Rights, Courts, Litigation, and the Struggle over Injury Compensation.* New York: Oxford University Press.

Barron, James. 2024. "Could 'Mitchell-Lama 2.0' Help New York's Housing Crisis?" *New York Times*, March 13.

Batlan, Felice. 2015. *Women and Justice for the Poor: A History of Legal Aid, 1863–1945.* New York: Cambridge University Press.

Béland, Daniel, Andrea Louise Campbell, and R. Kent Weaver. 2022. *Policy Feedback: How Policies Shape Politics.* New York: Cambridge University Press.

Bell, Derrick A., Jr. 1980. "Brown v. Board of Education and the Interest-Convergence Dilemma." *Harvard Law Review* 93 (3): 518–33.

Benfer, Emily, Peter Hepburn, Valerie Nazarro, Leah Robinson, Jamila Michener, and Danya E. Keene. 2025. "Disrupting the U.S. Eviction System: A Descriptive Analysis of Tenant Right to Counsel Law and Praxis 2017–2024." *Housing Policy Debate* 1–26. https://doi.org/10.1080/10511482.2025.2467136.

Bezdek, Barbara. 1991. "Silence in the Court: Participation and Subordination of Poor Tenants' Voices in Legal Process." *Hofstra Legal Review* 20: 533–608.

Blount, David C., Katharine Elder, Samantha Fu, Kaela Girod, Jessica Perez, and Bill Pitkin. 2023. "Pursuing Housing Justice: Interventions for Impact." Urban Institute. https://www.urban.org/apps/pursuing-housing-justice-interventions-impact.

Borsuk, Alan J., and Tom Kertscher. 2023. "So Simple, So Complex, So Human." Marquette Today. https://today.marquette.edu/2023/11/so-simple-so-complex-sohuman/.

Brady, David, Agnes Blome, and Hanna Kleider. 2016. "How Politics and Institutions Shape Poverty and Inequality." In *The Oxford Handbook of the Social Science of Poverty*, edited by David Brady and Linda M. Burton, 117–40. New York: Oxford University Press.

Brady, David, Ryan M. Finnigan, and Sabine Hübgen. 2017. "Rethinking the Risks of Poverty: A Framework for Analyzing Prevalences and Penalties." *American Journal of Sociology* 123 (3): 740–86.

Brady, Henry E., Sidney Verba, and Kay Lehman Schlozman. 1995. "Beyond SES: A Resource Model of Political Participation." *American Political Science Review* 89 (2): 271–94.

Brenner, Ryan, Ingrid Gould Ellen, Sophie House, Ellie Lochhead, and Katherine O'Regan. 2023. "Half the Battle Is Just Showing Up: Non-Answers and Default Judgments in Non-Payment Eviction Cases across New York State, 2016–2022." NYU Furman Center. https://furmancenter.org/files/publications/Half_the_Battle_is_Just_Showing_Up_V3_(1).pdf.

Brito, Tonya L., David Pate Jr., and Jia-Hui Stefanie Wong. 2014. "'I Do for My Kids': Negotiating Race and Racial Inequality in Family Court." *Fordham Law Review* 83: 3027.

Brito, Tonya L., Kathryn A. Sabbeth, Jessica K. Steinberg, and Lauren Sudeall. 2022. "Racial Capitalism in the Civil Courts." *Columbia Law Review* 122 (5): 1243–86.

Brown, Heath. 2021. *Homeschooling the Right: How Conservative Education Activism Erodes the State*. New York: Columbia University Press.

Brown, Wendy. 1995. *States of Injury: Power and Freedom in Late Modernity*. Princeton, NJ: Princeton University Press.

———. 2015. *Undoing the Demos: Neoliberalism's Stealth Revolution*. Cambridge, MA: MIT Press.

Burawoy, Michael. 1991. *Ethnography Unbound: Power and Resistance in the Modern Metropolis*. Berkeley: University of California Press.

Burbank, Stephen B., and Sean Farhang. 2017. *Rights and Retrenchment*. London: Cambridge University Press.

Burch, Traci. 2013. *Trading Democracy for Justice: Criminal Convictions and the Decline of Neighborhood Political Participation*. Chicago: University of Chicago Press.

Burden, Barry C., and Amber Wichowsky. 2014. "Economic Discontent as a Mobilizer: Unemployment and Voter Turnout." *Journal of Politics* 76 (4): 887–98.

Bureau of Labor Statistics. 2024. "Consumer Expenditures—2023." News Release, September 25. https://www.bls.gov/news.release/pdf/cesan.pdf.

Burstein, Paul. 2017. "Legal Mobilization as a Social Movement Tactic: The Struggle for Equal Employment Opportunity." In *Law and Social Movements*, edited by Michal McCann, 301–25. Abingdon, UK: Routledge.

Calacal, Celisa. 2023. "This Election, KC Tenants Power Gets Its First Shot at Shifting the Balance of Power in Kansas City." KCUR. https://www.kcur.org/politics-elections-and-government/2023-06-19/this-election-kc-tenants-power-gets-its-first-shot-at-shifting-the-balance-of-power-in-kansas-city

Callison, Kevin, Davida Finger, and Isabella M. Smith. 2022. "COVID-19 Eviction Moratoriums and Eviction Filings: Evidence from New Orleans." *Housing and Society* 49 (1): 1–9.

Cameron, Charles M., Jeffrey A. Segal, and Donald Songer. 2000. "Strategic Auditing in a Political Hierarchy: An Informational Model of the Supreme Court's Certiorari Decisions." *American Political Science Review* 94 (1): 101–16.

Campbell, Andrea Louise. 2003. *How Policies Make Citizens: Senior Political Activism and the American Welfare State.* Princeton, NJ: Princeton University Press.

Carter, April. 2005. *Direct Action and Democracy Today.* Cambridge, UK: Polity.

Caulfield, Richard H. 1971. "Tenant Unions: Growth of a Vehicle for Change in Low-Income Housing." *UCD Law Review* 3 (1): 1–30.

Chiappetta, Casey, and Octavia Howell. 2022. "Eviction Court Outcomes in Philadelphia Differ by Type of Landlord." Pew. https://www.pewtrusts.org/en/research-and-analysis/articles /2022/11/02/eviction-court-outcomes-in-philadelphia-differ-by-type-of-landlord.

Chu, Dion, Matthew R. Greenfield, and Peter Zuckerman. 2013. "Measuring the Justice Gap: Flaws in the Interstate Allocation of Civil Legal Services Funding and a Proposed Remedy." *Pace Law Review* 33: 965.

Chua, Lynette J., and David M. Engel. 2019. "Legal Consciousness Reconsidered." *Annual Review of Law and Social Science* 15: 335–53.

Consortium for the National Equal Justice Library. 2019. "US Civil Legal Aid: Overview." https://legalaidhistory.org/current-overview/us-legal-aid/us-civil-legal-aid-overview/.

Craig, Stephen C. 1979. "Efficacy, Trust, and Political Behavior: An Attempt to Resolve a Lingering Conceptual Dilemma." *American Politics Quarterly* 7 (2): 225–39.

Craig, Stephen C., Richard G. Niemi, and Glenn E. Silver. 1990. "Political Efficacy and Trust: A Report on the NES Pilot Study Items." *Political Behavior* 12: 289–314.

Crenshaw, Kimberlé Williams. 1988. "Toward a Race-Conscious Pedagogy in Legal Education." *National Black Law Journal* 11: 1.

Cruz Nichols, Vanessa, Alana M. W. LeBrón, and Francisco I. Pedraza. 2018. "Spillover Effects: Immigrant Policing and Government Skepticism in Matters of Health for Latinos." *Public Administration Review* 78 (3): 432–43.

Culpepper, Pepper D. 2010. *Quiet Politics and Business Power: Corporate Control in Europe and Japan.* Cambridge: Cambridge University Press.

Cunningham, Jamein P. 2016. "An Evaluation of the Federal Legal Services Program: Evidence from Crime Rates and Property Values." *Journal of Urban Economics* 92: 76–90.

Cunningham, Jamein P., and Rob Gillezeau. 2018. "The Effects of the Neighborhood Legal Services Program on Riots and the Wealth of African Americans." *RSF: The Russell Sage Foundation Journal of the Social Sciences* 4 (6): 144–57.

Danzon, Patricia M. 1984. "Tort Reform and the Role of Government in Private Insurance Markets." *Journal of Legal Studies* 13: 517–49.

Davis, Martha F. 1993. *Brutal Need: Lawyers and the Welfare Rights Movement, 1960–1973.* New Haven, CT: Yale University Press.

de Figueiredo, John M., and Rui J. P. de Figueiredo Jr. 2002. "The Allocation of Resources by Interest Groups: Lobbying, Litigation and Administrative Regulation." *Business and Politics* 4 (2): 161–81.

Desmond, Matthew. 2023. *Poverty, by America.* New York: Crown.

Desmond, Matthew, and Monica Bell. 2015. "Housing, Poverty, and the Law." *Annual Review of Law and Social Science* 11 (1): 15–35.

Dowdall, Emily, Jacob Rosch, Janine Simmons, and Michelle Schmitt. 2021. *Debt Collection in Philadelphia*. Reinvestment Fund. https://clsphila.org/wp-content/uploads/2021/03/ReinvestmentFund_2021_PHL-Debt-Collection-Final-report.pdf.

Eakeley, Douglas S. 1997. "Role of the Legal Services Corporation in Preserving Our National Commitment to Equal Access to Justice." *Annual Survey of American Law* 1997:741–45.

Elsesser, Charles. 2012. "Community Lawyering—The Role of Lawyers in the Social Justice Movement." *Loyola Journal of Public Interest Law* 14:375.

Enns, Peter K. 2016. *Incarceration Nation: How the United States Became the Most Punitive Democracy in the World*. New York: Cambridge University Press.

Eskridge, William N., Jr., and John Ferejohn. 1992. "The Article 1, Section 7 Game." *Georgetown Law Journal* 8:523–64.

Estrada-Correa, Vanesa, and Martin Johnson. 2012. "Foreclosure Depresses Voter Turnout: Neighborhood Disruption and the 2008 Presidential Election in California." *Social Science Quarterly* 93 (3): 559–76.

Farhang, Sean. 2010. *The Litigation State: Public Regulation and Private Lawsuits in the United States*. Princeton, NJ: Princeton University Press.

Feldman, Roberta M., and Susan Stall. 2004. *The Dignity of Resistance: Women Residents' Activism in Chicago Public Housing*. Cambridge: Cambridge University Press.

Fields, Desiree. 2015. "Contesting the Financialization of Urban Space: Community Organizations and the Struggle to Preserve Affordable Rental Housing in New York City." *Journal of Urban Affairs* 37 (2): 144–65.

———. 2017. "Unwilling Subjects of Financialization." *International Journal of Urban and Regional Research* 41 (4): 588–603.

Fields, Desiree, and Elora Lee Raymond. 2021. "Racialized Geographies of Housing Financialization." *Progress in Human Geography* 45 (6): 1625–45.

Fields, Desiree, and Sabina Uffer. 2016. "The Financialisation of Rental Housing: A Comparative Analysis of New York City and Berlin." *Urban Studies* 53 (7): 1486–502.

Flavin, Patrick, and Gregory Shufeldt. 2020. "Explaining State Preemption of Local Laws: Political, Institutional, and Demographic Factors." *Publius: The Journal of Federalism* 50 (2): 280–309.

Fleming-Klink, Isaiah, Brian J. McCabe, and Eva Rosen. 2023. "Navigating an Overburdened Courtroom: How Inconsistent Rules, Shadow Procedures, and Social Capital Disadvantage Tenants in Eviction Court." *City & Community* 22 (3): 220–45.

Forman, James, Jr. 2017. *Locking Up Our Own: Crime and Punishment in Black America*. New York: Farrar, Straus and Giroux.

Fortner, Michael Javen. 2015. "Beyond Criminal Justice Reform." *Dissent* 62 (4): 51–53.

Franko, William W. 2021. "How State Responses to Economic Crisis Shape Income Inequality and Financial Well-being." *State Politics & Policy Quarterly* 21 (1): 31–54.

Franko, William W., and Christopher Witko. 2018. *The New Economic Populism: How States Respond to Economic Inequality*. New York: Oxford University Press.

Fraser, Nancy. 2014. *Justice Interruptus: Critical Reflections on the "Postsocialist" Condition*. Abingdon, UK: Routledge.

Freund, David M. P. 2007. *Colored Property: State Policy and White Racial Politics in Suburban America*. Chicago: University of Chicago Press.

Galanter, Marc. 1974. "Why the Haves Come Out Ahead: Speculations on the Limits of Legal Change." *Law & Society Review* 9: 95.

Ganz, Marshall. 2009. *Why David Sometimes Wins: Leadership, Organization, and Strategy in the California Farm Worker Movement*. New York: Oxford University Press.

Garcia-Rios, Sergio, Nazita Lajevardi, Kassra A. R. Oskooii, and Hannah L. Walker. 2023. "The Participatory Implications of Racialized Policy Feedback." *Perspectives on Politics* 21 (3): 932–50.

Gelly, Rafael, and Pablo Spiller. 1990. "A Rational Choice Theory of Supreme Court Statutory Decisions." *Journal of Law Economics and Organization* 6: 263.

General Accounting Office. 1969. "Effectiveness and Administration of the Legal Services Program under Title II of the Economic Opportunity Act of 1964." Personal Papers of Albert H. Corbett, box 5, Lyndon Baines Johnson Presidential Library.

Genn, Hazel. 1999. *Paths to Justice: What People Do and Think about Going to Law*. London: Bloomsbury Publishing.

Gerstle, Gary. 2017. *American Crucible: Race and Nation in the Twentieth Century*. Princeton, NJ: Princeton University Press.

Gibson, S., M. Hamilton, E. Stevens, M. Moffet, H. Caspers, and E. Taylor, eds. 2024. "CSP Stat." National Center for State Courts. www.courtstatistics.org.

Gillespie, Andra, and Melissa R. Michelson. 2011. "Participant Observation and the Political Scientist: Possibilities, Priorities, and Practicalities." *PS: Political Science & Politics* 44 (2): 261–65.

Glaser, Barney G., and Anselm L. Strauss. 1967. *The Discovery of Grounded Theory: Strategies for Qualitative Research*. Chicago: Aldine Publishing Company.

Golio, A. J., Grace Daniels, Russell Moran, Y. Frank Southall, and Tricia Lamoza. 2023. "Eviction Court Outcomes and Access to Procedural Knowledge: Evidence from a Tenant-Focused Intervention in New Orleans." *Housing Policy Debate* 33 (6): 1443–62.

Goodman, Christopher B., Megan E. Hatch, and Bruce D. McDonald III. 2021. "State Preemption of Local Laws: Origins and Modern Trends." *Perspectives on Public Management and Governance* 4 (2): 146–58.

Gordon, Jennifer. 2007. "The Lawyer Is Not the Protagonist: Community Campaigns, Law, and Social Change." *California Law Review* 95 (5): 2133–46.

Gottschalk, Marie. 2006. *The Prison and the Gallows: The Politics of Mass Incarceration in America*. New York: Cambridge University Press.

———. 2011. "The Past, Present and Future of Mass Incarceration in the United States." *Criminology & Public Policy* 10: 483.

———. 2016. *Caught: The Prison State and the Lockdown of American Politics*. Princeton, NJ: Princeton University Press.

Grumbach, Jacob M. 2022. *Laboratories against Democracy: How National Parties Transformed State Politics*. Princeton, NJ: Princeton University Press.

Grumbach, Jacob M., and Jamila Michener. 2022. "American Federalism, Political Inequality, and Democratic Erosion." *ANNALS of the American Academy of Political and Social Science* 699 (1): 143–55.

Hacker, Jacob S. 2006. *The Great Risk Shift*. New York: Oxford University Press.

Hacker, Jacob S., Alexander Hertel-Fernandez, Paul Pierson, and Kathleen Thelen. 2022. "The American Political Economy: Markets, Power, and the Meta Politics of US Economic Governance." *Annual Review of Political Science* 25: 197–217.

Hadfield, Gillian. 2010. "Higher Demand, Lower Supply—A Comparative Assessment of the Legal Resource Landscape for Ordinary Americans." *Fordham Urban Law Journal* 37: 129.

Hague Institute for Innovation of Law and the Institute for the Advancement of the American Legal System. 2021. "Justice Needs and Satisfaction in the United States of America." file:/// Users/mes123/Downloads/Justice-Needs-and-Satisfaction-in-the-US-web.pdf.

Hamilton, Miriam. 2024. "Civil Case Trends." National Center for State Courts. https://www .courtstatistics.org/__data/assets/pdf_file/0020/104186/CLHL-Civil-Trends.pdf.

Han, Hahrie, Matthew Baggetta, and Jennifer Oser. 2024. "Organizing and Democracy: Understanding the Possibilities for Transformative Collective Action." *Annual Review of Political Science* 27: 245–62.

Han, Hahrie, Elizabeth McKenna, and Michelle Oyakawa. 2021. *Prisms of the People: Power and Organizing in Twenty-First-Century America.* Chicago: University of Chicago Press.

Hanley, Caroline, Kathryn Howell, and Benjamin Teresa. 2024. "Power in the Court: Legal Argumentation and the Hierarchy of Credibility in Eviction Hearings." *Socius* 10: 23780231241266510.

Haselswerdt, Jake, and Jamila Michener. 2019. "Disenrolled: Retrenchment and Voting in Health Policy." *Journal of Health Politics, Policy and Law* 44 (3): 423–54.

Hasen, Richard L. 2013. "The 2012 Voting Wars, Judicial Backstops, and the Resurrection of Bush v. Gore." *George Washington Law Review* 81: 1865.

Hepburn, Peter, Renee Louis, Joe Fish, Emily Lemmerman, Anne Kat Alexander, Timothy A. Thomas, Robert Koehler, Emily Benfer, and Matthew Desmond. 2021. "US Eviction Filing Patterns in 2020." *Socius* 7. https://doi.org/10.1177/23780231211009983.

Hertel-Fernandez, Alexander. 2018. "Policy Feedback as Political Weapon: Conservative Advocacy and the Demobilization of the Public Sector Labor Movement." *Perspectives on Politics* 16 (2): 364–79.

Hicks, William D., Carol Weissert, Jeffrey Swanson, Jessica Bulman-Pozen, Vladimir Kogan, Lori Riverstone-Newell, Jaclyn Bunch, et al. 2018. "Home Rule Be Damned: Exploring Policy Conflicts between the Statehouse and City Hall." *PS: Political Science & Politics* 51 (1): 26–38.

Hoffman, David A., and Anton Strezhnev. 2023. "Longer Trips to Court Cause Evictions." *Proceedings of the National Academy of Sciences* 120 (2): e2210467120.

Holder, Sarah, Kriston Capps, and Mackenzie Hawkins. 2023. "In Housing Court, a Scramble for Eviction Lawyers." *Bloomberg*, April 27.

Houseman, Alan W. 2001. "Civil Legal Assistance for Low-Income Persons: Looking Back and Looking Forward." *Fordham Urban Law Journal* 29 (3): 1213–44.

———. 2015. *Civil Legal Aid in the United States: An Update for 2015.* Georgetown University Law Library. https://repository.library.georgetown.edu/bitstream/handle/10822/761858 /Houseman_Civil_Legal_Aid_US_2015.pdf.

———. 2015. "Clinton Bamberger Dies: The Loss of an Icon." National Legal Aid and Defender Association. https://www.nlada.org/tribute-clinton-bamberger.

Houseman, Alan W., and Elisa Minoff. 2014. *The Anti-Poverty Effects of Civil Legal Aid*. https://legalaidhistory.org/wp-content/uploads/CNEJL-Anti-Povert-Impact-CLA-2015.pdf.

Houseman, Alan W., and Linda E. Perle. 2007. *Securing Equal Justice for All: A Brief History of Civil Legal Assistance in the United States*. Center for Law and Social Policy. https://www.clasp.org/sites/default/files/publications/2018/05/2018_securingequaljustice.pdf.

Hyman, Louis. 2011. *Debtor Nation: The History of America in Red Ink*. Princeton, NJ: Princeton University Press.

Iacus, Stefano M., Gary King, and Giuseppe Porro. 2012. "Causal Inference without Balance Checking: Coarsened Exact Matching." *Political Analysis* 20 (1): 1–24.

"Illegal Raids on Legal Services." 1983. Opinion. *New York Times*, September 8, A22.

Jacobi, Tonja. 2009. "The Role of Politics and Economics in Explaining Variation in Litigation Rates in the U.S. States." *Journal of Legal Studies* 38 (1): 205–33.

Jacobs, Lawrence R., and Suzanne Mettler. 2018. "When and How New Policy Creates New Politics: Examining the Feedback Effects of the Affordable Care Act on Public Opinion." *Perspectives on Politics* 16 (2): 345–63.

Johnson, Austin P., Kenneth J. Meier, and Kristen M. Carroll. 2017. "Forty Acres and a Mule: Housing Programs and Policy Feedback for African-Americans." *Politics, Groups, and Identities* 6 (4): 612–30.

Johnson, Earl. 1974. *Justice and Reform: The Formative Years of the OEO Legal Services Program*. New York: Russell Sage Foundation.

Johnson, Nia. 2021. "Hear Us: A National Tenants' Bill of Rights Is Foundational for Race Equity." *Next City*, November 18. https://perma.cc/69ZX-EFN7.

Joint Center for Housing Studies of Harvard University. 2024. *The State of the Nation's Housing 2024*. https://www.jchs.harvard.edu/sites/default/files/reports/files/Harvard_JCHS_The_State_of_the_Nations_Housing_2024.pdf.

Jung, Jiwook, and Tom VanHeuvelen. 2024. "Power Resources of Labor and the State Politics of Downsizing." *Socio-Economic Review* 22 (3): 1501–30.

Juravich, Nick. 2017. "'We the Tenants': Resident Organizing in New York City's Public Housing, 1964–1978." *Journal of Urban History* 43 (3): 400–420.

Kagan, Robert A. 1991. "Adversarial Legalism and American Government." *Journal of Policy Analysis and Management* 10 (3): 369–406.

———. 2019. *Adversarial Legalism: The American Way of Law*. 2nd ed. Cambridge, MA: Harvard University Press.

Karp, Michael. 2014. "The St. Louis Rent Strike of 1969: Transforming Black Activism and American Low-Income Housing." *Journal of Urban History* 40 (4): 648–70.

Keller, Bryan, and Zach Branson. 2024. "Defining, Identifying, and Estimating Causal Effects with the Potential Outcomes Framework: A Review for Education Research." *Asia Pacific Education Review* 25 (3): 575–94.

Kennedy, Duncan, Karl Klare, and Michael Turk. 2023. "A Wagner Act for Tenant Unions." Law and Political Economy Project. https://lpeproject.org/blog/a-wagner-act-for-tenant-unions/.

Kepes, Jacob Scott, and Alex M. Kempler. 2024. "'The System Is So Messed Up': Neutrality and Efficiency in an Eviction Courtroom." *Socius* 10: 23780231241286928.

Kerner Commission. 1968. *Report of the National Advisory Commission on Civil Disorders.* Washington, DC: US Government Printing Office.

Kessler, Mark. 1987. *Legal Services for the Poor: A Comparative and Contemporary Analysis of Interorganizational Politics.* New York: Greenwood Press.

King, Desmond S., and Rogers M. Smith. 2005. "Racial Orders in American Political Development."*American Political Science Review* 99 (1): 75–92.

Klearman, Sarah. 2022. "The S.F. Board of Supervisors Just Passed Unprecedented Protections for Tenants' Unions." *San Francisco Business Times,* February 16. https://www.bizjournals.com/sanfrancisco/news/2022/02/16/peskin-tenant-organizations-rights.html.

Kohl, Sebastian. 2021. "Too Much Mortgage Debt? The Effect of Housing Financialization on Housing Supply and Residential Capital Formation." *Socio-Economic Review* 19 (2): 413–40.

Korpi, Walter. (1978) 2022. *The Working Class in Welfare Capitalism: Work, Unions and Politics in Sweden.* London: Routledge.

Kousser, Thad, Jamila Michener, and Caroline Tolbert, eds. 2024. *Politics in the American States: A Comparative Analysis.* 12th ed. Washington, DC: Congressional Quarterly Press.

Law, Anna O. 2010. *The Immigration Battle in American Courts.* New York: Cambridge University Press.

Lawrence, Susan E. 2014. *The Poor in Court: The Legal Services Program and Supreme Court Decision Making.* Princeton, NJ: Princeton University Press.

Legal Aid Society. 2024. "What You Need to Know about New York's Good Cause Eviction Law." https://legalaidnyc.org/get-help/housing-problems/what-you-need-to-know-about-new-yorks-good-cause-eviction-law/.

Legal Services Alabama. 2023. *2023 Annual Report.* https://www.flipsnack.com/877B7ACC5A8/lsa-2023-annual-report.html.

———. 2024. "We Are Legal Aid in Alabama." https://legalservicesalabama.org/wp-content/uploads/2024/03/2024-Justice-Gap-Legal-Aid-at-a-Glance-1.pdf.

Legal Services Corporation (LSC). 1997. "Preserving LSC's New Congressional Framework." First Lady's Office, William J. Clinton Presidential Library.

———. 2021. Eviction Laws Database: State/Territory Dataset. Prepared by the Center for Public Health Law Research at Temple University's Beasley School of Law. https://www.lsc.gov/initiatives/effect-state-local-laws-evictions/lsc-eviction-laws-database.

———. 2022. *The Justice Gap Report.* https://justicegap.lsc.gov/the-report/.

———. 2023. *By the Numbers: The Data Underlying Legal Aid Programs.* https://lsc-live.app.box.com/s/h2bajpr3gps4s4a1iio6fwiddhmu1nwb.

———. 2024. Congressional Appropriations. https://www.lsc.gov/about-lsc/who-we-are/congressional-oversight/congressional-appropriations.

Legal Services Program (LSP), Office of Economic Opportunity. 1966a. "Guidelines for Legal Services Programs." Personal Papers of Bernard Louis Boutin, box 10, Lyndon Baines Johnson Presidential Library.

———. 1966b. "Report of the Legal Services Program to the American Bar Association." White House Central Files, box 41, Lyndon Baines Johnson Presidential Library.

Leighley, Jan E., and Jonathan Nagler. 2014. *Who Votes Now?: Demographics, Issues, Inequality, and Turnout in the United States.* Princeton, NJ: Princeton University Press.

Lerman, Amy E., and Vesla M. Weaver. 2014. *Arresting Citizenship: The Democratic Consequences of American Crime Control*. Chicago: University of Chicago Press.

Lewis, Nemoy. 2022. *The Uneven Racialized Impacts of Financialization*. Homeless Hub. https:// homelesshub.ca/sites/default/files/attachments/Lewis-Financialization-Racialized -Impacts-ofha-en.pdf.

Libgober, Brian. 2025. "Race and the Political Economy of Civil Justice." In *Rethinking Lawyer's Monopoly: Access to Justice and the Future of Legal Services*, edited by David Engstrom and Nora Freeman Engstrom. Cambridge: Cambridge University Press.

Lima, Valesca. 2020. "The Financialization of Rental Housing: Evictions and Rent Regulation." *Cities* 105: 102787.

Lind, E. Allan, and Tom R. Tyler. 1988. *The Social Psychology of Procedural Justice*. Berlin: Springer Science+Business Media.

Loffredo, Stephen. 2001. "Poverty Law and Community Activism: Notes from a Law School Clinic." *University of Pennsylvania Law Review* 150:173.

Lopez, Gerald P. 1992. *Rebellious Lawyering: One Chicano's Vision of Progressive Law Practice*. Boulder, CO: Westview Press.

———. 1996. "An Aversion to Clients: Loving Humanity and Hating Human Beings." *Harvard Civil Rights–Civil Liberties Law Review* 31: 315.

MacCoun, Robert J. 2005. "Voice, Control, and Belonging: The Double-Edged Sword of Procedural Fairness." *Annual Review of Law and Social Science* 1 (1): 171–201.

Madden, David, and Peter Marcuse. 2016. *In Defense of Housing: The Politics of Crisis*. London: Verso Books.

Marks, F. Raymond, Kirk Leswig, and Barbara A. Fortinsky. 1972. *The Lawyer, the Public, and Professional Responsibility*. Chicago: American Bar Foundation.

Martinez, Marayna. 2024. "How Does the Racial Composition of High Schools Affect Political Participation among Students of Color?" *Politics, Groups, and Identities*, 1–36.

Marx, Karl. (1844) 1926. "On the Jewish Question." In *Selected Essays*, translated by H. J. Stenning, 40–96. New York: Leonard Parsons.

Massey, Douglas S., and Nancy A. Denton. 1993. "Segregation and the Making of the Underclass." *Urban Sociology Reader* 2: 191–201.

McIntosh, Wayne V. 1990. *The Appeal of Civil Law: A Political-Economic Analysis of Litigation*. Champaign: University of Illinois Press.

McNollgast. 1990. "Positive and Normative Models of Procedural Rights: An Integrative Approach to Administrative Procedures." *Journal of Law, Economics, & Organization* 6: 307–32.

———. 1994. "Politics and the Courts: A Positive Theory of Judicial Doctrine and the Rule of Law." *Southern California Law Review* 68: 1631.

Melnick, R. Shep. 1983. "Deadlines, Common Sense, and Cynicism." *Brookings Review* 2 (1): 21–24.

———. 2010. *Between the Lines: Interpreting Welfare Rights*. Washington, DC: Brookings Institution Press.

Mettler, Suzanne. 2005. *Soldiers to Citizens: The GI Bill and the Making of the Greatest Generation*. New York: Oxford University Press.

———. 2011. *The Submerged State: How Invisible Government Policies Undermine American Democracy.* Chicago: University of Chicago Press.

———. 2016. "The Policyscape and the Challenges of Contemporary Politics to Policy Maintenance." *Perspectives on Politics* 14 (2): 369–90.

Mettler, Suzanne, and Mallory SoRelle. 2023. "Policy Feedback Theory." In *Theories of the Policy Process,* edited by Chris Weible and Paul Sabatier, 151–81. 5th ed. New York: Routledge.

Mettler, Suzanne, and Joe Soss. 2004. "The Consequences of Public Policy for Democratic Citizenship: Bridging Policy Studies and Mass Politics." *Perspectives on Politics* 2 (1): 55–73.

Michener, Jamila. 2018. *Fragmented Democracy: Medicaid, Federalism, and Unequal Politics.* New York: Cambridge University Press.

———. 2019a. "Medicaid and the Policy Feedback Foundations for Universal Healthcare." *ANNALS of the American Academy of Political and Social Science* 685 (1): 116–34.

———. 2019b. "Policy Feedback in a Racialized Polity." *Policy Studies Journal* 47 (2): 423–50.

———. 2020. "Power from the Margins: Grassroots Mobilization and Urban Expansions of Civil Legal Rights." *Urban Affairs Review* 56 (5): 1390–422.

———. 2022. "Civil Justice, Local Organizations, and Democracy." *Columbia Law Review* 122 (5): 1389–422.

———. 2023a. "Legal Aid and Social Policy: Managing a Political Economy of Scarcity." *Annals of the American Academy of Political and Social Science* 706 (1): 137–58.

———. 2023b. "Policy Feedback in the Pandemic: Lessons from Three Key Policies." Roosevelt Institute. https://rooseveltinstitute.org/publications/policy-feedback-in-the-pandemic/#:~:text=Three%20pivotal%20federal%20policies%20included,of%20federal%20student%20loan%20debts.

———. 2023c. "Racism, Power, and Health Equity: The Case of Tenant Organizing." *Health Affairs* 42 (10): 1318–24.

———. 2023d. "Entrenching Inequity, Eroding Democracy: State Preemption of Local Housing Policy." *Journal of Health Politics, Policy and Law* 48 (2): 157–85.

———. 2024. "Racial, Economic, and Gender Inequity in the States." In *Politics in the American States: A Comparative Analysis,* edited by Thad Kousser, Jamila Michener, and Caroline Tolbert, 1–22. 12th ed. Washington, DC: Congressional Quarterly Press.

———. 2025a. "Building Power for Health: The Grassroots Politics of Sustaining and Strengthening Medicaid." *Journal of Health Politics, Policy and Law* 50 (2): 189–221.

———. 2025b. "Beyond Access: Power, Organizing, and Civil Legal Inequality." In *Rethinking Lawyer's Monopoly: Access to Justice and the Future of Legal Services,* edited by David Engstrom and Nora Freeman Engstrom. Cambridge: Cambridge University Press.

———. 2025c. "Housing Insecurity and U.S. Economic Policies: Lessons from Tenant Organizing." Washington Center for Equitable Growth. https://equitablegrowth.org/housing-insecurity-and-u-s-economic-policies-lessons-from-tenant-organizing/#:~:text=I%20argue%20that%20tenant%20organizing,the%20worse%20excesses%20of%20populism.

Michener, Jamila, and Mallory SoRelle. 2022. "Politics, Power, and Precarity: How Tenant Organizations Transform Local Political Life." *Interest Groups & Advocacy* 11 (2): 209–36.

Michener, Jamila, Mallory SoRelle, and Chloe Thurston. 2022. "From the Margins to the Center: A Bottom-up Approach to Welfare State Scholarship." *Perspectives on Politics* 20 (1): 154–69.

Milkman, Ruth. 2024. "Power Resource Theory and the 21st Century US Labor Movement." *Stato e mercato* 44 (1): 39–66.

Miller, Lisa L. 2008. *The Perils of Federalism: Race, Poverty, and the Politics of Crime Control.* New York: Oxford University Press.

Milloy, Ross E. 1997. "Suit Fights Absentee Vote by Soldiers at Texas Base." *New York Times,* March 2. First Lady's Office, William J. Clinton Presidential Library.

Moffett-Bateau, Alex J. 2023. "Strategies of Resistance in the Everyday: The Political Approaches of Black Women Living in a Public Housing Development in Chicago." *Journal of Women, Politics & Policy* 44 (4): 525–47.

———. 2024. *Redefining the Political: Black Feminism and the Politics of Everyday Life.* Philadelphia: Temple University Press.

Morgenson, Gretchen. 2023. "These Tenants Fought One of America's Largest Corporate Landlords—and Scored Some Wins." *NBC News,* July 5.

Murakawa, Naomi. 2014. *The First Civil Right: How Liberals Built Prison America.* New York: Oxford University Press.

National Center for Access to Justice. 2021. "Justice Index." https://ncaj.org/state-rankings /justice-index/attorney-access.

National Coalition for a Civil Right to Counsel. 2025. *The Right to Counsel for Tenants Fighting Eviction: Enacted Legislation.* http://civilrighttocounsel.org/uploaded_files/283/RTC _Enacted_Legislation_in_Eviction_Proceedings_FINAL.pdf.

National Legal Aid Funding Data. 2024. American Bar Association. https://www.americanbar .org/groups/legal_services/abarray-national-legal-aid-funding-data/

Navarrete, Cristián. 2024. "Answering 'Why' beyond Causality: Exploring (Non)causal Explanation in Qualitative Research." Authorea. doi:10.31124/advance.172427543.34805937/v2.

Nickles, Peter J., Lucie E. White, and Luke W. Cole. 2001. "PANEL 3: Creating Models for Progressive Lawyering in the 21st Century." *Journal of Law and Policy* 9 (2): 4.

Nixon, Richard. 1971. "Special Message to the Congress Proposing Establishment of a Legal Services Corporation." American Presidency Project. https://www.presidency.ucsb.edu /documents/special-message-the-congress-proposing-establishment-legal-services -corporation.

Novkov, Julie. 2001. *Constituting Works, Protecting Women: Gender, Law, and Labor in the Progressive Era and New Deal Years.* Ann Arbor: University of Michigan Press.

———. 2002. "Racial Constructions: The Legal Regulation of Miscegenation in Alabama, 1890–1934." *Law and History Review* 20 (2): 225–77.

Office for Access to Justice. "About ATJ." Accessed 2023. https://www.justice.gov/atj/about-atj.

Ojeda, Christopher, Jamila Michener, and Jake Haselswerdt. 2024. ("The Politics of Personal Crisis: How Negative Life Events Affect Political Participation." *Political Behavior* 46:2611–30.

Omi, Michael, and Howard Winant. 1986. *Racial Formation in the United States: From the 1960s to the 1990s.* New York: Routledge.

Orren, Karen, and Stephen Skowronek. 2004. *The Search for American Political Development.* Cambridge: Cambridge University Press.

Pacewicz, Josh. 2022. "What Can You Do with a Single Case? How to Think about Ethnographic Case Selection like a Historical Sociologist." *Sociological Methods & Research* 51 (3): 931–62.

Pacheco, Julianna, and Eric Plutzer. 2008. "Political Participation and Cumulative Disadvantage: The Impact of Economic and Social Hardship on Young Citizens." *Journal of Social Issues* 64 (3): 571–93.

Page, Joshua, and Joe Soss. 2021. "The Predatory Dimensions of Criminal Justice." *Science* 374 (6565): 291–94.

Partridge, Mark D., and Amanda L. Weinstein. 2013. "Rising Inequality in an Era of Austerity: The Case of the US." *European Planning Studies* 21 (3): 388–410.

Patashnik, Eric M., and Julian E. Zelizer. 2013. "The Struggle to Remake Politics: Liberal Reform and the Limits of Policy Feedback in the Contemporary American State." *Perspectives on Politics* 11 (4): 1071–87.

Petach, Luke. 2022. "Income Stagnation and Housing Affordability in the United States." *Review of Social Economy* 80 (3): 359–86.

Pierson, Paul. 1993. "When Effect Becomes Cause: Policy Feedback and Political Change?" *World Politics* 45 (4): 595–628.

———. 2004. *Politics in Time: History, Institutions, and Social Analysis.* Princeton, NJ: Princeton University Press.

Piomelli, Ascanio. 2006. "The Democratic Roots of Collaborative Lawyering." *Clinical Law Review* 12:541–614.

Piven, Frances Fox, and Richard Cloward. 2011. "The Weight of the Poor: A Strategy to End Poverty." *New Political Science* 33 (3): 271–84.

Powers, Lonnie A. 2015. "Civil Legal Assistance Is a Potent Anti-Poverty Tool." *Huffington Post*, April 26.

Quigley, William P. 1997. "The Demise of Law Reform and the Triumph of Legal Aid: Congress and the Legal Services Corporation from the 1960's to the 1990's." *Saint Louis University Public Law Review* 17 (2): 241–64.

Rahman, K. Sabeel, and Kathleen Thelen. 2022. "The Role of Law in the American Political Economy." In *The American Political Economy: Political, Markets, and Power*, edited by Jacob S. Hacker, Alexander Hertel-Fernandez, Paul Pierson, and Kathleen Thelen, 76–102. New York: Cambridge University Press.

Refslund, Bjarke, and Jens Arnholtz. 2022. "Power Resource Theory Revisited—The Perils and Promises of Our Understanding Contemporary Labour Politics." *Economic and Industrial Democracy* 43 (4): 1958–79.

Reich, David. 2021. "Additional Funding Needed for Legal Services Corporation." Center on Budget and Policy Priorities. https://www.cbpp.org/blog/additional-funding-needed-for-legal-service-corporation.

Rhode, Deborah L. 2004. *Access to Justice.* New York: Oxford University Press.

Riker, William H. 1964. *Federalism: Origin, Operation, Significance.* New York: Little, Brown and Company.

Riverstone-Newell, Lori. 2017. "The Rise of State Preemption Laws in Response to Local Policy Innovation." *Publius: The Journal of Federalism* 47 (3): 403–25.

Roberts, Dorothy. 2009. *Shattered Bonds: The Color of Child Welfare*. London: Hachette UK.

———. 2014. *Killing the Black Body: Race, Reproduction, and the Meaning of Liberty*. New York: Vintage.

Robinson, Cedric. 1983. *Black Marxism: The Making of the Black Radical Tradition*. Chapel Hill: University of North Carolina Press.

Robinson, John N., III. 2021. "Surviving Capitalism: Affordability as a Racial 'Wage' in Contemporary Housing Markets." *Social Problems* 68 (2): 321–39.

Rocha, Rene R., Benjamin R. Knoll, and Robert D. Wrinkle. 2015. "Immigration Enforcement and the Redistribution of Political Trust." *Journal of Politics* 77 (4): 901–13.

Rodriguez, Akira Drake. 2021. *Diverging Space for Deviants: The Politics of Atlanta's Public Housing*. Athens: University of Georgia Press.

Rosenstone, Steven J. 1982. "Economic Adversity and Voter Turnout." *American Journal of Political Science* 26 (1): 25–46.

Rosenthal, Aaron. 2021. "Submerged for Some? Government Visibility, Race, and American Political Trust." *Perspectives on Politics* 19 (4): 1098–114.

Rosino, Michael L. 2016. "Boundaries and Barriers: Racialized Dynamics of Political Power." *Sociology Compass* 10 (10): 939–51.

Rothstein, Richard. 2017. *The Color of Law: A Forgotten History of How Our Government Segregated America*. New York: Liveright Publishing.

Sabbeth, Kathryn A. 2021. "Erasing the 'Scarlet E' of Eviction Records." *Appeal*. https://theappeal.org/the-lab/report/erasing-the-scarlet-e-of-eviction-records/.

———. 2022. "Eviction Courts." *University of Saint Thomas Law Journal* 18 (2): 359–404.

Sandefur, Rebecca L. 2007. "Lawyers' Pro Bono Service and American-Style Civil Legal Assistance." *Law & Society Review* 41 (1): 79–112.

———. 2008. "Access to Civil Justice and Race, Class, and Gender Inequality." *Annual Review of Sociology* 34:339–58.

———. 2009. "Fulcrum Point of Equal Access to Justice: Legal and Nonlegal Institutions of Remedy." *Loyola of Los Angeles Law Review* 42 (4): 949–78.

———. 2016. "What We Know and Need to Know about the Legal Needs of the Public." *Southern Carolina Law Review* 67: 443.

———. 2019. "Access to What?" *Daedalus* 148 (1): 49–55.

———. 2020. "Legal Advice from Nonlawyers: Consumer Demand, Provider Quality, and Public Harms." *Stanford Journal of Civil Rights and Civil Liberties* 16: 283.

Sandefur, Rebecca L., and James Teufel. 2020. "Assessing America's Access to Civil Justice Crisis." *UC Irvine Law Review* 11:753–80.

Sandman, James J. 2015. "Management's Recommendation for LSC's FY 2017 Budget Request." Legal Services Corporation. https://perma.cc/748X-EB7G.

Satter, Beryl. 2009. *Family Properties: Race, Real Estate, and the Exploitation of Black Urban America*. New York: Metropolitan Books.

Schattschneider, Elmer E. 1935. *Politics, Pressures and the Tariff*. New York: Prentice Hall.

Schlafly, Phyllis. 1995. "Outgoing Tide for Legal Services Corp?" *Washington Times*, A21. First Lady's Office, William J. Clinton Presidential Library.

Schneider, Anne, and Helen Ingram. 1993. "Social Construction of Target Populations: Implications for Politics and Policy," *American Political Science Review* 87 (2): 334–47.

Schueler, McKenna. 2023. "Florida Gov. DeSantis Approves Another Industry-Backed Bill Gutting Local Tenant Protections." *Orlando Weekly*, June 29.

Scott, Randall W. 1979. "Housing Courts and Housing Justice: An Overview." *Urban Law Annual* 17: 3.

Seamster, Louise, and Raphaël Charron-Chénier. 2017. "Predatory Inclusion and Education Debt: Rethinking the Racial Wealth Gap." *Social Currents* 4 (3): 199–207.

Seawright, J. 2016a. "Better Multimethod Design: The Promise of Integrative Multimethod Research." *Security Studies* 25 (1): 42–49.

———. 2016b. *Multi-Method Social Science: Combining Qualitative and Quantitative Tools*. Cambridge: Cambridge University Press.

Seecharan, Justin. 2023. "Florida Second in Nation for Eviction and Foreclosure Moves." WMNF News, May 9. https://www.wmnf.org/florida-second-in-nation-for-eviction-and-foreclosure-moves/.

Seligman, Amanda I. 2005. *Block by Block: Neighborhoods and Public Policy on Chicago's West Side*. Chicago: University of Chicago Press.

Senate Report no. 599. 1965.

Seron, Carroll, Martin Frankel, Gregg Van Ryzin, and Jean Kovath. 2001. "The Impact of Legal Counsel on Outcomes for Poor Tenants in New York City's Housing Court: Results of a Randomized Experiment." *Law and Society Review* 35 (2): 419–34.

Sessa-Hawkins, Margaret, and Andrew Perez. 2017. "Dark Money Group Received Massive Donation in Fight against Obama's Supreme Court Nominee." *Maplight*, October 24.

Shah, Paru, and Amber Wichowsky. 2019. "Foreclosure's Fallout: Economic Adversity and Voter Turnout." *Political Behavior* 41 (4): 1099–115.

Shanahan, Colleen F., Jessica K. Steinberg, Alyx Mark, and Anna E. Carpenter. 2022. "The Institutional Mismatch of State Civil Courts." *Columbia Law Review* 122 (5): 1471–537.

Shaub, Max. 2021. "Acute Financial Hardship and Voter Turnout: Theory and Evidence from the Sequence of Bank Working Days." *American Political Science Review* 115 (4): 1258–74.

Sigafoos, Jennifer, and James Organ. 2021. "'What about the Poor People's Rights?' The Dismantling of Social Citizenship through Access to Justice and Welfare Reform Policy." *Journal of Law and Society* 48 (3): 362–85.

Skocpol, Theda. 1992. *Protecting Soldiers and Mothers: The Political Origins of Social Policy in the United States*. Cambridge, MA: Harvard University Press.

Skowronek, Stephen. 1982. *Building a New American State: The Expansion of National Administrative Capacities, 1877–1920*. Cambridge: Cambridge University Press.

Small, Mario Luis. 2009. "'How Many Cases Do I Need?' On Science and the Logic of Case Selection in Field-Based Research." *Ethnography* 10 (1): 5–38.

———. 2011. "How to Conduct a Mixed Methods Study: Recent Trends in a Rapidly Growing Literature." *Annual Review of Sociology* 37: 57–86.

Smith, Reginald H. 1919. *Justice and the Poor: A Study of the Present Denial of Justice to the Poor and of the Agencies Making More Equal Their Position before the Law, with Particular Reference to Legal Aid Work in the United States*. Stanford, CA: Carnegie Foundation for the Advancement of Teaching.

Smith, Rogers M. 1997. *Civic Ideals: Conflicting Visions of Citizenship in US History*. New Haven, CT: Yale University Press.

———. 2003. *Stories of Peoplehood: The Politics and Morals of Political Membership*. Cambridge: Cambridge University Press.

Sommerlad, Hilary. 2004. "Some Reflections on the Relationship between Citizenship, Access to Justice, and the Reform of Legal Aid." *Journal of Law and Society* 31 (3): 345–68.

SoRelle, Mallory E. 2016. "Politics of the Policyscape." In *Global Encyclopedia of Public Administration, Public Policy, and Governance*, edited by Ali Farazmand, 1–7. Cham, Switzerland: Springer International Publishing.

———. 2020. *Democracy Declined: The Failed Politics of Consumer Financial Protection*. Chicago: University of Chicago Press.

———. 2022. "From Personal Responsibility to Political Mobilization: Using Attribution Frames to Overcome Policy Feedback Effects." *American Politics Research* 50 (2): 173–85.

———. 2023. "Privatizing Financial Protection: Regulatory Feedback and the Politics of Financial Reform." *American Political Science Review* 117 (3): 1–19.

SoRelle, Mallory E., and Allegra Fullerton. 2024. "Policy Feedback Effects of Preemption." *Policy Studies Journal* 52 (2): 235–55.

SoRelle, Mallory E., and Serena Laws. 2023. "The Political Benefits of Student Loan Debt Relief." *Research & Politics* 10 (2): 205316802311740.

SoRelle, Mallory E., and Suzanne Mettler. 2021. "More than Meets the Eye: Government Social Provision and the Politics of 'Public Options.'" In *Politics, Policy, and Public Options*, edited by Ganesh Sitaraman and Anne Alstott, 6–19. Cambridge: Cambridge University Press.

SoRelle, Mallory E., and Jamila Michener. 2022. "Methods for Applying Policy Feedback Theory." In *Methods of the Policy Process*, edited by Christopher M. Weible and Samuel Workman, 80–104. New York: Routledge.

SoRelle, Mallory E., and Alexis N. Walker. 2016. "Partisan Preemption: The Strategic Use of Federal Preemption Legislation." *Publius: The Journal of Federalism* 46 (4): 486–509.

Soss, Joe. 1999. "Lessons of Welfare: Policy Design, Political Learning, and Political Action." *American Political Science Review* 93 (2): 363–80.

———. 2000. *Unwanted Claims: The Politics of Participation in the US Welfare System*. Ann Arbor: University of Michigan Press.

Soss, Joe, Richard Fording, and Sanford Schram. 2011. *Disciplining the Poor: Neoliberal Paternalism and the Persistent Power of Race*. Chicago: University of Chicago Press.

Soss, Joe, and Vesla Weaver. 2017. "Police Are Our Government: Politics, Political Science, and the Policing of Race–Class Subjugated Communities." *Annual Review of Political Science* 20: 565–91.

Spade, Dean. 2015. *Normal Life: Administrative Violence, Critical Trans Politics, and the Limits of Law*. Durham, NC: Duke University Press.

———. 2020. "Solidarity Not Charity: Mutual Aid for Mobilization and Survival." *Social Text* 38 (1): 131–51.

Spillman, Lyn. 2014. "Mixed Methods and the Logic of Qualitative Inference." *Qualitative Sociology* 37 (2): 189–205.

Staszak, Sarah. 2015. *No Day in Court: Access to Justice and the Politics of Judicial Retrenchment*. New York: Oxford University Press.

———. 2024. *Privatizing Justice: Arbitration and the Decline of Public Governance in the U.S.* New York: Oxford University Press.

Steinberg, Jessica K. 2014. "Demand Side Reform in the Poor People's Court." *Connecticut Law Review* 47: 741.

———. 2017. "Informal, Inquisitorial, and Accurate: An Empirical Look at a Problem-Solving Housing Court." *Law & Social Inquiry* 42 (4): 1058–90.

Streeck, Wolfgang. 2011. "Taking Capitalism Seriously: Towards an Institutionalist Approach to Contemporary Political Economy." *Socio-Economic Review* 9 (1): 137–67.

Sudeall, Lauren, and Daniel Pasciuti. 2021. "Praxis and Paradox: Inside the Black Box of Eviction Court." *Vanderbilt Law Review* 74 (5): 1365–434.

Super, David A. 2011. "The Rise and Fall of the Implied Warrant of Habitability." *California Law Review* 99: 389.

Táíwò, Olúfẹ́mi O., Anne E. Fehrenbacher, and Alexis Cooke. 2021. "Material Insecurity, Racial Capitalism, and Public Health." *Hastings Center Report* 51 (6): 17–22.

Tani, Karen M. 2016. *States of Dependency: Welfare, Rights, and American Governance, 1935–1972.* New York: Cambridge University Press.

Taylor, Keeanga Yamahtta. 2013. *Rats, Riots and Revolution: Black Housing in the 1960s.* Chicago: Haymarket Books.

———2019. *Race for Profit: How Banks and the Real Estate Industry Undermined Black Home-ownership.* Chapel Hill: University of North Carolina Press.

Teufel, James, Shannon Mace, Jordan Michman, Daniel Atkins, and David J. Dausey. 2015. "Legal Aid Inequities Predict Health Disparities." *Hamline Law Review* 38: 329.

Thibaut, John W., and Laurens Walker. 1975. *Procedural Justice: A Psychological Analysis.* Hillsdale, NJ: L. Erlbaum Associates.

———. 1978. "A Theory of Procedure." *California Law Review* 66: 541–66.

Thomas, Cal. 1992. "Unlimited Clinton Partnership?" *Washington Times.* First Lady's Office, William J. Clinton Presidential Library.

Thurston, Chloe N. 2018. *At the Boundaries of Homeownership: Credit, Discrimination, and the American State.* Cambridge: Cambridge University Press.

———. 2023. "How Should We Govern Housing Markets in a Moral Political Economy?" *Daedalus* 152 (1): 194–97.

Trounstine, Jessica. 2018. *Segregation by Design: Local Politics and Inequality in American Cities.* Cambridge: Cambridge University Press.

Tushnet, Mark. 2009. *Weak Courts, Strong Rights: Judicial Review and Social Welfare Rights in Comparative Constitutional Law.* Princeton, NJ: Princeton University Press.

Tyler, Tom R. 1988. "What Is Procedural Justice-Criteria Used by Citizens to Assess the Fairness of Legal Procedures." *Law & Society Review* 22: 103.

Tyler, Tom R., and Kathleen M. McGraw. 1986. "Ideology and the Interpretation of Personal Experience: Procedural Justice and Political Quiescence." *Journal of Social Issues* 42 (2): 115–28.

US House, Committee on Education and Labor. 1973. *Establishment of a Legal Services Corporation.* 93rd Congress, February 21–March 1.

US House, Committee on Judiciary. 1985. *Legal Services Corporation Authorization.* 99th Congress, April 17–18.

———. 1995. *Reauthorization of the Legal Services Corporation.* 104th Congress, May 16–July 27.

US Senate, Committee on Labor and Public Welfare. 1970. *Legal Services Program of the Office of Economic Opportunity*. 91st Congress, October 7–9.

Villazor, Rose Cuison. 2004. "Community Lawyering: An Approach to Addressing Inequalities in Access to Health Care for Poor, of Color and Immigrant Communities." *New York University Journal of Legislation and Public Policy* 8 (1): 35–62.

Vivero, Mauricio. 2001. "From 'Renegade' Agency to Institution of Justice: The Transformation of the Legal Services Corporation." *Fordham Urban Law Journal* 29 (3): 1323–48.

Waldron, Jeremy. 1993. *Liberal Rights: Collected Papers 1981–1991*. New York: Cambridge University Press.

Walker, Hannah L. 2020. *Mobilized by Injustice: Criminal Justice Contact, Political Participation, and Race*. New York: Oxford University Press.

Wallat, Katherine S. 2019. "Reconceptualizing Access to Justice." *Marquette Law Review* 103: 581.

Weaver, Vesla M. 2007. "Frontlash: Race and the Development of Punitive Crime Policy." *Studies in American Political Development* 21 (2): 230–65.

Weaver, Vesla M., and Gwen Prowse. 2020. "Racial Authoritarianism in US Democracy." *Science* 369 (6508): 1176–78.

Webster, Betsy. 2023. "KC Tenants Leader Wins Council Seat." KCTV, June 20. https://www.kctv5.com/2023/06/21/kc-tenants-political-arm-celebrates-wins-election-night/.

Weingast, Barry R. 2002. "Self-Enforcing Constitutions: With an Application to American Democratic Stability."

Westwood, Howard C. 1971. "Getting Justice for the Freedman." *Howard Law Journal* 16:492–537.

White, Lucie E. 1988. "Mobilization of the Margins of the Lawsuit: Making Space for Clients to Speak." *New York University Review of Law & Social Change* 16 (4): 535–64.

Whitlow, John. 2018. "Beyond Access to Justice: Challenging the Neoliberal Roots of Hypergentrification." Law and Political Economy Project. https://lpeproject.org/blog/beyond-access-to-justice-challenging-the-neoliberal-roots-of-hyper-gentrification.

———. 2022. "Law and Countervailing Tenant Power in the Real Estate State." Law and Political Economy Project. https://lpeproject.org/authors/john-whitlow/.

———. 2023 "Toward Housing Justice: Law, Tenant Power, and the Decommodification of Urban Property." *University of Pennsylvania Journal of Law and Social Change* 27 (3): 17–204.

Wijburg, Gertjan. 2021. "The De-Financialization of Housing: Towards a Research Agenda." *Housing Studies* 36 (8): 1276–93.

Williams, Rhonda Y. 2004. *The Politics of Public Housing: Black Women's Struggles against Urban Inequality*. New York: Oxford University Press.

WJP Rule of Law Index 2024. 2024. World Justice Project. https://worldjusticeproject.org/rule-of-law-index/.

Wolfinger, James. 2009. "The Limits of Black Activism: Philadelphia's Public Housing in the Depression and World War II." *Journal of Urban History* 35 (6): 787–814.

Yin, Robert K. 2009. *Case Study Research: Design and Methods*. Thousand Oaks, CA: Sage Publications.

Yoshino, Kenji. 2007. *Covering: The Hidden Assault on Our Civil Rights*. New York: Random House.

Zackin, Emily, and Chloe N. Thurston. 2024. *The Political Development of American Debt Relief.* Chicago: University of Chicago Press.

Zemans, Frances K. 1983. "Legal Mobilization: The Neglected Role of the Law in the Political System." *American Political Science Review* 77 (3): 690–703.

Zimmerman, Joseph F. 2008. "Congressional Devolution of Power." In *The Federal Nation: Perspectives on American Federalism,* edited by Iwan W. Morgan and Philip J. Davies, 103–26. New York: Palgrave Macmillan.

Zimmerman, Nourit, and Tom R. Tyler. 2009. "Between Access to Counsel and Access to Justice: A Psychological Perspective." *Fordham Urban Law Journal* 37: 47.

INDEX

American Bar Association (ABA), 96–97,
99–100, 105
arbitration, 63, 150
access to justice, 8, 10–13, 15, 16n18, 19–25,
34–36, 44–45, 55–56, 92–94, 98–99, 133, 187,
195–207, 209, 212–14; bills, 46–54, 117–26.
See also justice gap, legal counsel: access to

backup center, ix, 103, 109, 116, 123
Bamberger Jr., E. Clinton, 92, 100–101
Barr, Bob, 114

causal inference, 8n4, 18nn19 and 20, 18–19,
65–66, 237–39
citizenship, 17, 22n22, 25, 55–56, 60–63,
69–74, 79, 86–87, 92–93, 128, 141–42,
197–99, 207, 209
city council, 163–64, 176, 185, 210
civil courts, 13–14, 24, 36, 94, 130–32, 145,
158–60, 165, 175–77, 180–81, 183–84,
227–29; specialized, 39–40, 39n7; structure
of, 36–40. *See also* housing: court
civil justice problems. *See* civil legal problems
civil legal problems, 10–12, 15–18, 23–26,
57–62, 64–74, 79–87, 136, 166, 196–198,
202, 207, 209–10
civil rights, 11, 14n14, 22n22, 62, 64, 92,
94–95, 112, 128–29, 137–41, 168; for
tenants, 77, 152–53, 168–69, 172–73,
177–78, 185, 205, 210–12
class action, 43, 88, 94, 102, 104–5, 114, 116
Clinton, Bill, 112–113
Clinton, Hillary Rodham, 110, 113, 236

code enforcement, 39n7, 78, 80–81,
88–89, 191–92
collective action, 6–8, 14–17, 14n14, 24–25,
92, 95–96, 101–2, 135, 167, 172–73, 186–87,
200–7, 209–10. *See also* organizing
community lawyering, 170–75, 177. *See also*
impact litigation, poverty lawyers
court support, 77, 175–79, 183
COVID-19, 4, 6–7, 26, 75–77, 79–80, 83–86,
120, 157–60, 172, 178, 186, 190, 200–201,
204–5, 230, 236n11
cy pres, 43

debt: collection, 10–11, 26, 42n9, 66–67, 93,
103, 128; rental arrears, 28–30, 57–59,
83–84, 88–89, 146–47, 149, 157–60, 213;
Debt Collective, 207
default judgement, 15, 38–39, 158
disability, 1, 52–55, 77n17, 153–54
domestic violence survivors, 52–55,
69n11, 123–25
Durant, William Clark, 111–12

Economic Opportunity Act, 89, 99–100
ethnography, 8–9, 9n5, 75–77, 152, 227–30,
232, 234, 237–39
eviction, 27–34, 37–39, 57–59, 61, 67, 77, 82,
84–86, 88–89, 102, 112, 114–15, 130–33,
145–49, 151–54, 157–62, 165, 170–87,
188–95, 199–204, 210–12, 228; process,
37–39, 144–47, 159–60, 178; blockade,
77, 181–83; good cause, 28, 28n2;
moratorium, 26, 178–83

259

A NOTE ON THE TYPE

This book has been composed in Arno, an Old-style serif typeface in the classic Venetian tradition, designed by Robert Slimbach at Adobe.